GW01607775

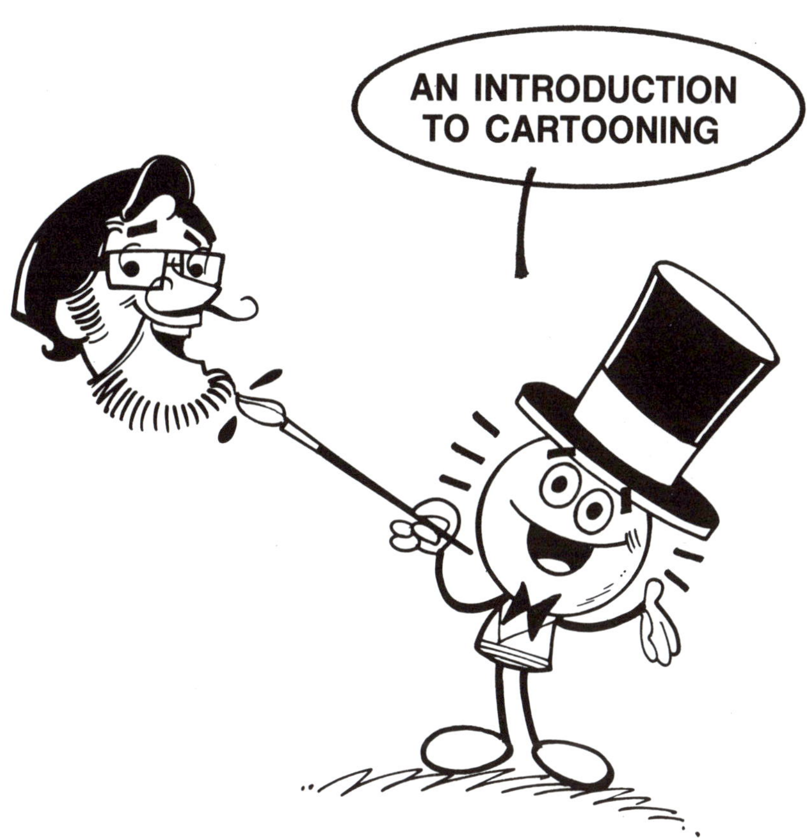
AN INTRODUCTION
TO CARTOONING

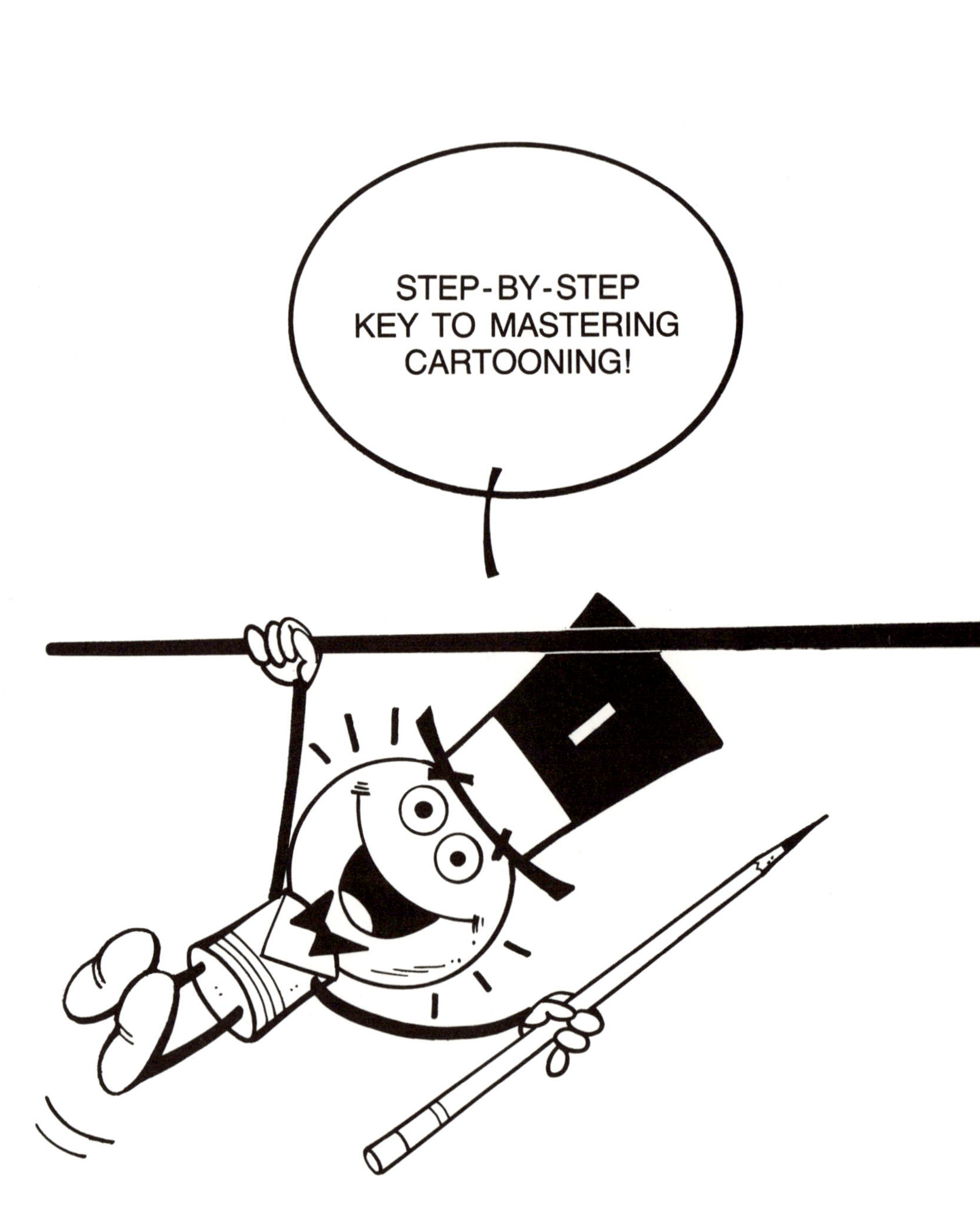
STEP-BY-STEP
KEY TO MASTERING
CARTOONING!

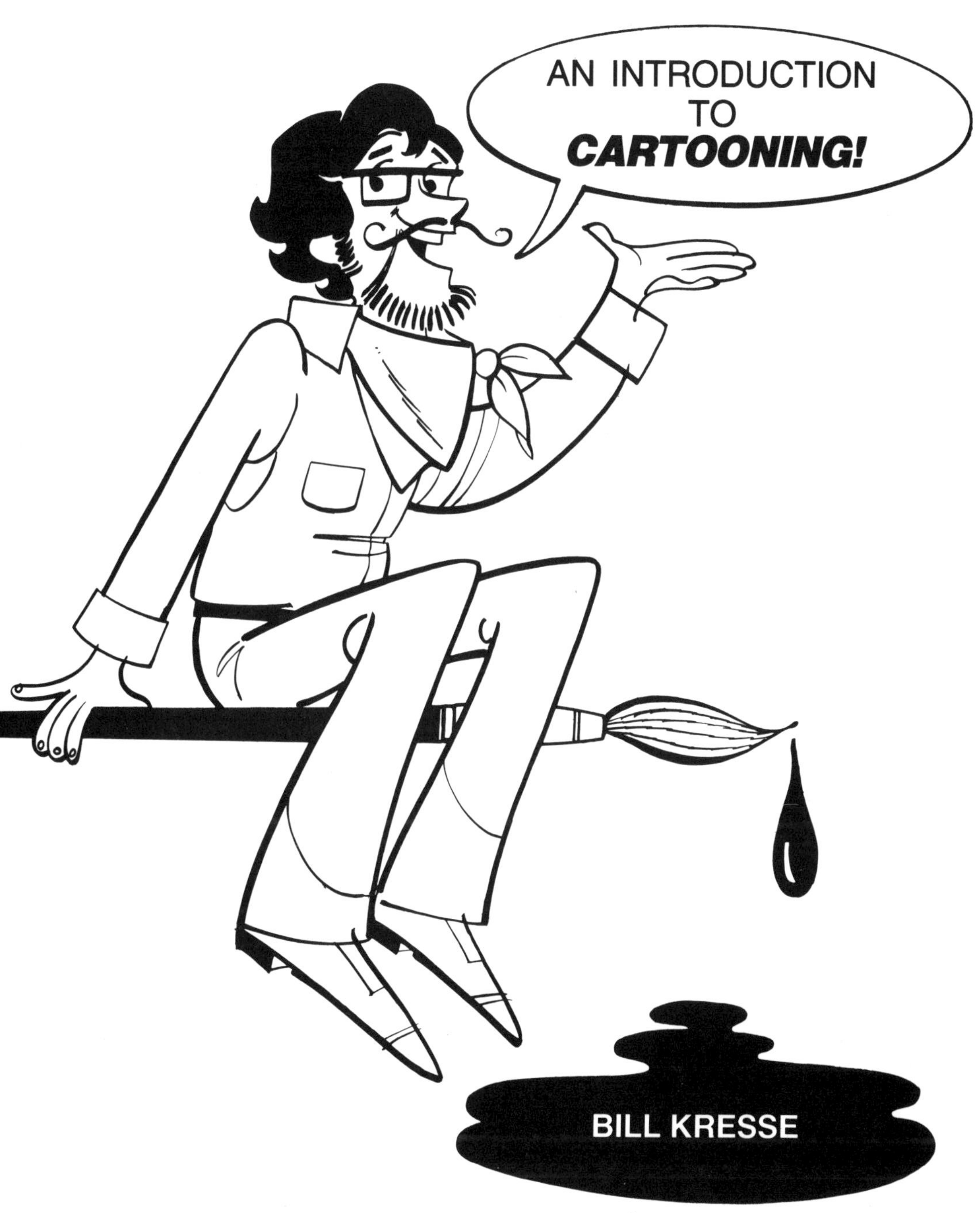

ARCO PUBLISHING, INC.
NEW YORK

Published by Arco Publishing, Inc.
215 Park Avenue South, New York, N.Y. 10003

Library of Congress Cataloging in Publication Data

Kresse, Bill.
An introduction to cartooning.

1. Cartooning. I. Title.
NC1320.K73 1984 741.5 83-22384
ISBN 0-668-05885-4 (Paper Edition)

Printed in the United States of America

10 9 8 7 6 5 4 3 2 1

DEDICATED TO:
CARTOONISTS EVERYWHERE, PAST, PRESENT, AND VERY IMPORTANTLY . . . FUTURE; TO BEAUTIFUL, SWEET LORRAINE AND HANDSOME LITTLE DANDIE, WHO ARE A CONSTANT SOURCE OF INSPIRATION, AND TO BORIS...WHO IS A GOOD FRIEND, GOOD BOOSTER, AND CARTOON APPRECIATOR!

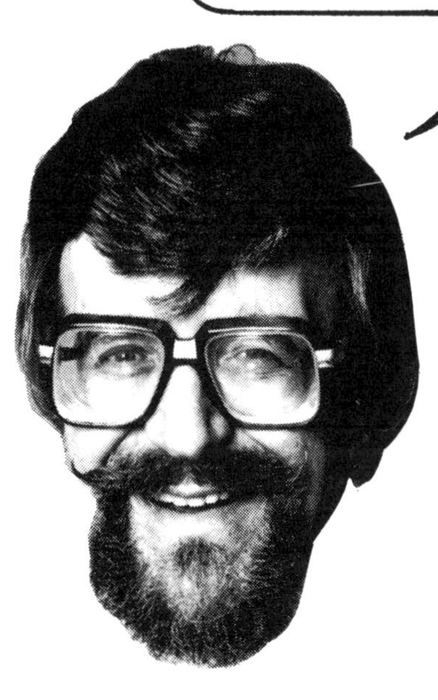

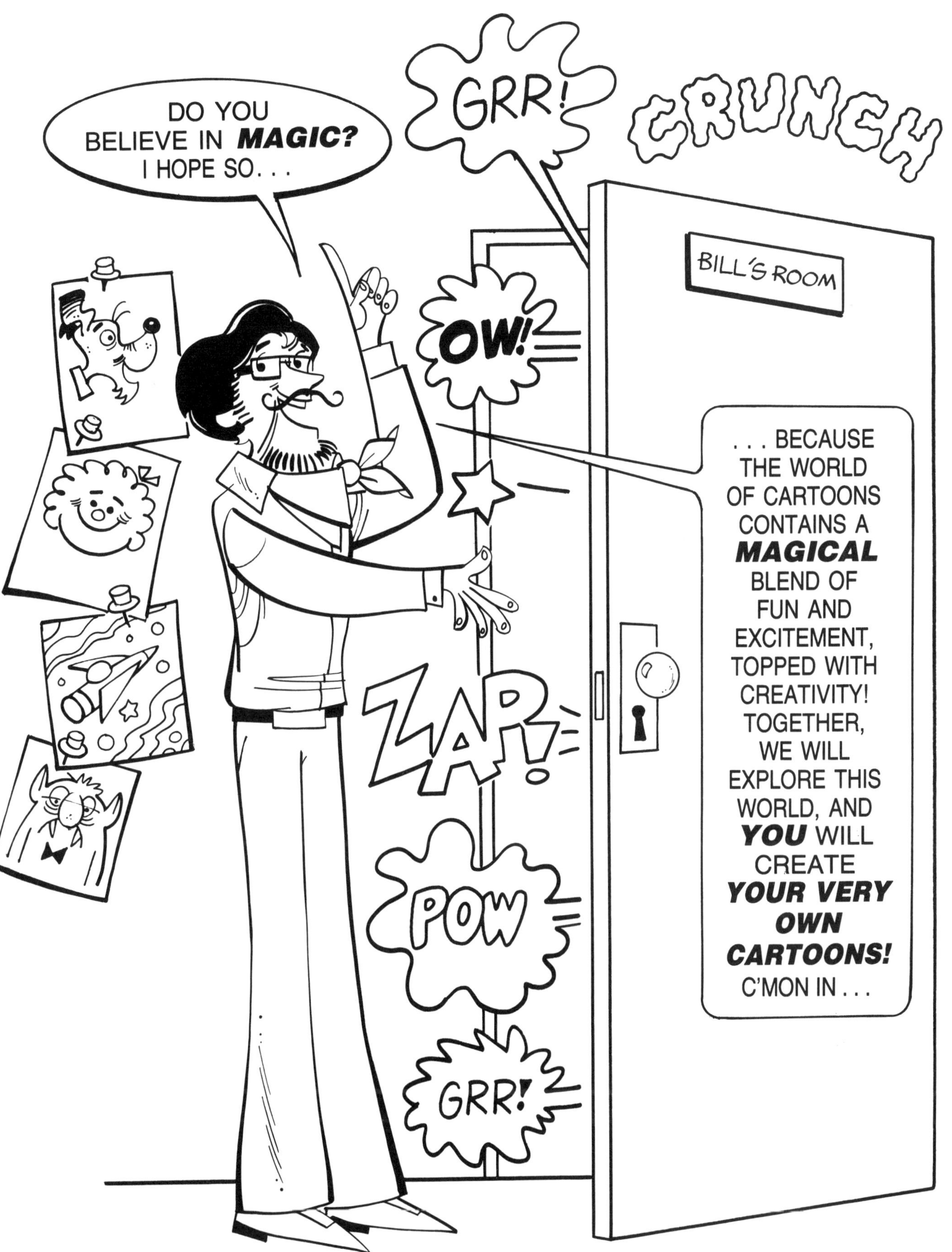
DO YOU BELIEVE IN **MAGIC?** I HOPE SO. . .
GRR!
CRUNCH
BILL'S ROOM
OW!
. . . BECAUSE THE WORLD OF CARTOONS CONTAINS A **MAGICAL** BLEND OF FUN AND EXCITEMENT, TOPPED WITH CREATIVITY! TOGETHER, WE WILL EXPLORE THIS WORLD, AND **YOU** WILL CREATE **YOUR VERY OWN CARTOONS!** C'MON IN . . .
ZAP!
POW
GRR!

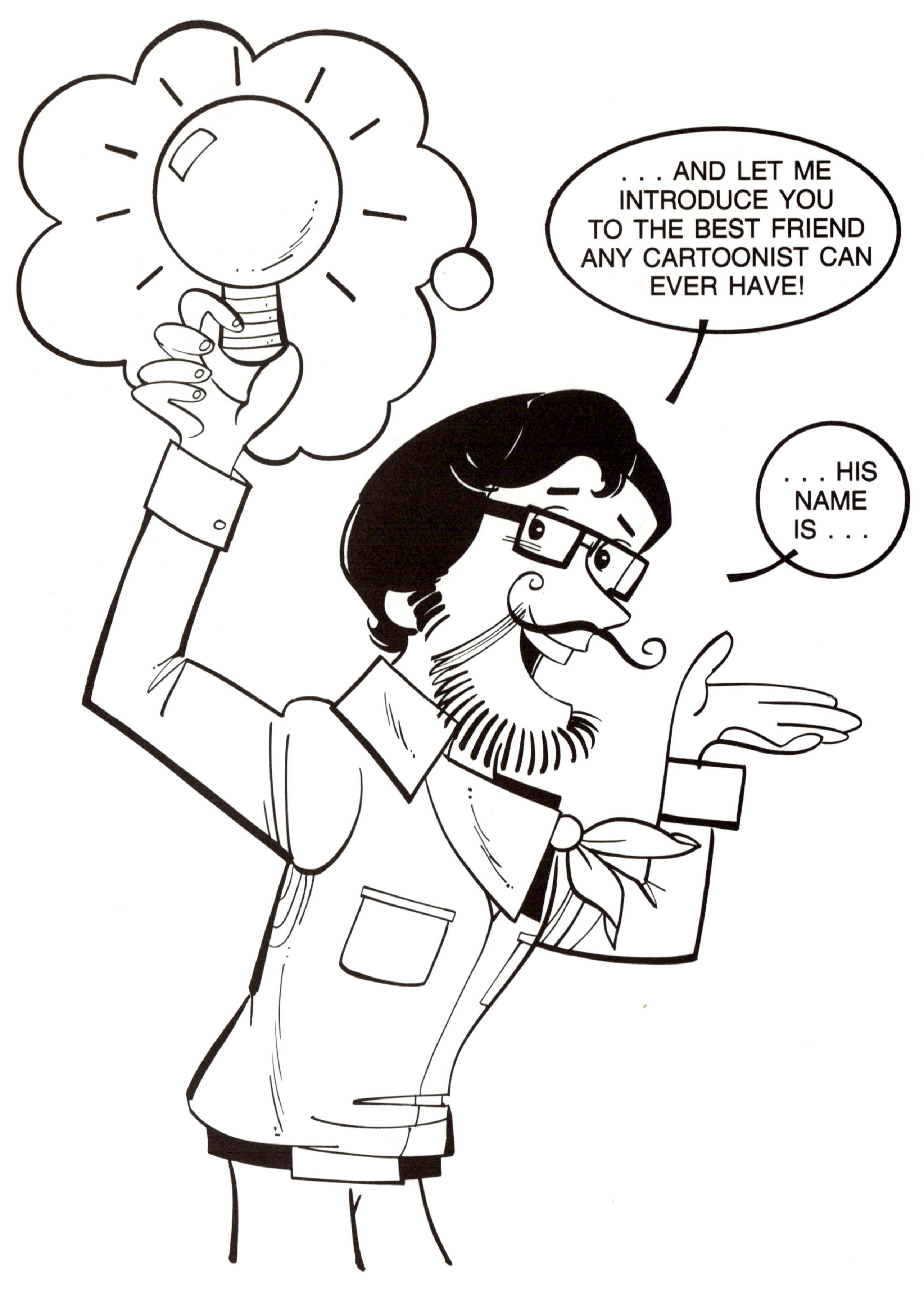
. . . AND LET ME INTRODUCE YOU TO THE BEST FRIEND ANY CARTOONIST CAN EVER HAVE!
. . . HIS NAME IS . . .

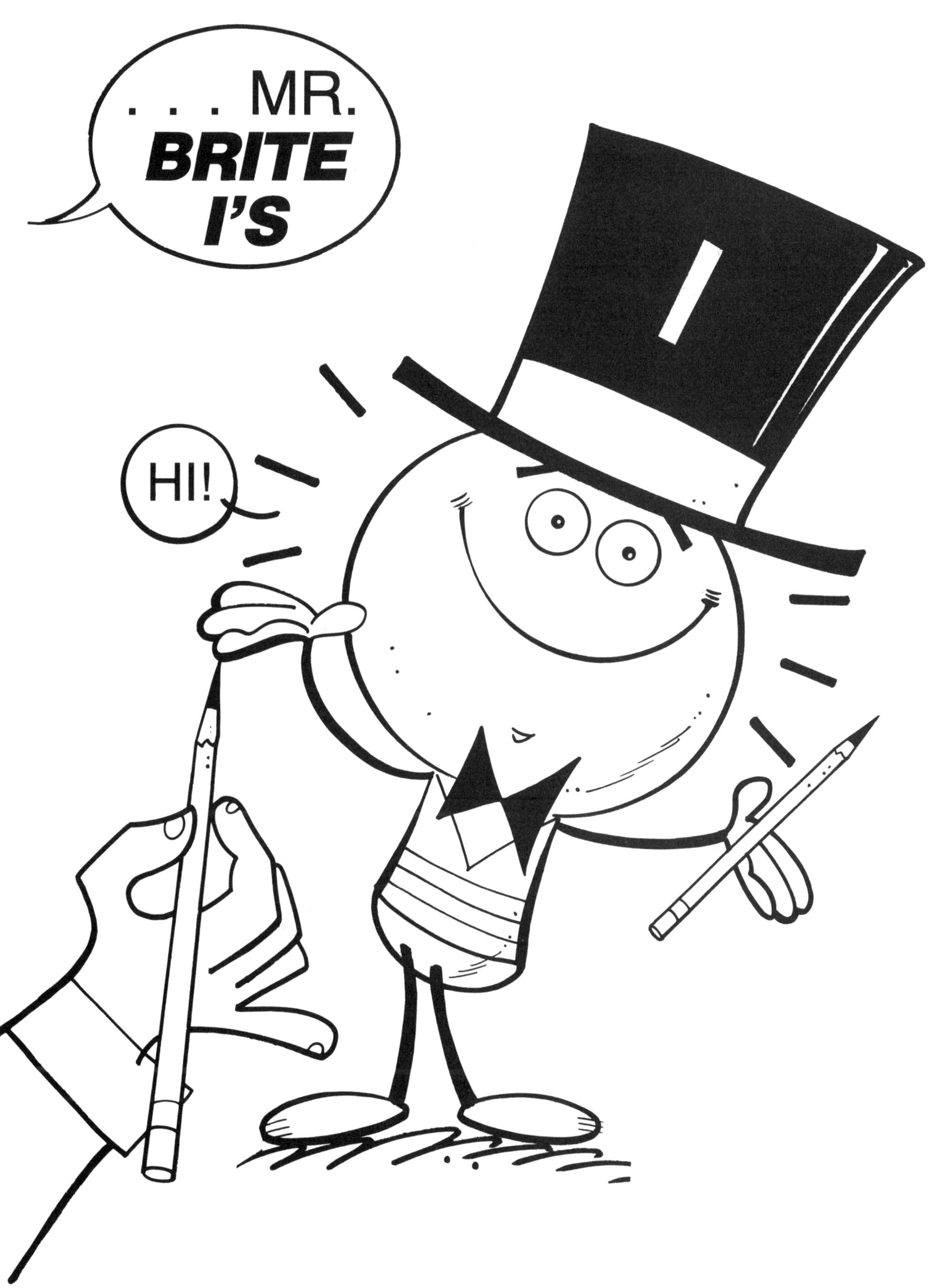
. . . MR.
BRITE
I'S
HI!

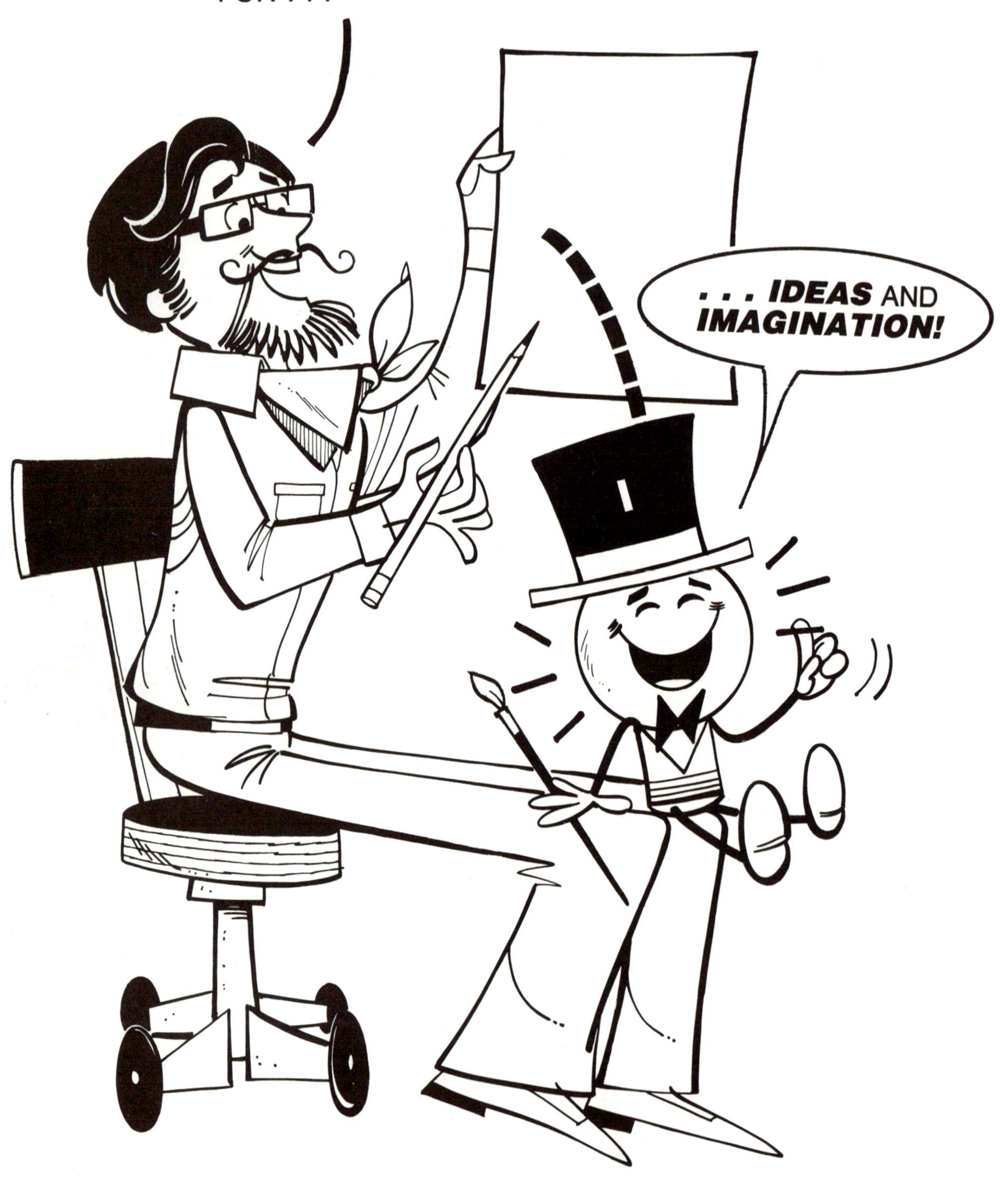
HE'S **VERY IMPORTANT** BECAUSE THE ***I's*** IN HIS NAME STAND FOR . . .
. . . **IDEAS** AND **IMAGINATION!**
I

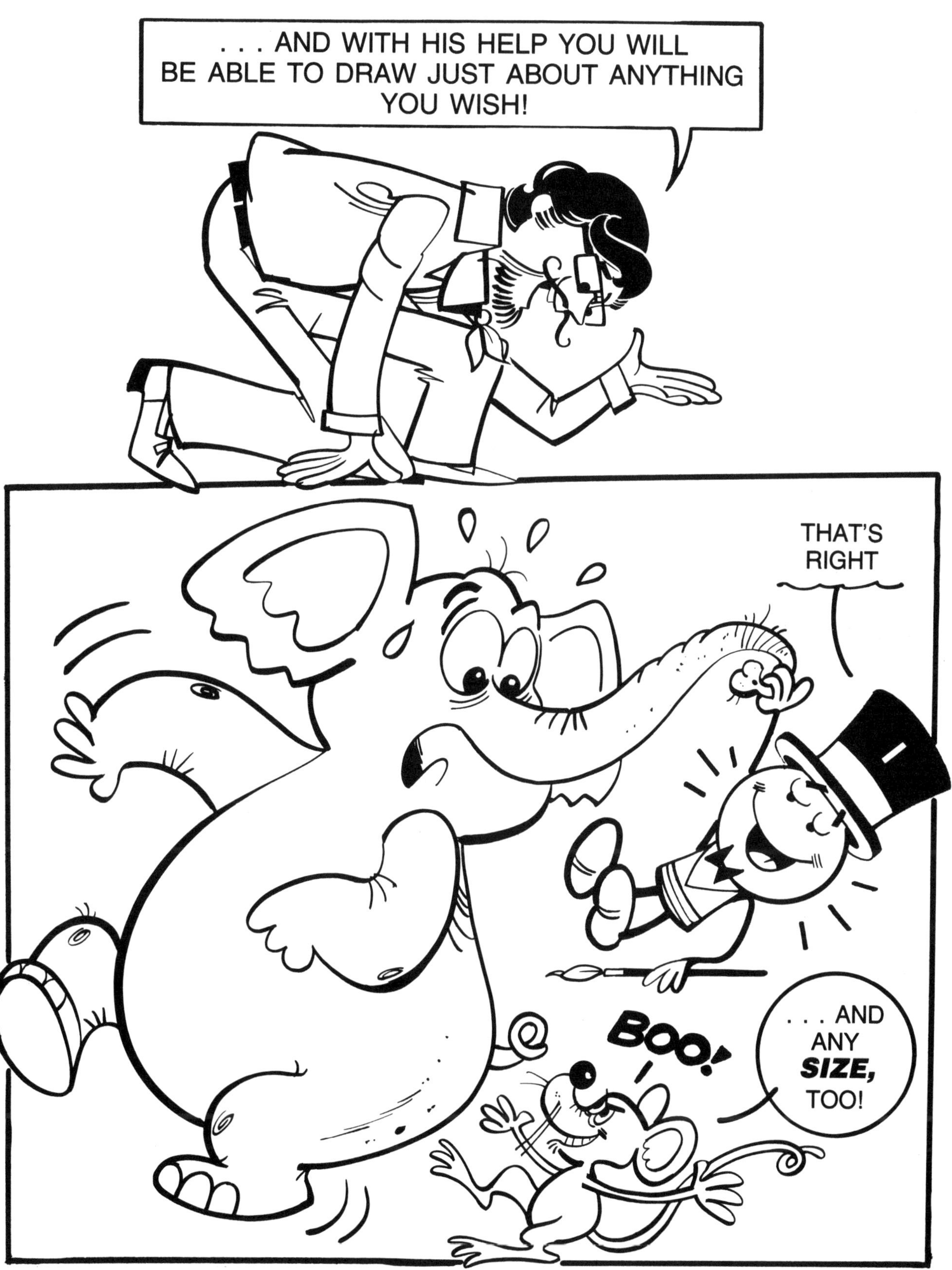
. . . AND WITH HIS HELP YOU WILL BE ABLE TO DRAW JUST ABOUT ANYTHING YOU WISH!
THAT'S RIGHT
BOO!
. . . AND ANY **SIZE,** TOO!

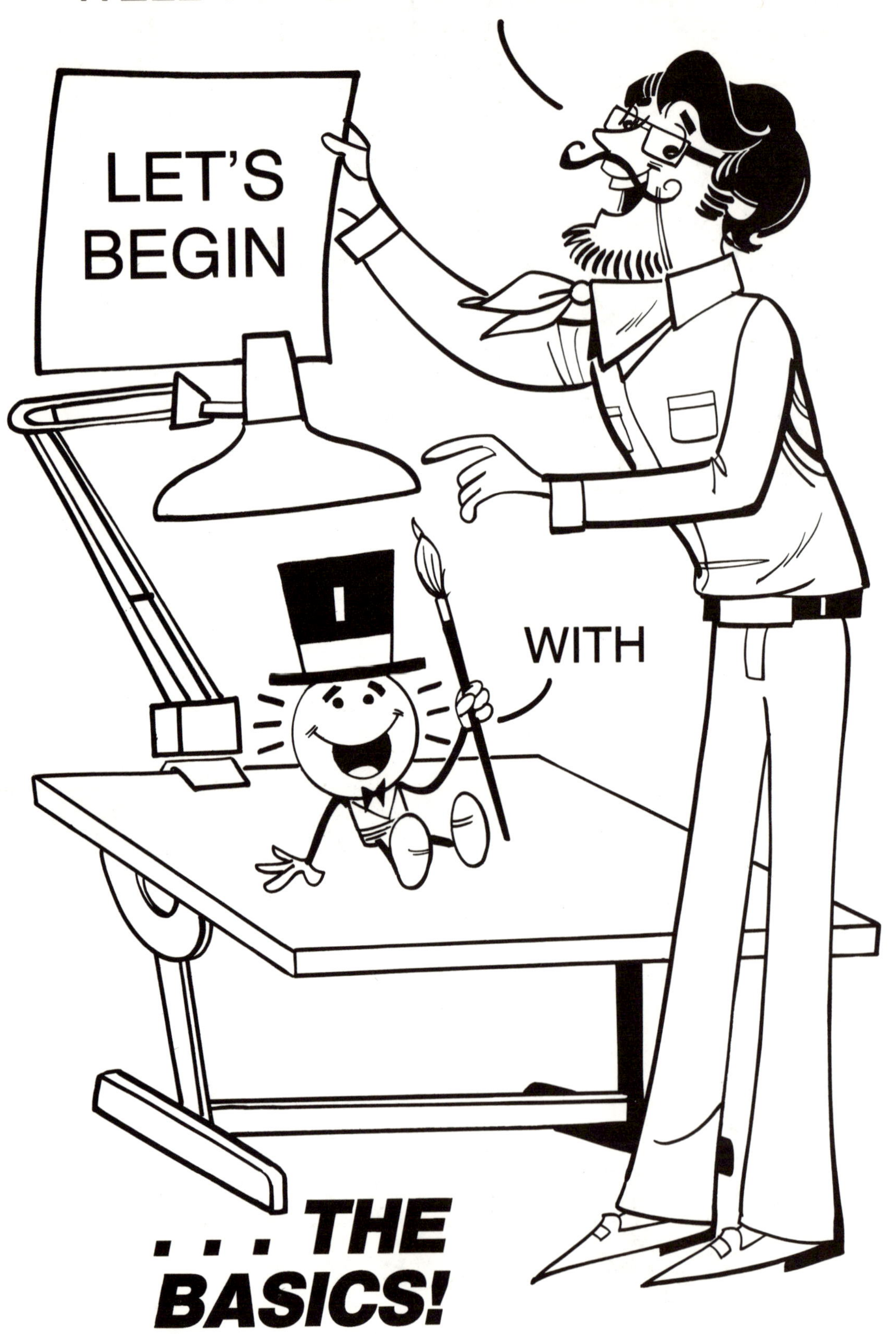
WELL . . . ***IF YOU'RE READY . . .***
LET'S BEGIN
WITH
. . . THE BASICS!

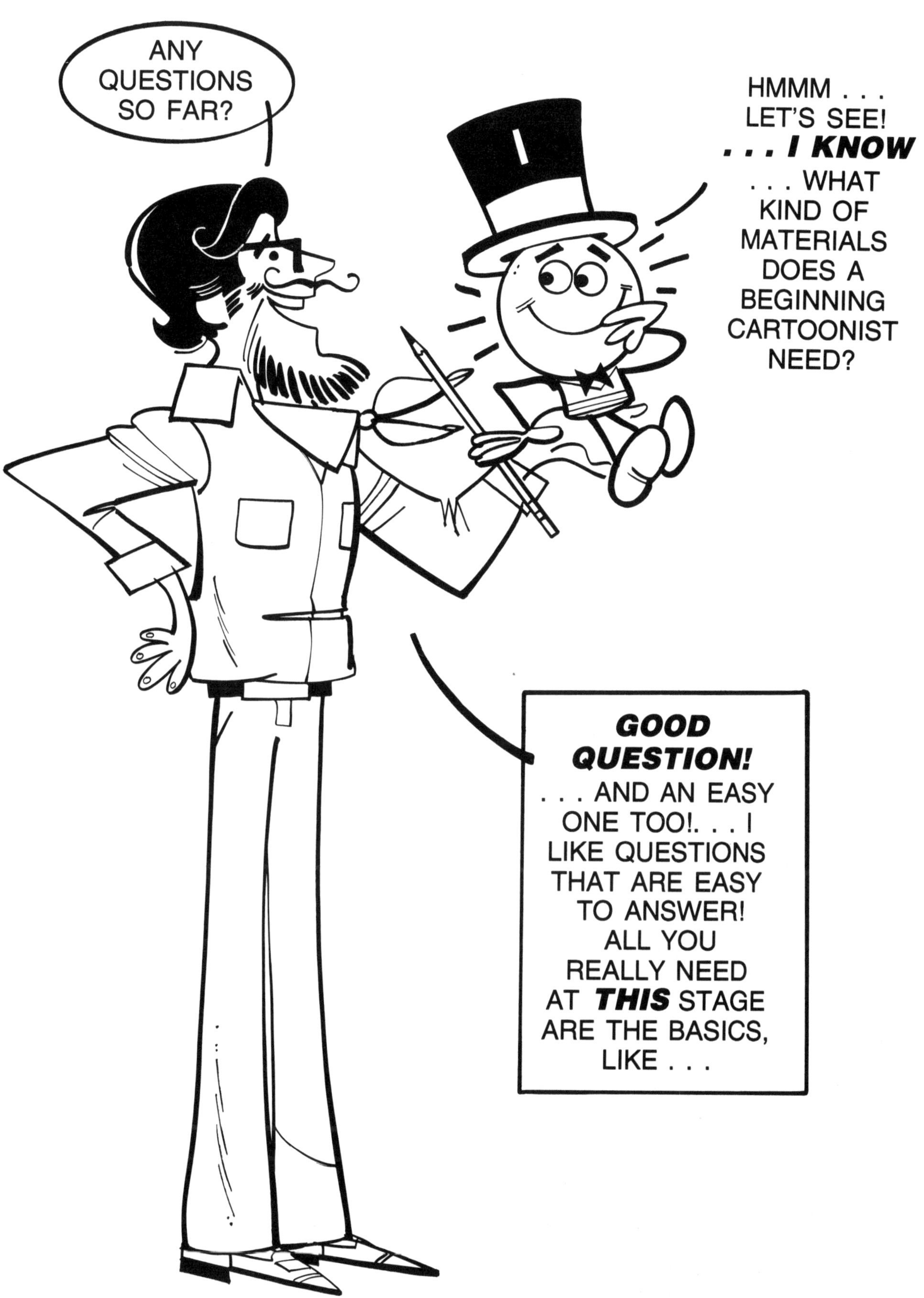
ANY QUESTIONS SO FAR?
HMMM . . . LET'S SEE! . . . I KNOW . . . WHAT KIND OF MATERIALS DOES A BEGINNING CARTOONIST NEED?
GOOD QUESTION! . . . AND AN EASY ONE TOO!. . . I LIKE QUESTIONS THAT ARE EASY TO ANSWER! ALL YOU REALLY NEED AT THIS STAGE ARE THE BASICS, LIKE . . .

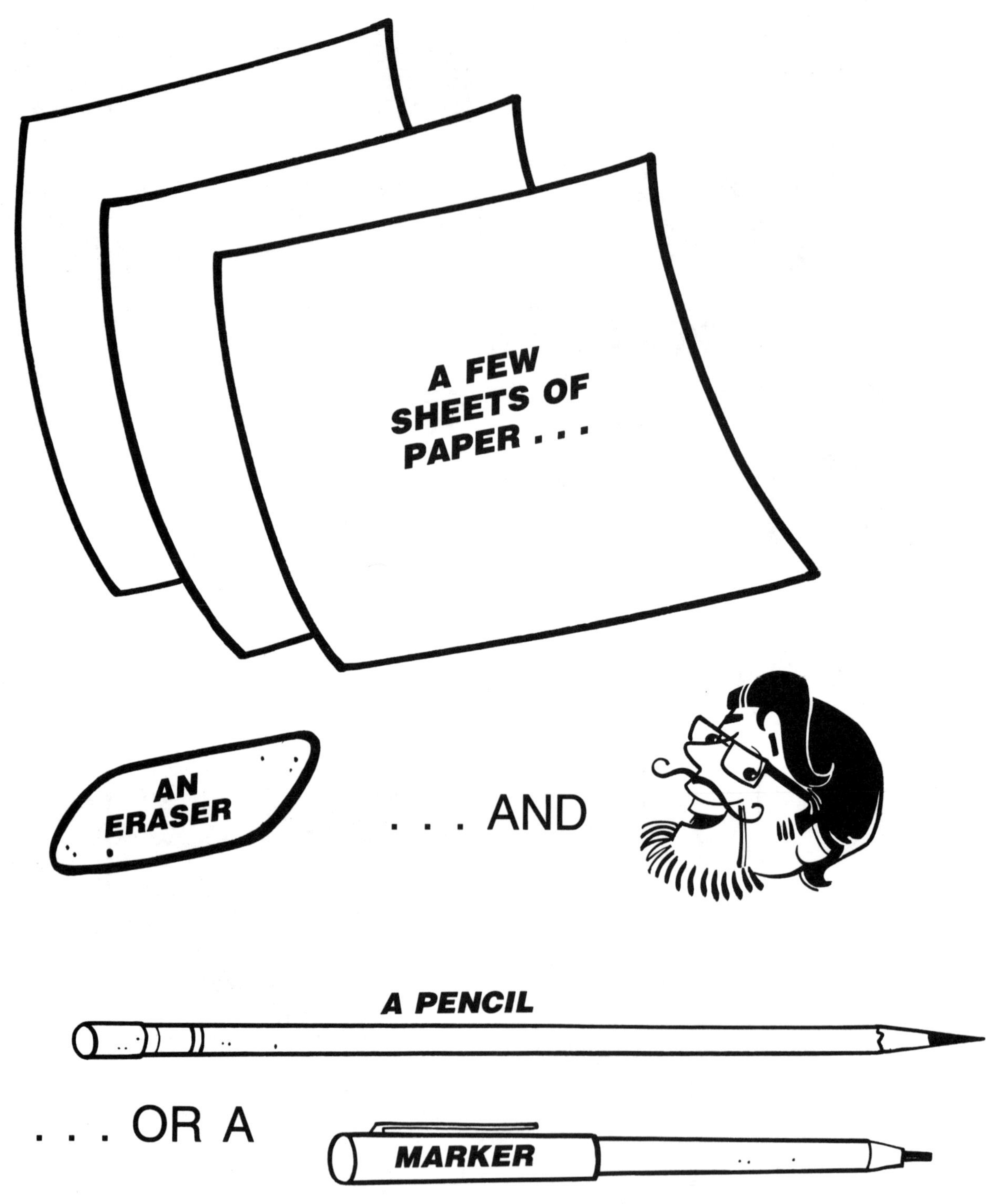

. . . AND YOU'RE ALL SET!

FOR NOW, LET'S NOT WORRY ABOUT SIZE . . .

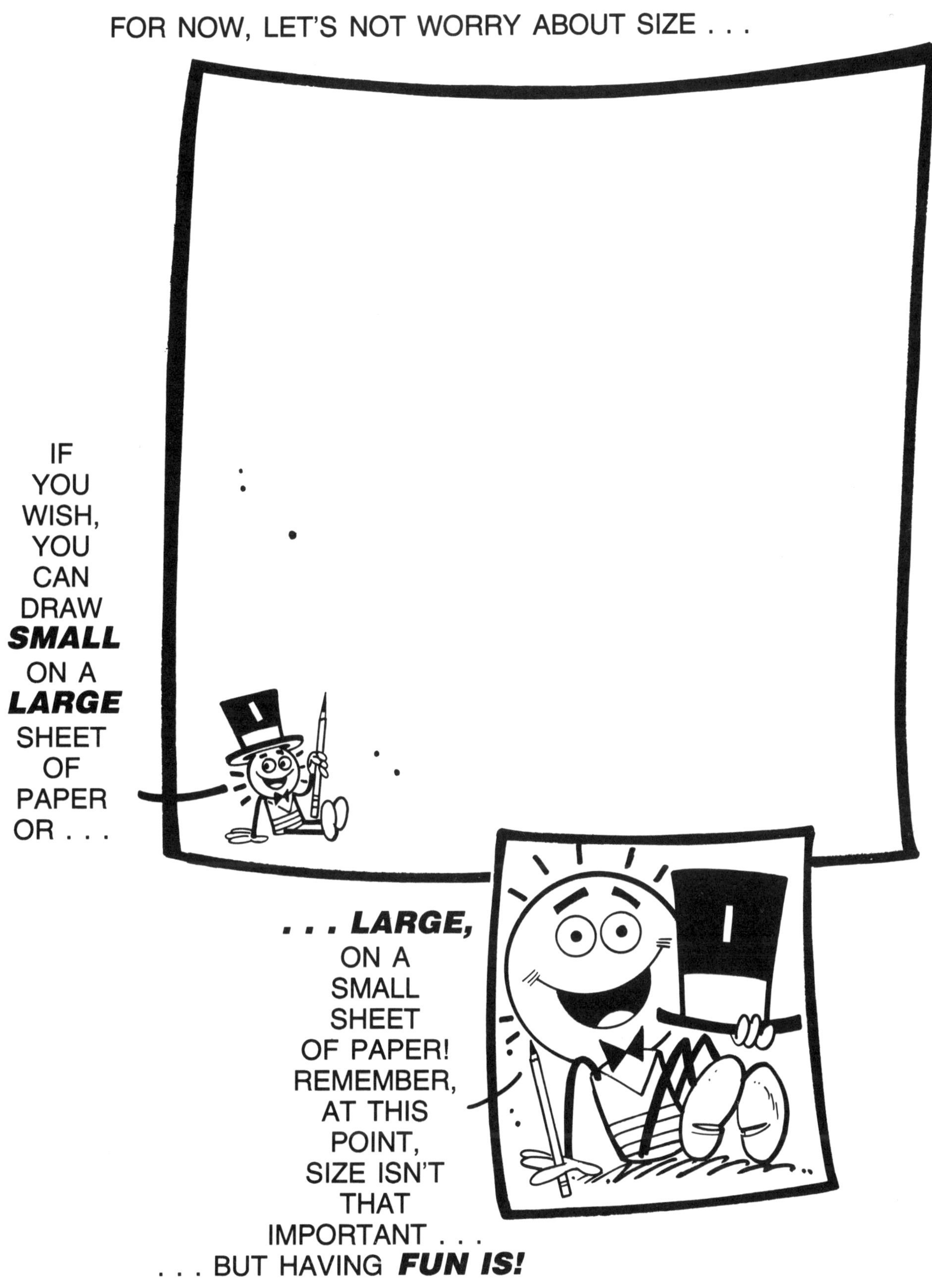

IF YOU WISH, YOU CAN DRAW ***SMALL*** ON A ***LARGE*** SHEET OF PAPER OR . . .

. . . LARGE, ON A SMALL SHEET OF PAPER! REMEMBER, AT THIS POINT, SIZE ISN'T THAT IMPORTANT . . .

. . . BUT HAVING ***FUN IS!***

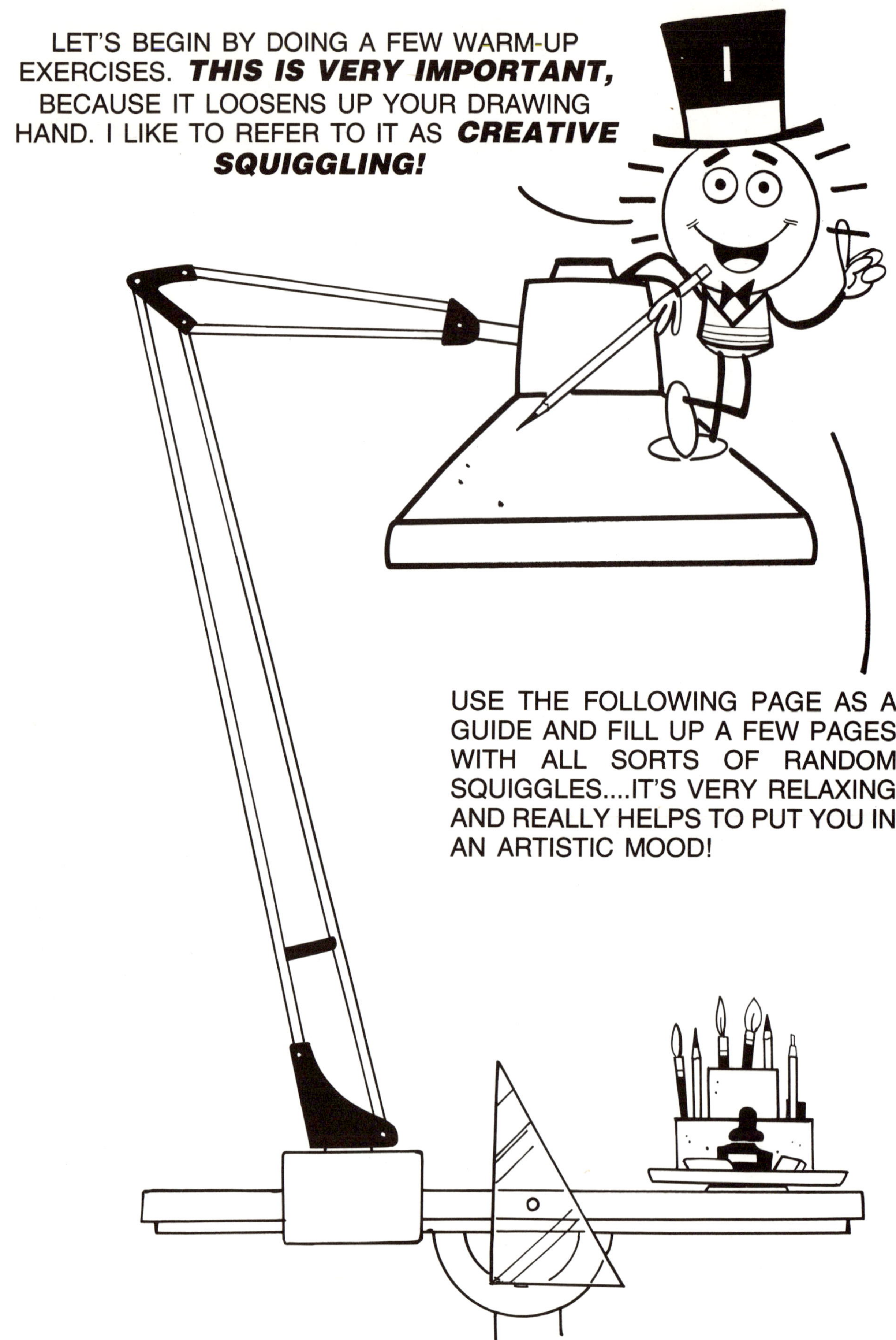
LET'S BEGIN BY DOING A FEW WARM-UP EXERCISES. ***THIS IS VERY IMPORTANT,*** BECAUSE IT LOOSENS UP YOUR DRAWING HAND. I LIKE TO REFER TO IT AS ***CREATIVE SQUIGGLING!***
USE THE FOLLOWING PAGE AS A GUIDE AND FILL UP A FEW PAGES WITH ALL SORTS OF RANDOM SQUIGGLES....IT'S VERY RELAXING AND REALLY HELPS TO PUT YOU IN AN ARTISTIC MOOD!

WHEW!...NOT BAD, IF I SAY SO MYSELF. . .
NOW, HOW'S ABOUT TRYING A FEW
PAGES ON YOUR OWN!

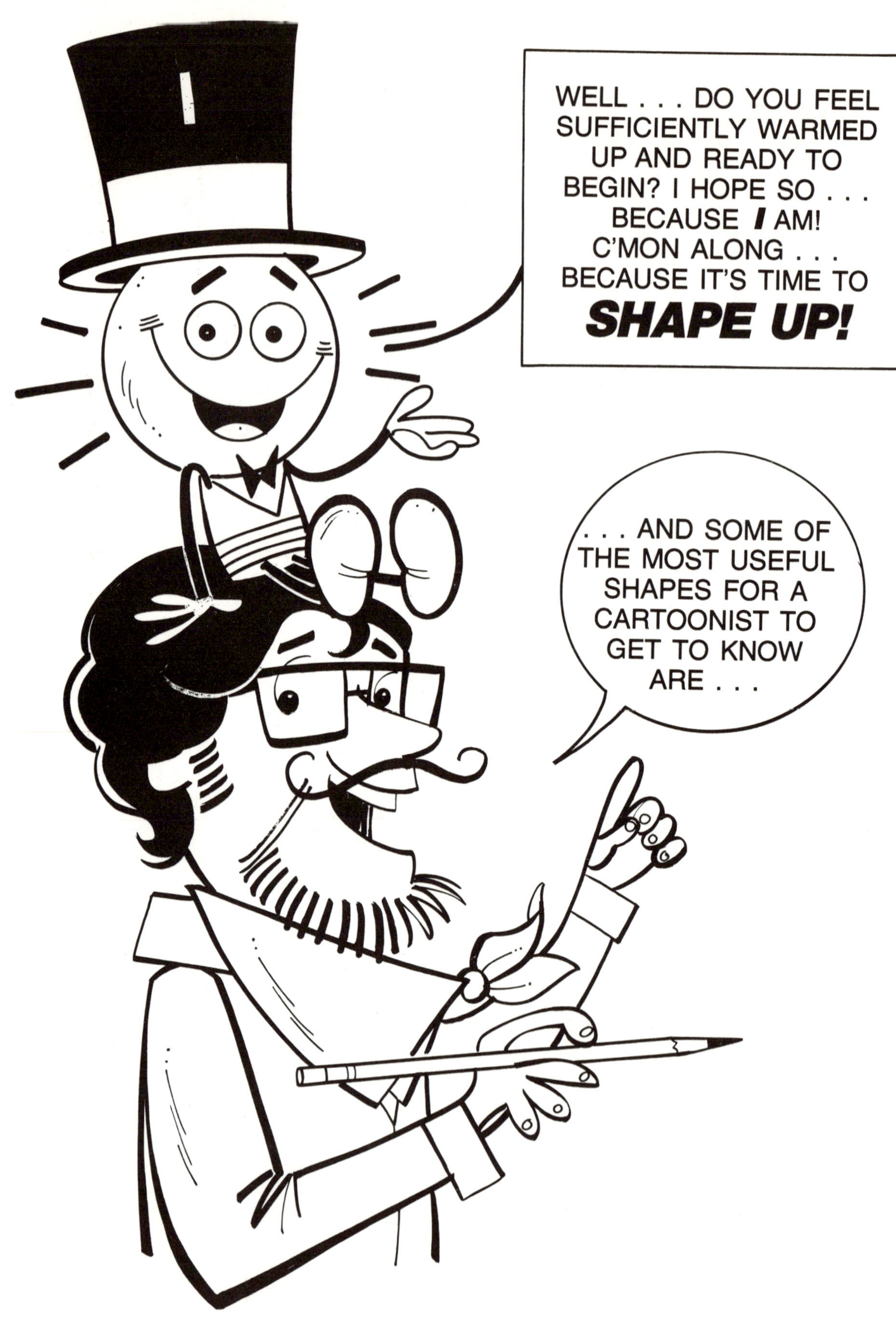
WELL . . . DO YOU FEEL SUFFICIENTLY WARMED UP AND READY TO BEGIN? I HOPE SO . . . BECAUSE ***I*** AM! C'MON ALONG . . . BECAUSE IT'S TIME TO ***SHAPE UP!***
. . . AND SOME OF THE MOST USEFUL SHAPES FOR A CARTOONIST TO GET TO KNOW ARE . . .

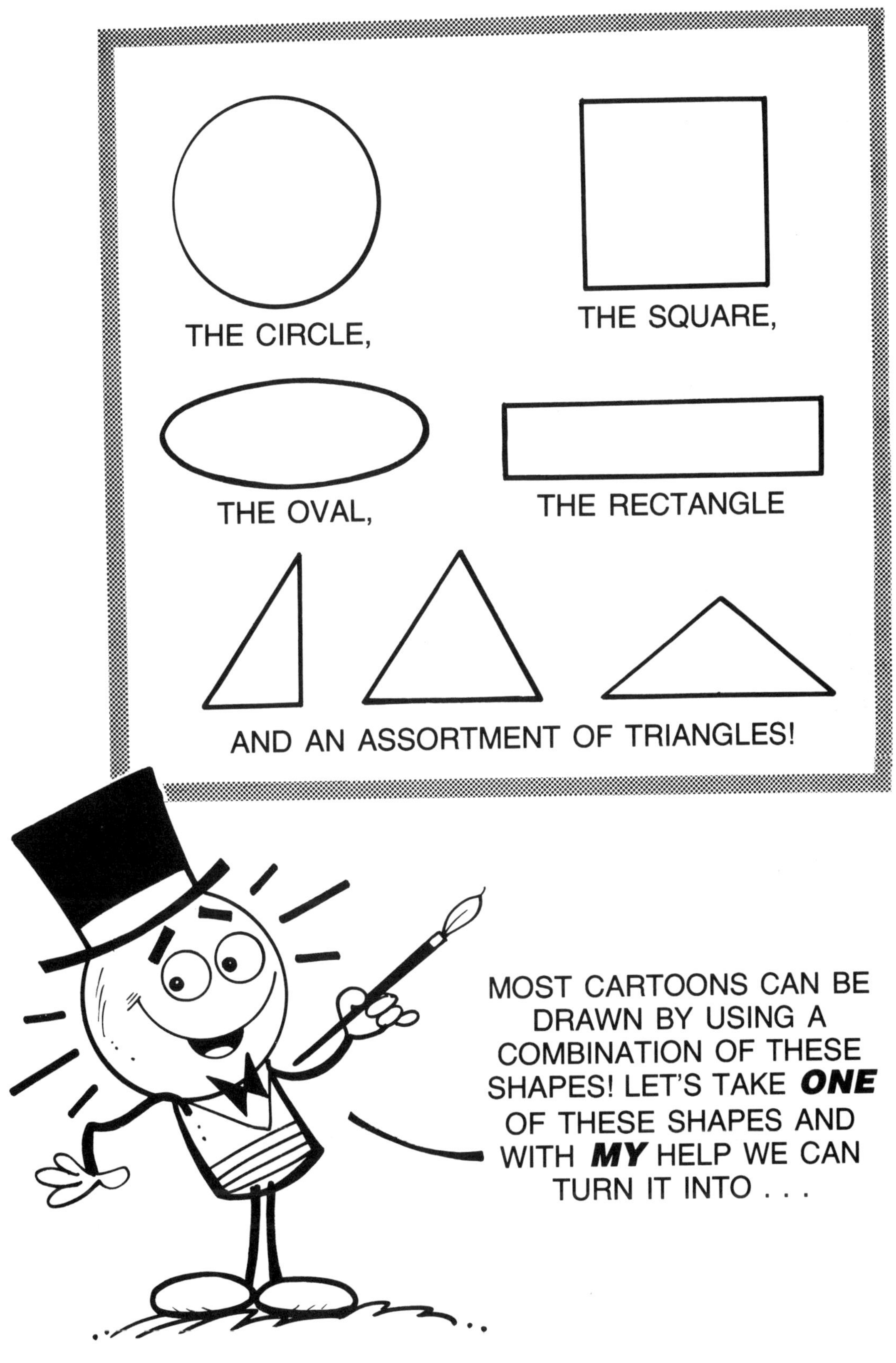

MOST CARTOONS CAN BE DRAWN BY USING A COMBINATION OF THESE SHAPES! LET'S TAKE ***ONE*** OF THESE SHAPES AND WITH ***MY*** HELP WE CAN TURN IT INTO . . .

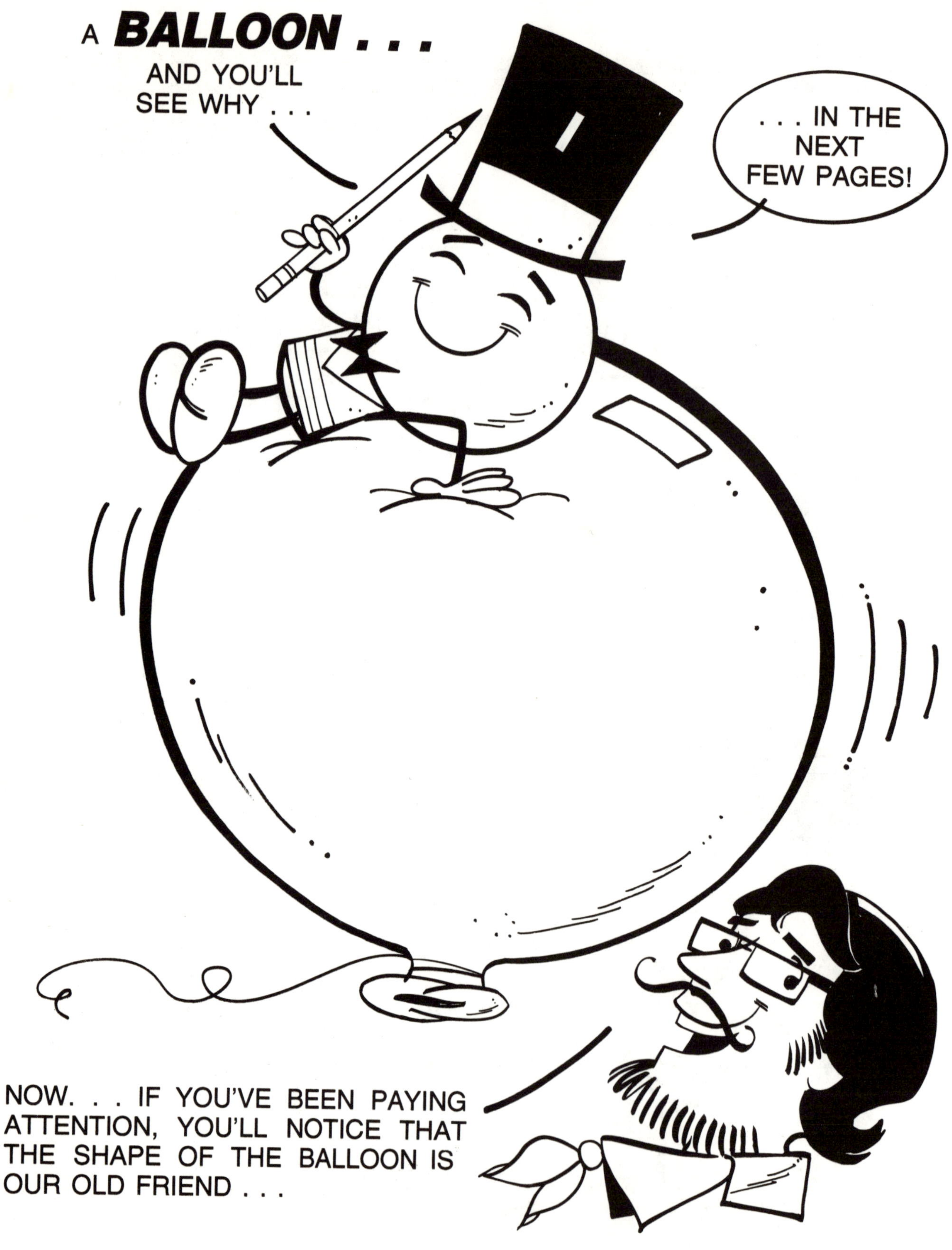
A BALLOON . . .
AND YOU'LL SEE WHY . . .
. . . IN THE NEXT FEW PAGES!
NOW. . . IF YOU'VE BEEN PAYING ATTENTION, YOU'LL NOTICE THAT THE SHAPE OF THE BALLOON IS OUR OLD FRIEND . . .

. . . THE CIRCLE, WHICH WILL GIVE YOU A ***HEAD START*** IN DRAWING ***YOUR FIRST CARTOON!*** THIS IS ANOTHER WAY OF SAYING A GOOD WAY TO ***START*** IS WITH THE ***HEAD.*** NO, NOT A HEAD OF LETTUCE, I MEAN A ***REAL*** HEAD . . . OR . . . AT LEAST, A REAL ***CARTOON*** HEAD!

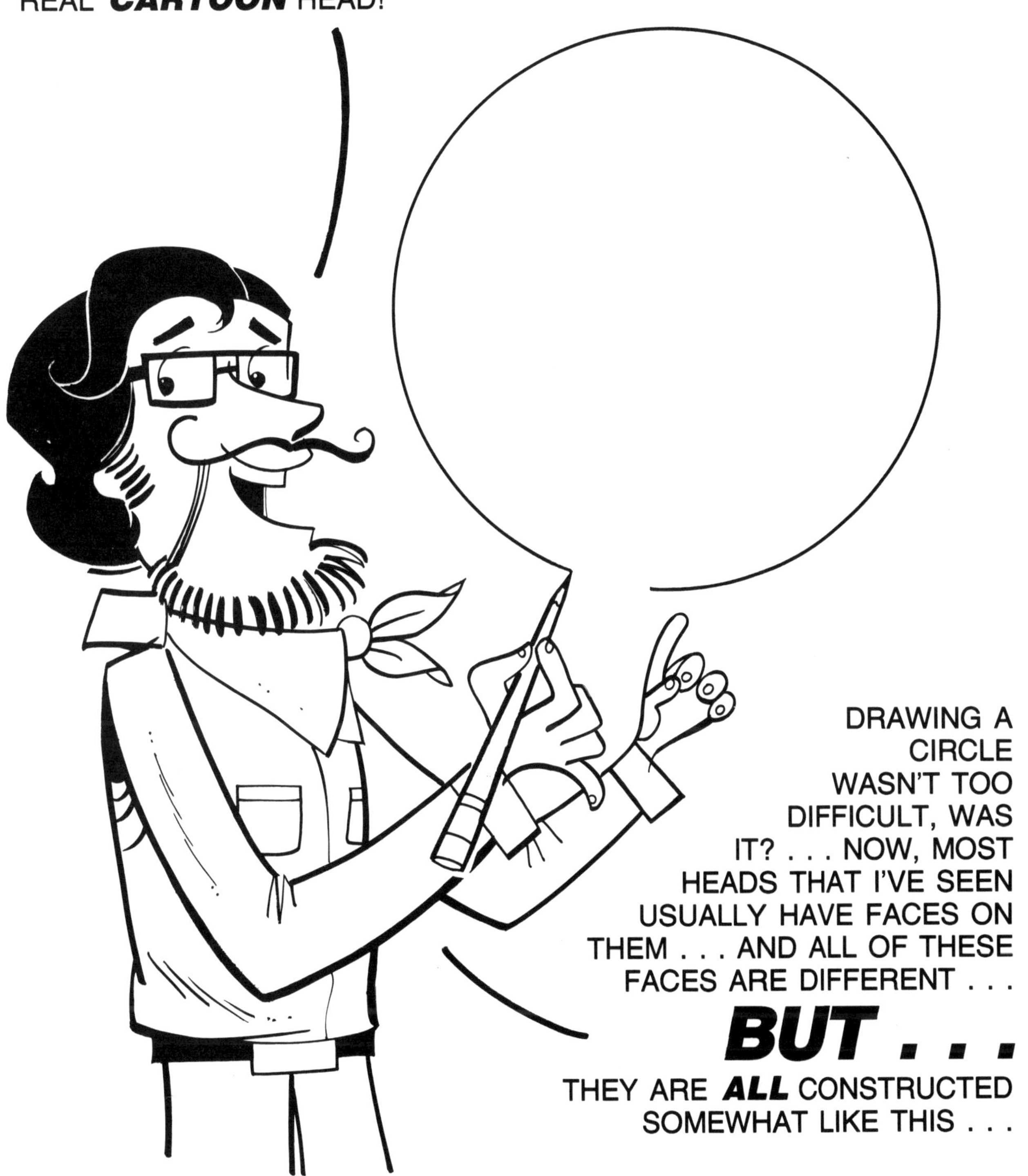

DRAWING A CIRCLE WASN'T TOO DIFFICULT, WAS IT? . . . NOW, MOST HEADS THAT I'VE SEEN USUALLY HAVE FACES ON THEM . . . AND ALL OF THESE FACES ARE DIFFERENT . . .

BUT . . .

THEY ARE ***ALL*** CONSTRUCTED SOMEWHAT LIKE THIS . . .

FIRST WE CAN DRAW AN IMAGINARY LINE THROUGH THE CENTER OF OUR CIRCLE . . .

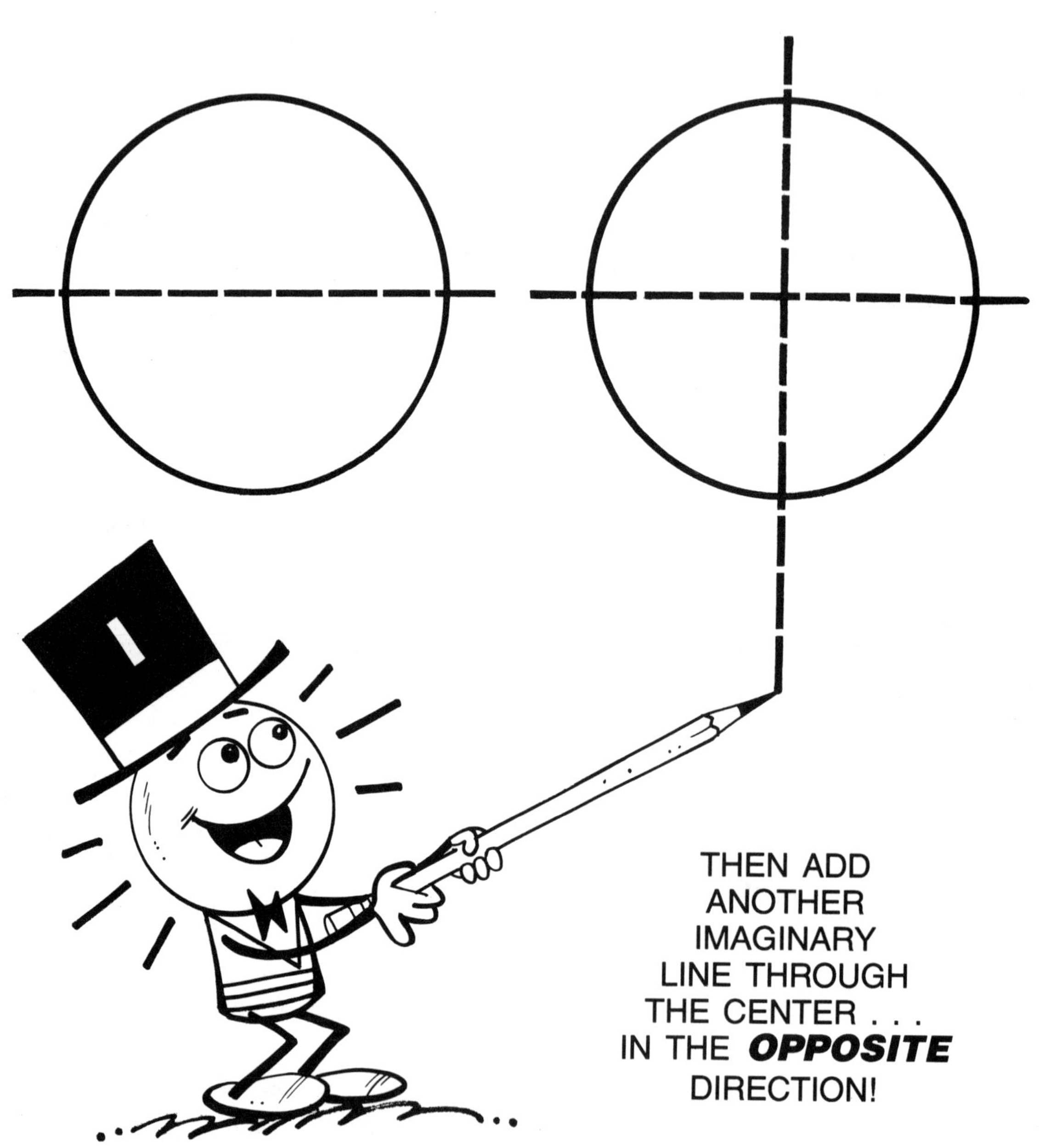

THEN ADD ANOTHER IMAGINARY LINE THROUGH THE CENTER . . . IN THE ***OPPOSITE*** DIRECTION!

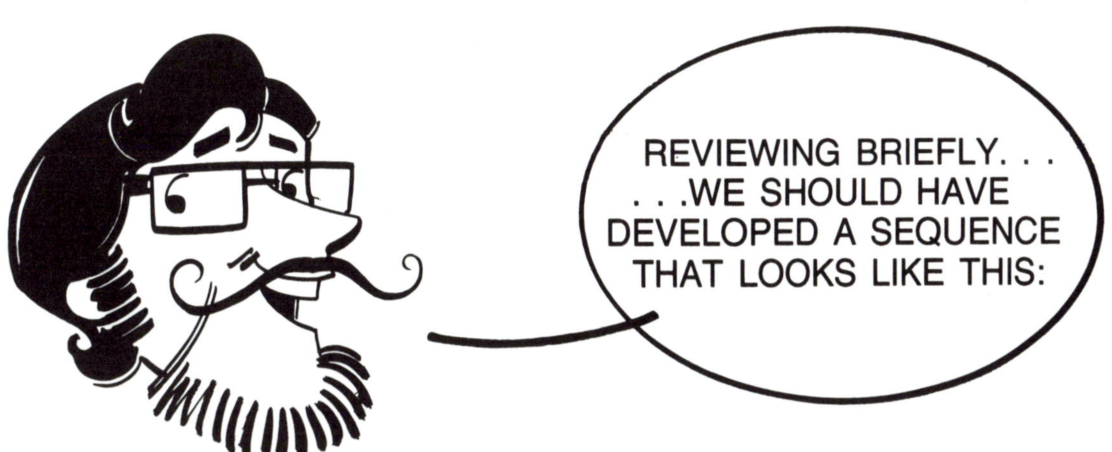

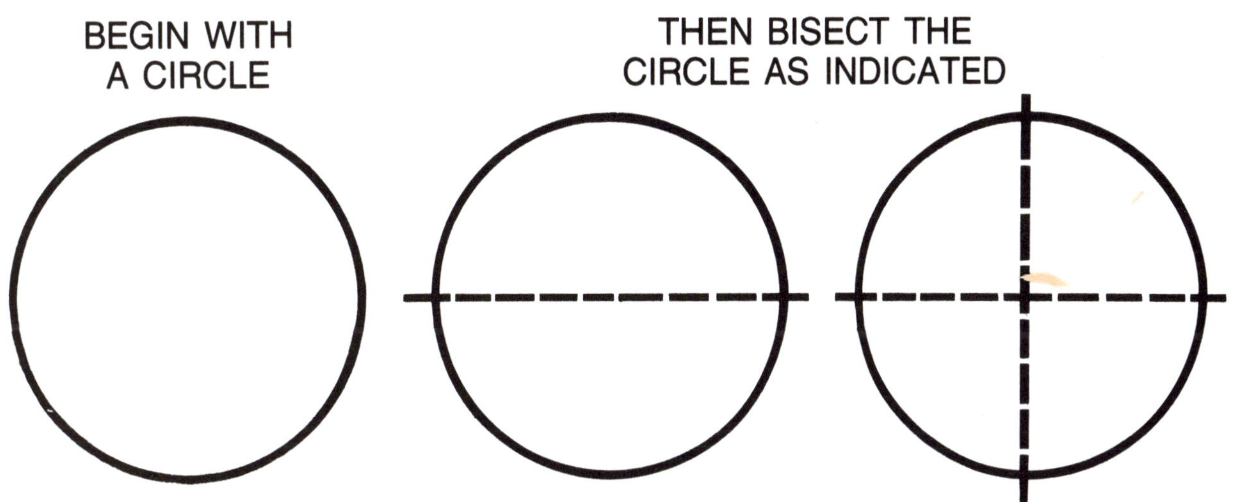

AND ON THIS CIRCLE WE CAN PLACE A FEW VERY FAMILIAR OBJECTS, LIKE:

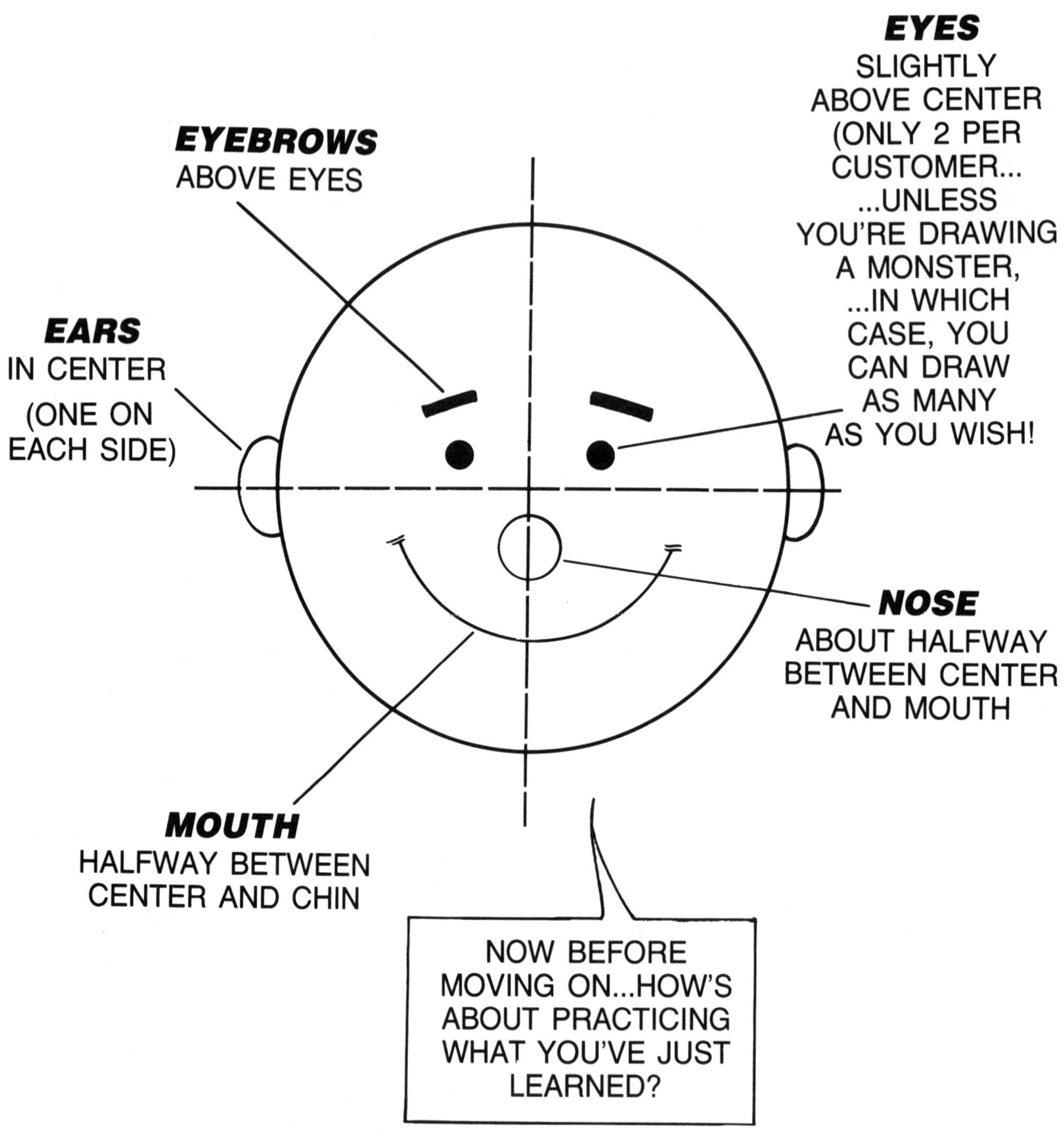
EYES
SLIGHTLY ABOVE CENTER (ONLY 2 PER CUSTOMER... ...UNLESS YOU'RE DRAWING A MONSTER, ...IN WHICH CASE, YOU CAN DRAW AS MANY AS YOU WISH!
EYEBROWS
ABOVE EYES
EARS
IN CENTER
(ONE ON EACH SIDE)
NOSE
ABOUT HALFWAY BETWEEN CENTER AND MOUTH
MOUTH
HALFWAY BETWEEN CENTER AND CHIN
NOW BEFORE MOVING ON...HOW'S ABOUT PRACTICING WHAT YOU'VE JUST LEARNED?

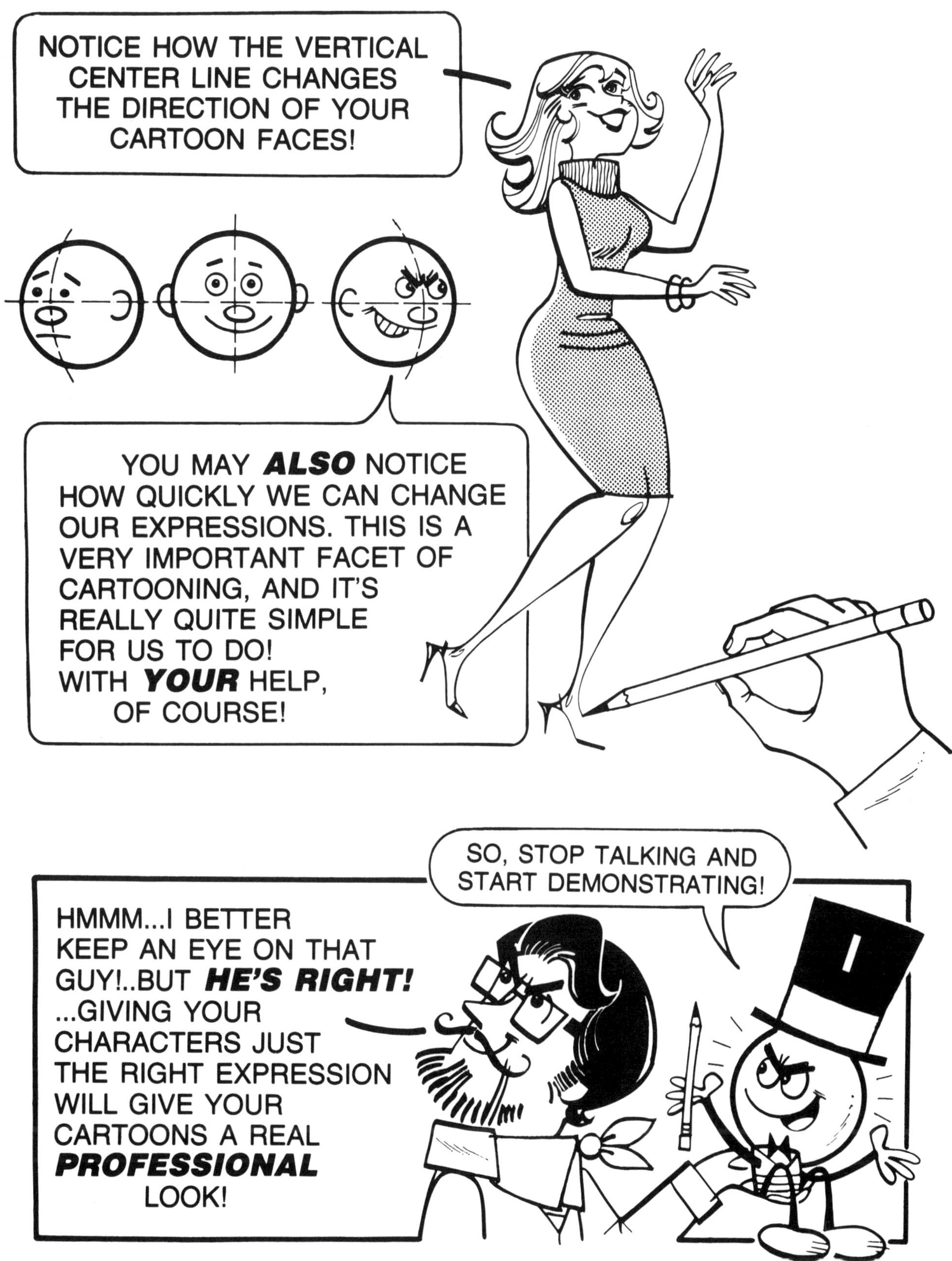
NOTICE HOW THE VERTICAL CENTER LINE CHANGES THE DIRECTION OF YOUR CARTOON FACES!
YOU MAY ***ALSO*** NOTICE HOW QUICKLY WE CAN CHANGE OUR EXPRESSIONS. THIS IS A VERY IMPORTANT FACET OF CARTOONING, AND IT'S REALLY QUITE SIMPLE FOR US TO DO! WITH ***YOUR*** HELP, OF COURSE!
SO, STOP TALKING AND START DEMONSTRATING!
HMMM...I BETTER KEEP AN EYE ON THAT GUY!..BUT ***HE'S RIGHT!*** ...GIVING YOUR CHARACTERS JUST THE RIGHT EXPRESSION WILL GIVE YOUR CARTOONS A REAL ***PROFESSIONAL*** LOOK!

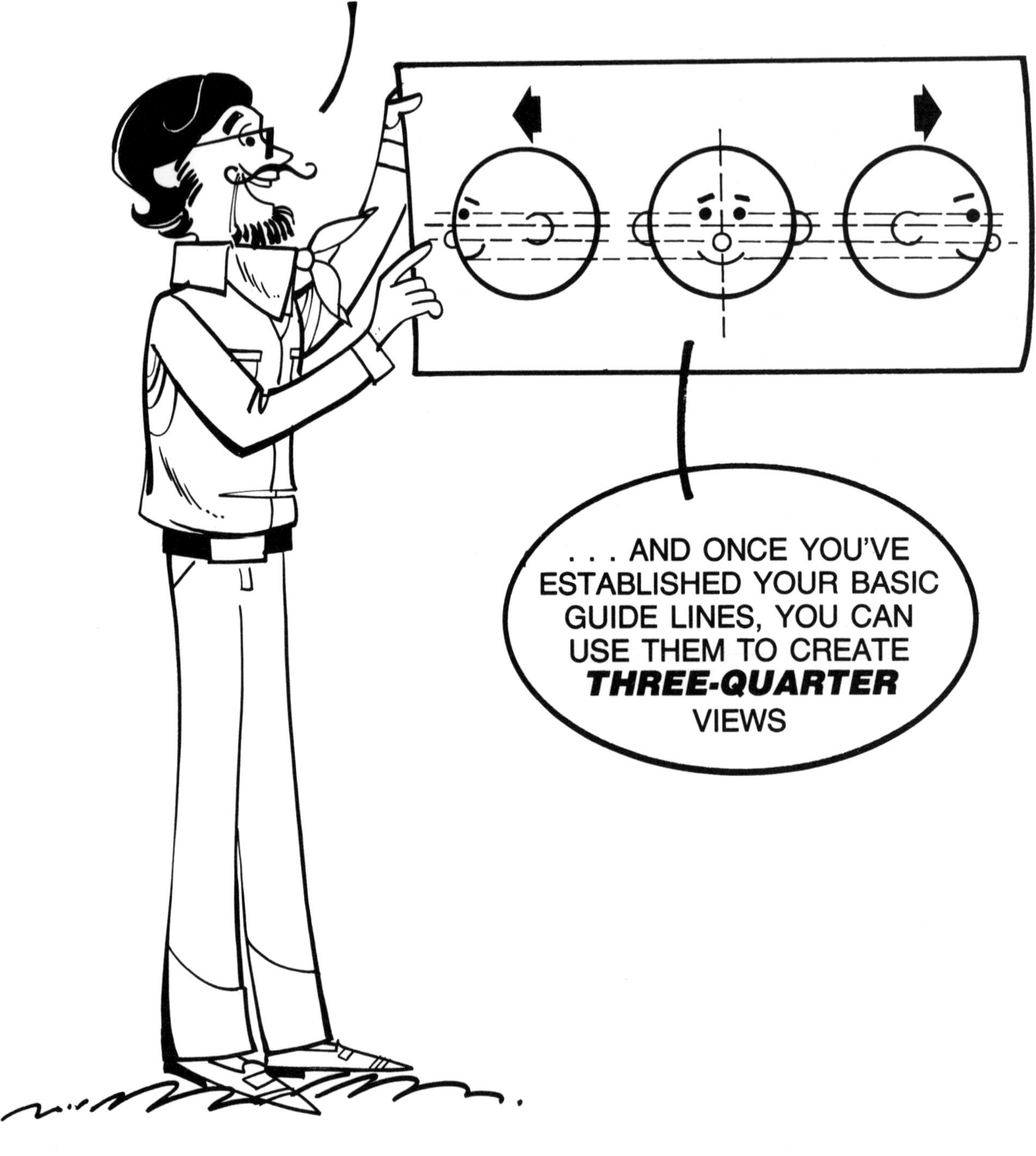
O.K.! O.K.! WATCH THIS! NOTICE HOW THESE FEATURES THAT WE'VE JUST DISCUSSED REMAIN IN THE SAME PLACE, REGARDLESS OF THE DIRECTION OUR CARTOON CHARACTER DECIDES TO TURN HIS HEAD...
. . . AND ONCE YOU'VE ESTABLISHED YOUR BASIC GUIDE LINES, YOU CAN USE THEM TO CREATE ***THREE-QUARTER*** VIEWS

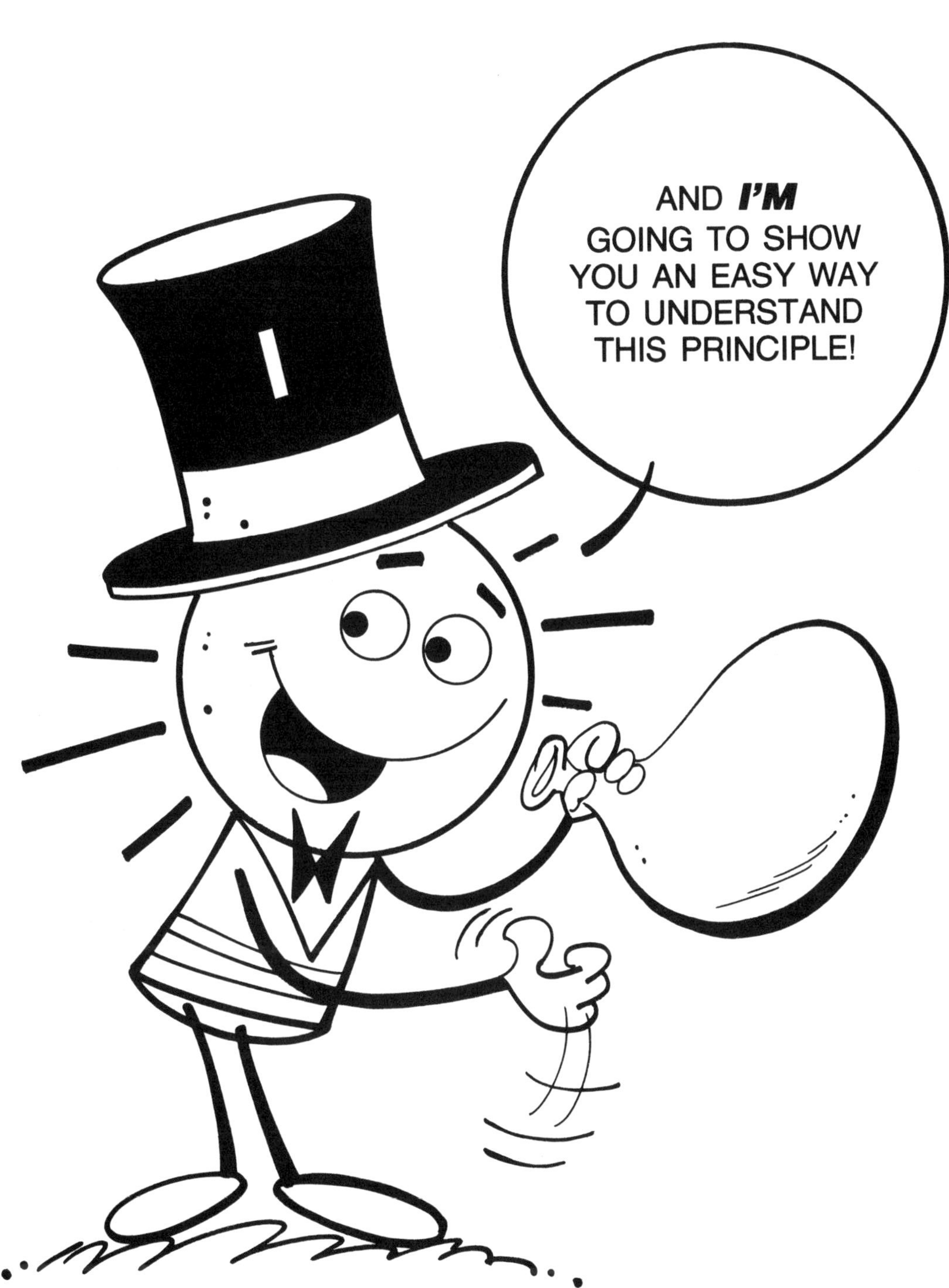
AND ***I'M*** GOING TO SHOW YOU AN EASY WAY TO UNDERSTAND THIS PRINCIPLE!

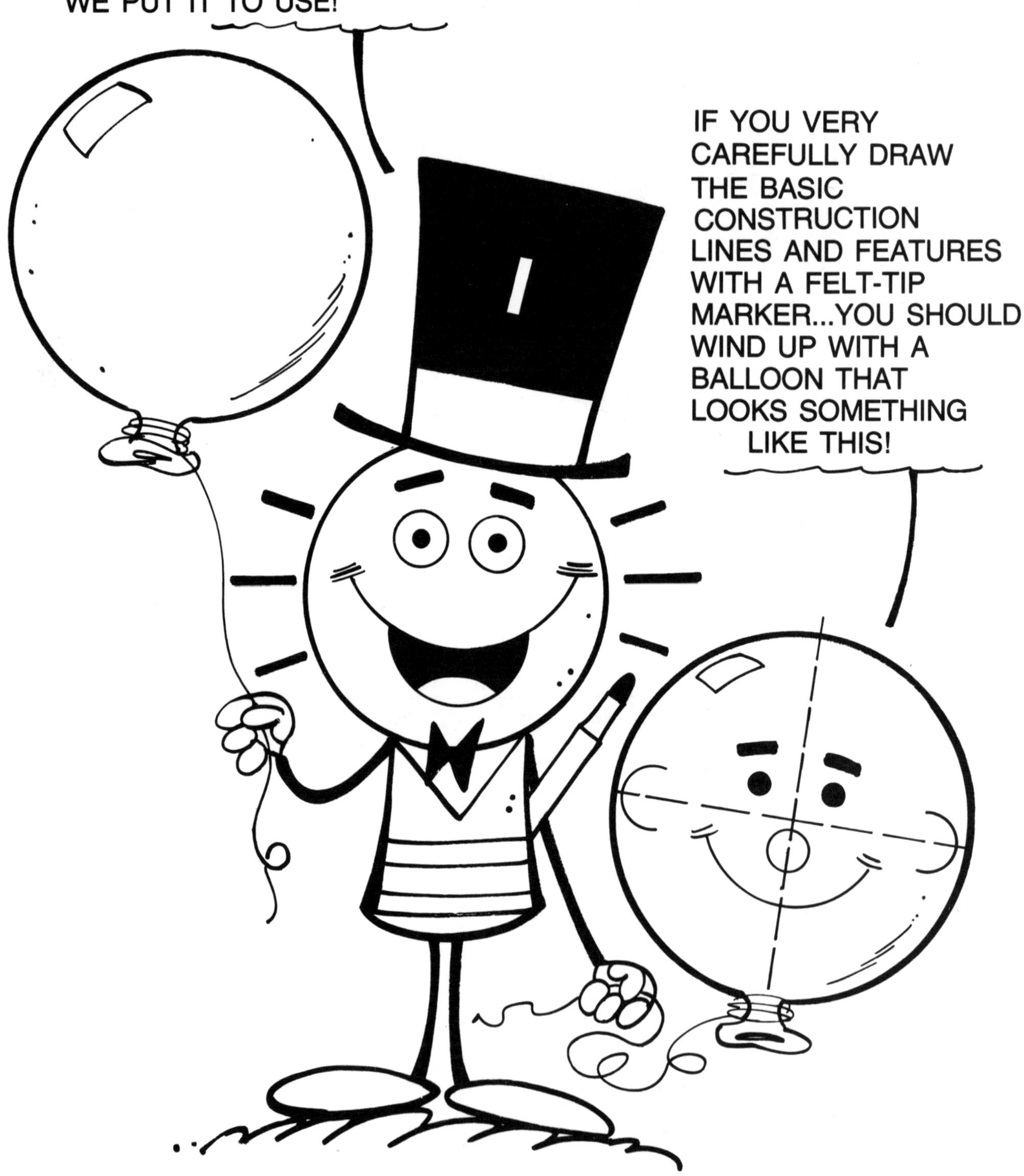
REMEMBER THAT BALLOON WE DISCUSSED A FEW PAGES AGO...WELL, HERE'S WHERE WE PUT IT TO USE!
IF YOU VERY CAREFULLY DRAW THE BASIC CONSTRUCTION LINES AND FEATURES WITH A FELT-TIP MARKER...YOU SHOULD WIND UP WITH A BALLOON THAT LOOKS SOMETHING LIKE THIS!

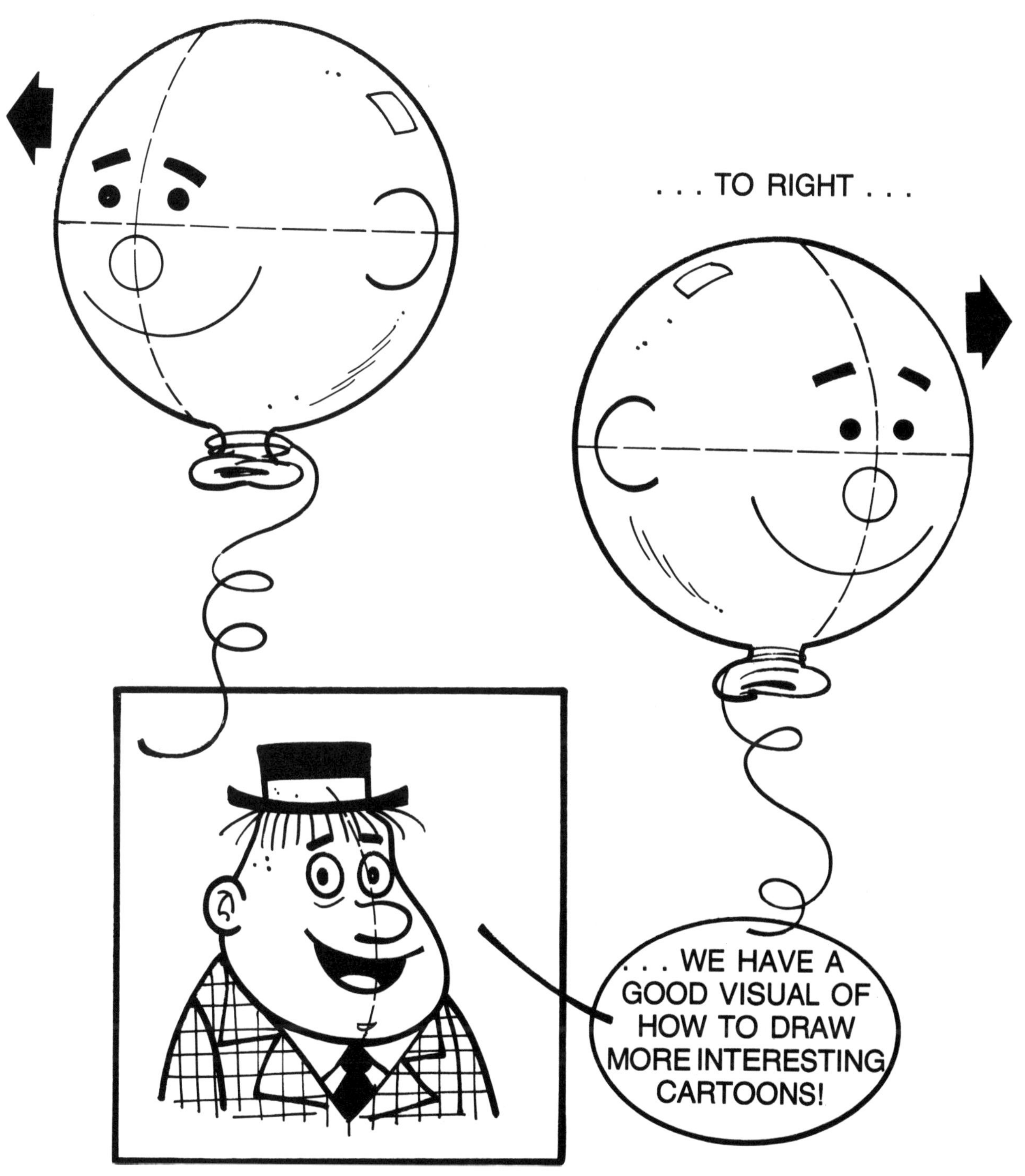
BY WATCHING
WHAT HAPPENS
WHEN WE TURN
OUR FRIEND
FROM LEFT . . .
. . . TO RIGHT . . .
. . . WE HAVE A
GOOD VISUAL OF
HOW TO DRAW
MORE INTERESTING
CARTOONS!

THIS SEEMS LIKE A GOOD TIME TO PUT ALL THIS INFORMATION TO PRACTICAL USE . . .

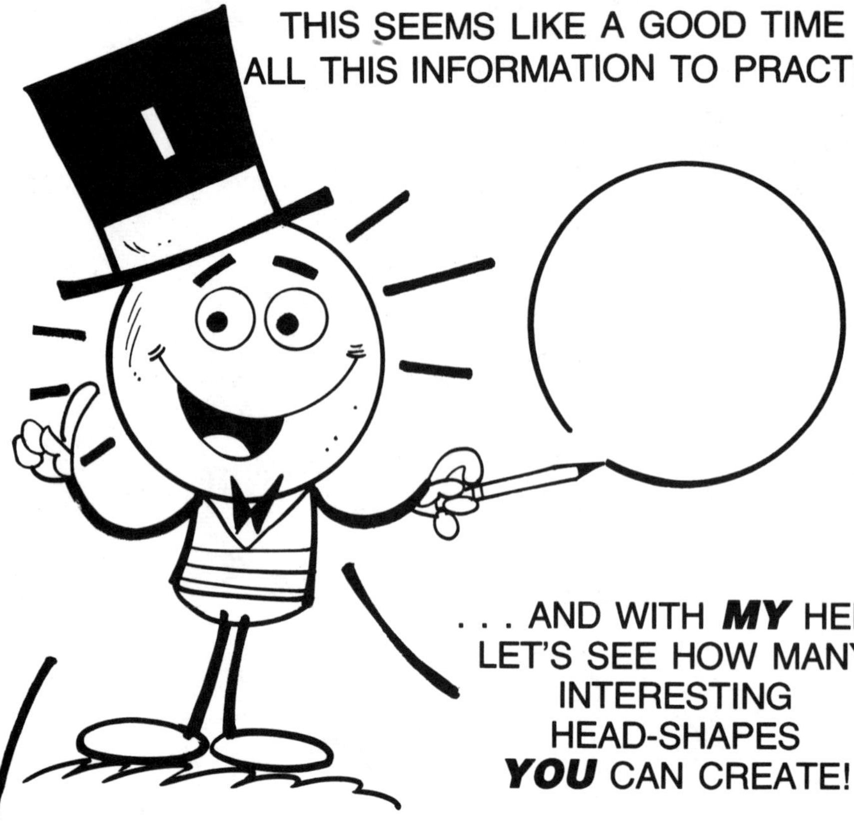

. . . AND WITH ***MY*** HELP LET'S SEE HOW MANY INTERESTING HEAD-SHAPES ***YOU*** CAN CREATE!

TRY TO ***IMAGINE*** THAT OUR CIRCLE IS VERY SOFT AND PLIABLE AND CAN BE PUSHED AND PULLED INTO ALL SORTS OF SHAPES. FOR INSTANCE:

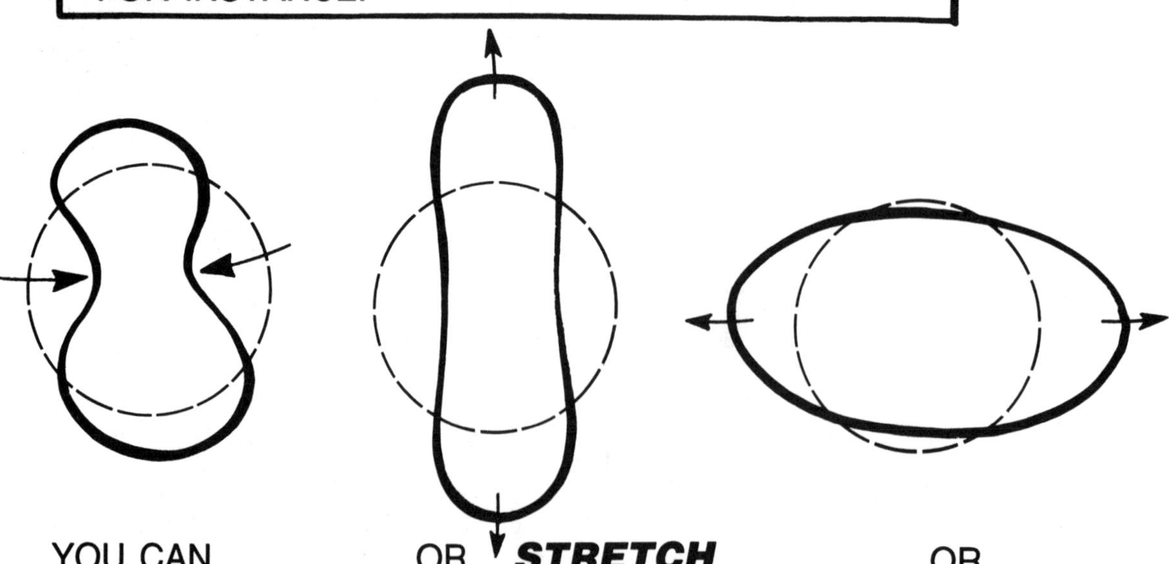

YOU CAN ***SCRUNCH*** IT . . .

. . . OR ***STRETCH*** IT ***THIS*** WAY . . .

. . . OR ***THAT*** WAY!

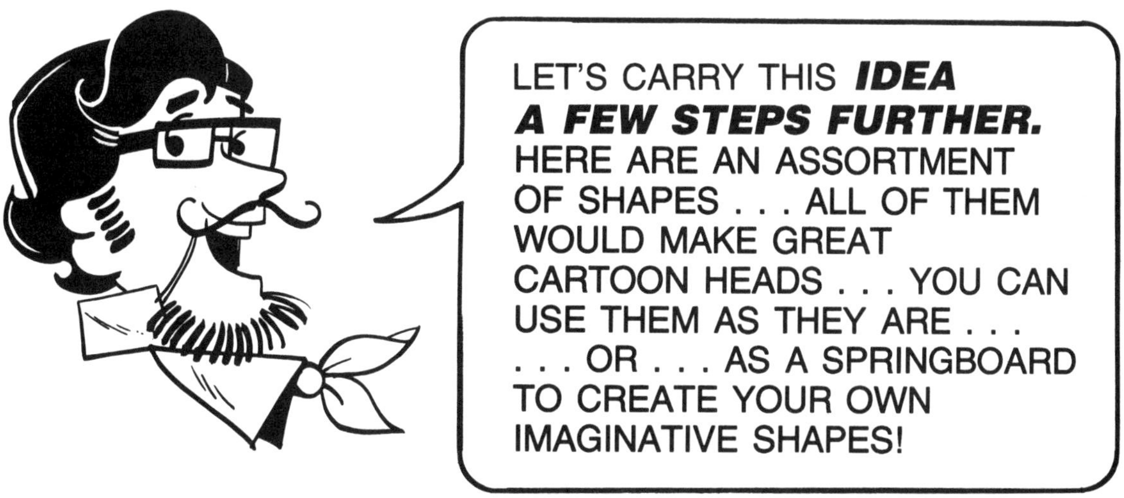

LET'S CARRY THIS ***IDEA***
A FEW STEPS FURTHER.
HERE ARE AN ASSORTMENT OF SHAPES . . . ALL OF THEM WOULD MAKE GREAT CARTOON HEADS . . . YOU CAN USE THEM AS THEY ARE . . .
. . . OR . . . AS A SPRINGBOARD TO CREATE YOUR OWN IMAGINATIVE SHAPES!

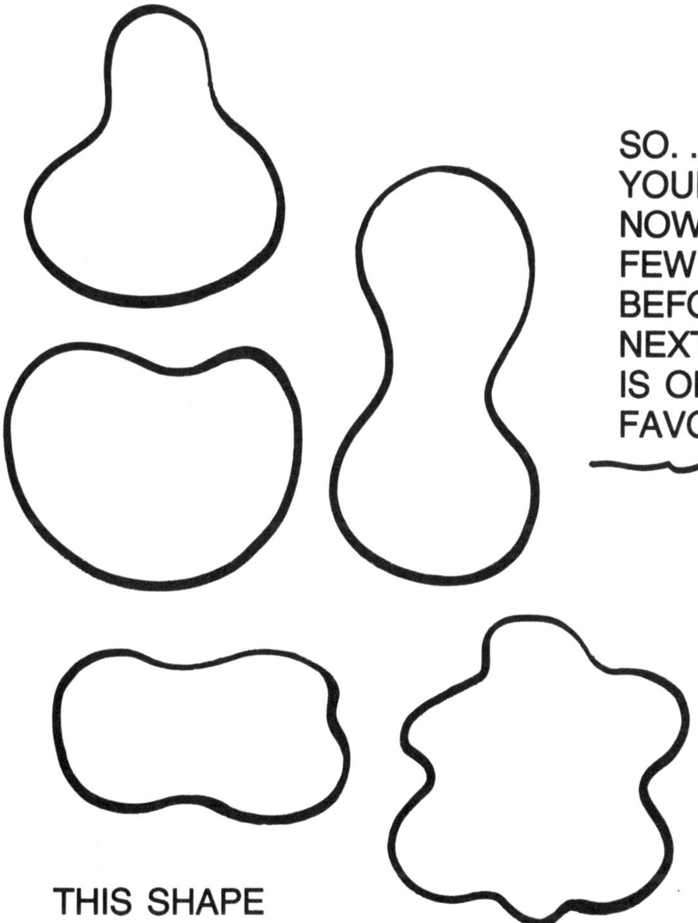

SO. . . HOW'S ABOUT EXERCISING YOUR CREATIVITY RIGHT NOW BY DESIGNING A FEW PERSONAL SHAPES BEFORE MOVING ON TO THE NEXT PAGE . . . WHICH IS ONE OF MY FAVORITES!

THIS SHAPE WOULD MAKE A FINE-LOOKING MONSTER

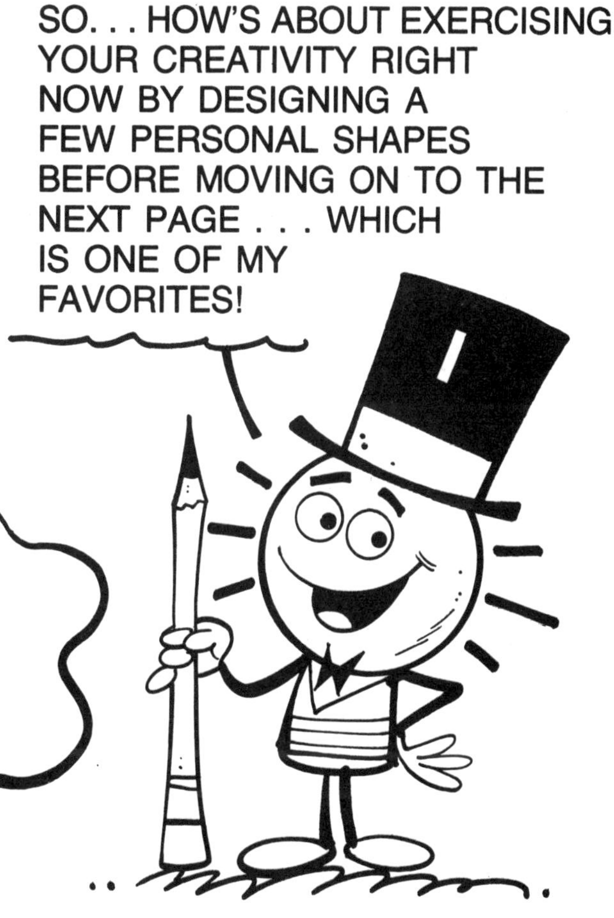

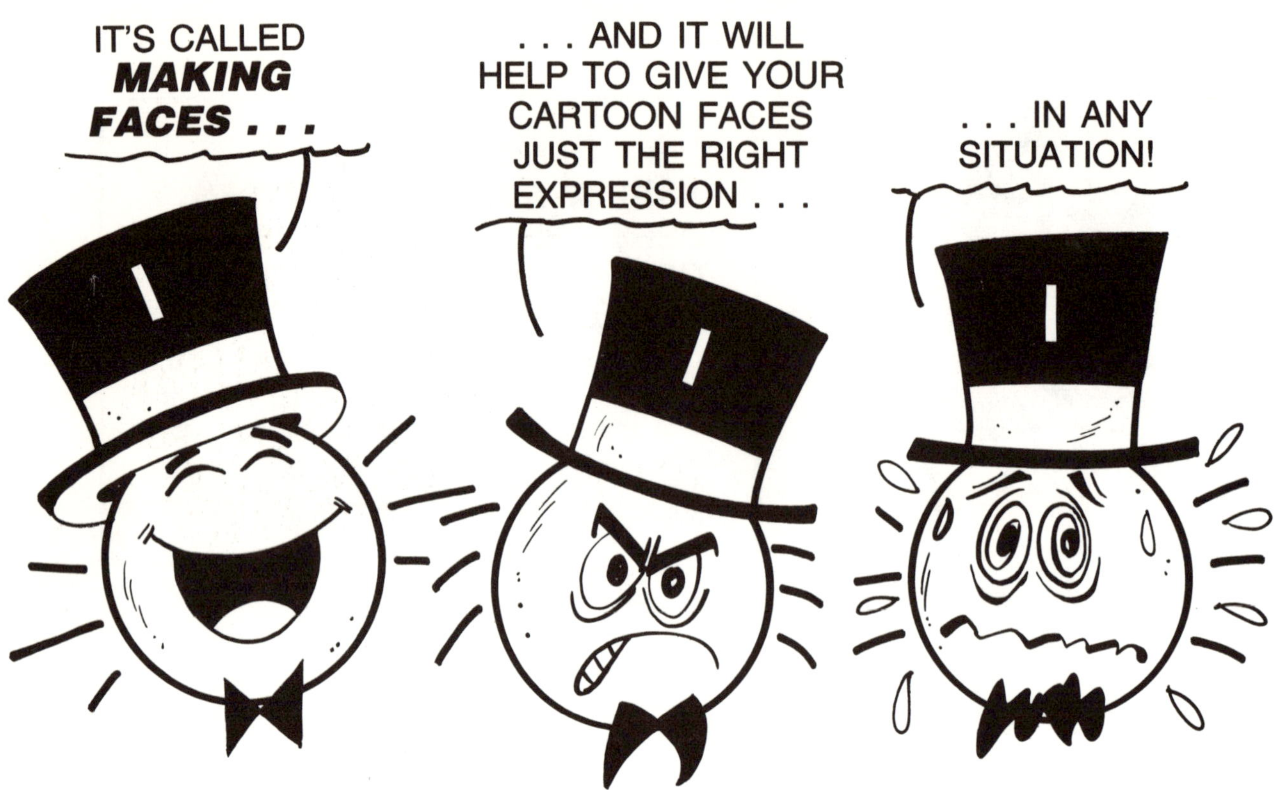
IT'S CALLED
MAKING
FACES . . .
. . . AND IT WILL
HELP TO GIVE YOUR
CARTOON FACES
JUST THE RIGHT
EXPRESSION . . .
. . . IN ANY
SITUATION!

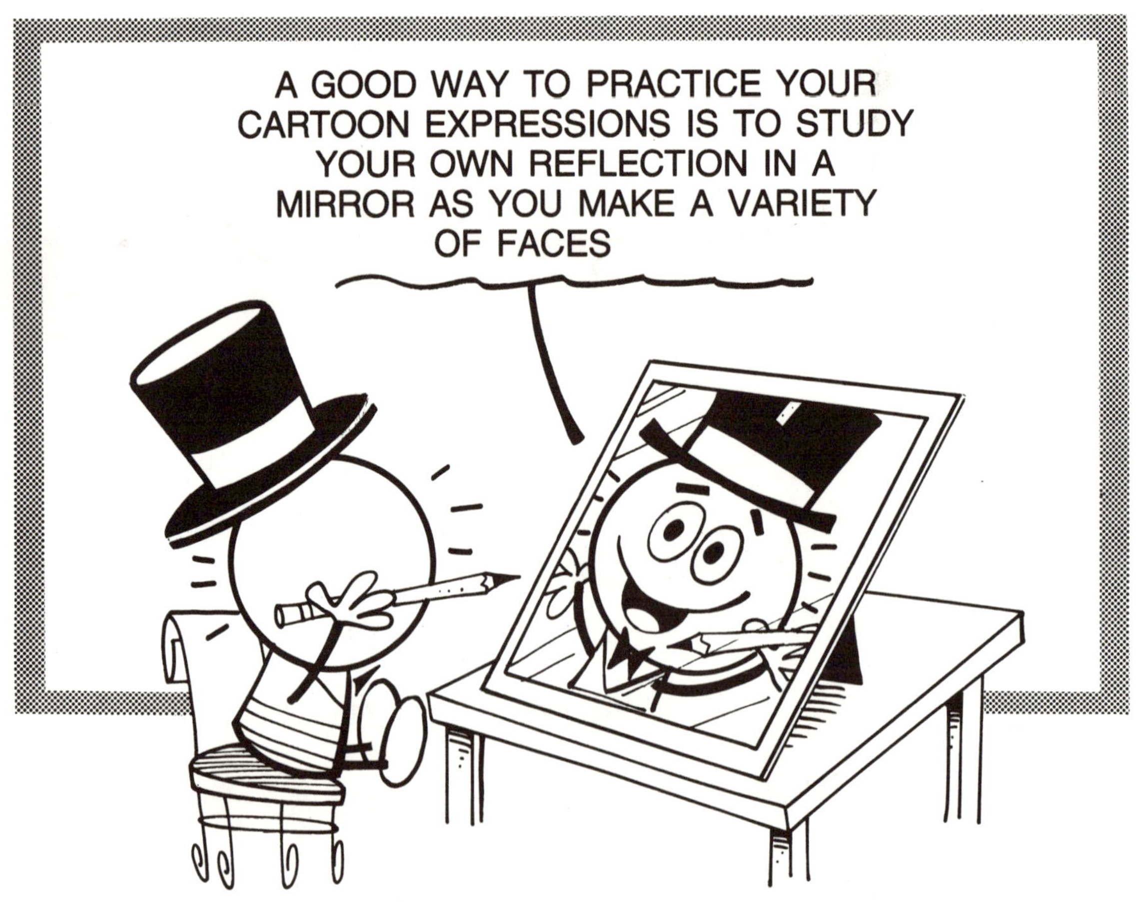
A GOOD WAY TO PRACTICE YOUR
CARTOON EXPRESSIONS IS TO STUDY
YOUR OWN REFLECTION IN A
MIRROR AS YOU MAKE A VARIETY
OF FACES

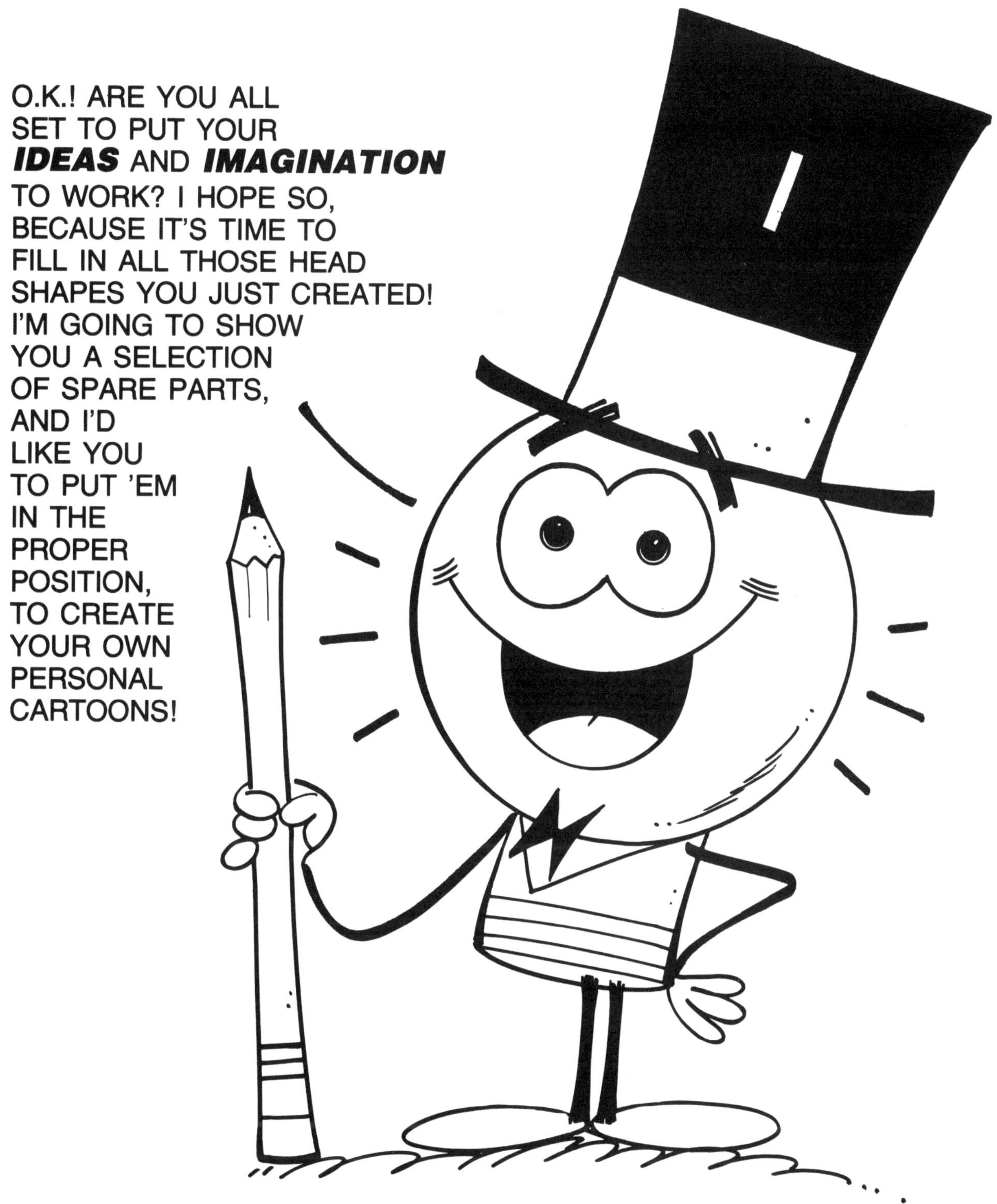
O.K.! ARE YOU ALL SET TO PUT YOUR ***IDEAS*** AND ***IMAGINATION*** TO WORK? I HOPE SO, BECAUSE IT'S TIME TO FILL IN ALL THOSE HEAD SHAPES YOU JUST CREATED! I'M GOING TO SHOW YOU A SELECTION OF SPARE PARTS, AND I'D LIKE YOU TO PUT 'EM IN THE PROPER POSITION, TO CREATE YOUR OWN PERSONAL CARTOONS!

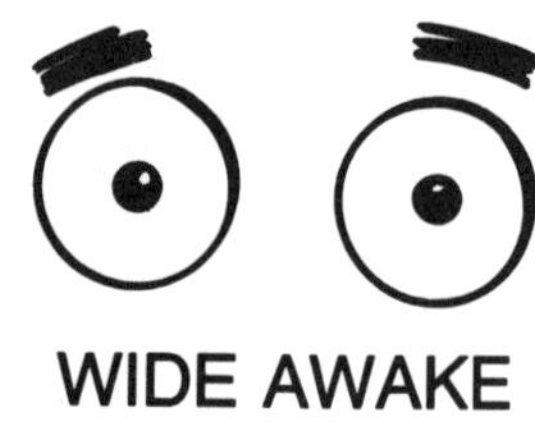

WIDE AWAKE

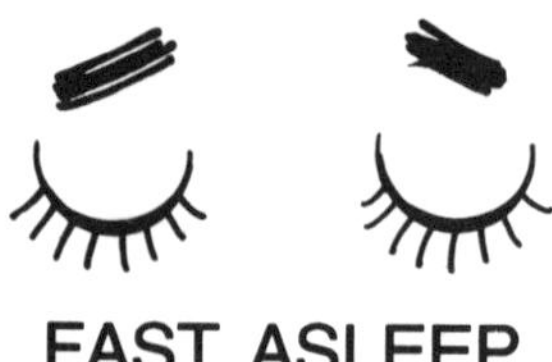

FAST ASLEEP

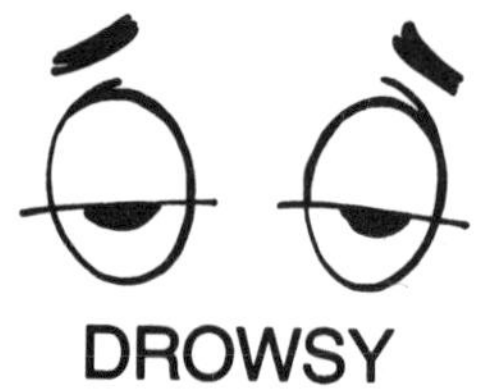

DROWSY

HAPPY

LET'S BEGIN WITH

EYES!

MOST OF US USUALLY HAVE TWO AND BY NOW YOU SHOULD KNOW EXACTLY WHERE TO PLACE THEM! PERHAPS ***YOU*** CAN CREATE A FEW OF YOUR OWN!

ANGRY

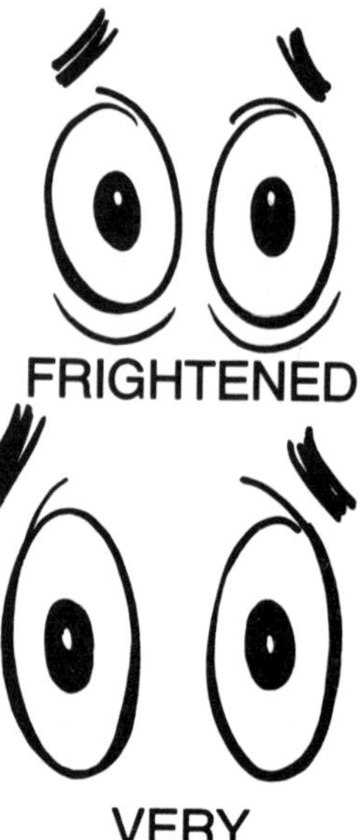

FRIGHTENED

VERY FRIGHTENED

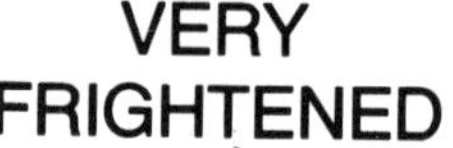

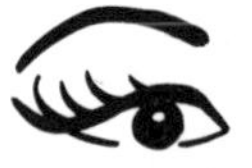

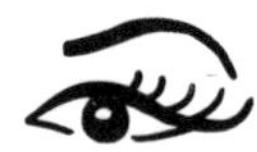

SEXY

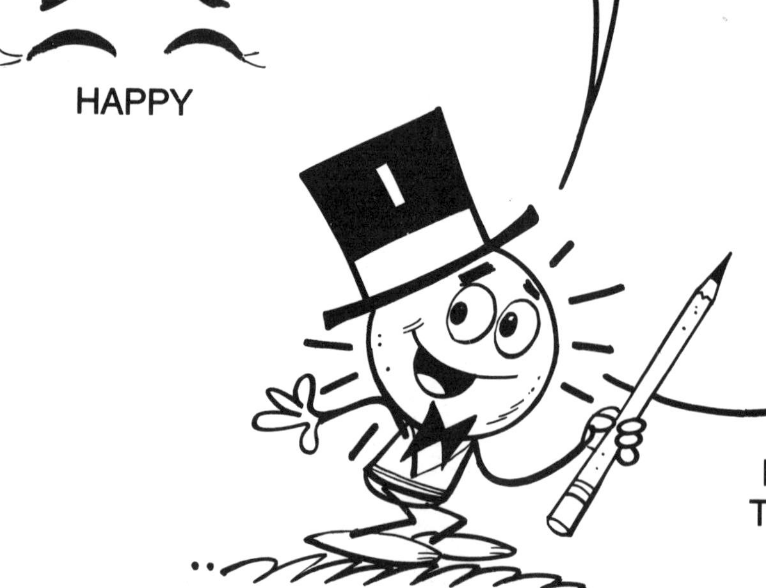

NOTICE HOW IMPORTANT EYEBROWS ARE IN SHOWING EXPRESSION! PRACTICE SOME OF THESE EYES BEFORE MOVING ON TO . . .

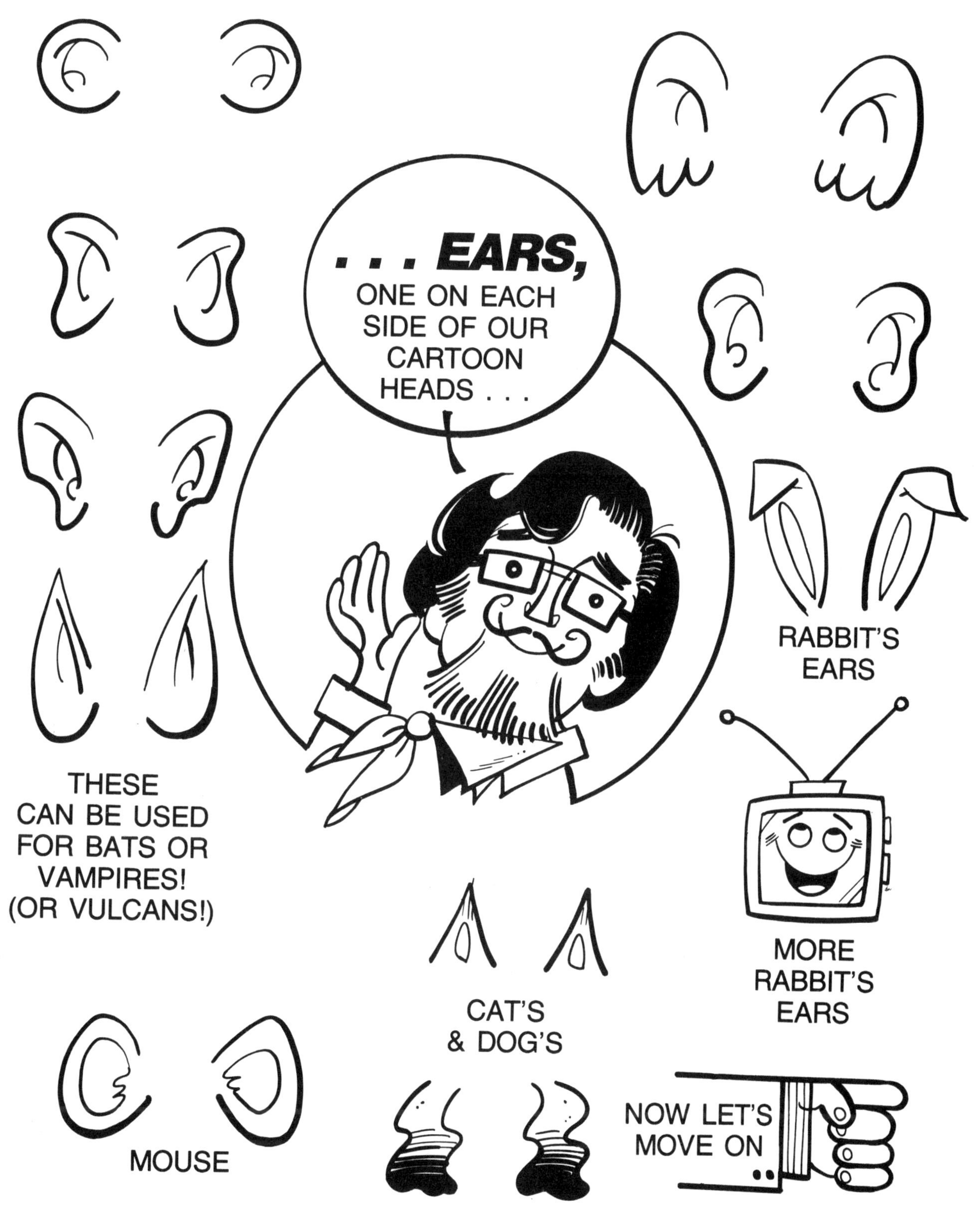
. . . EARS,
ONE ON EACH SIDE OF OUR CARTOON HEADS . . .
RABBIT'S EARS
THESE CAN BE USED FOR BATS OR VAMPIRES! (OR VULCANS!)
MORE RABBIT'S EARS
CAT'S & DOG'S
MOUSE
NOW LET'S MOVE ON . .

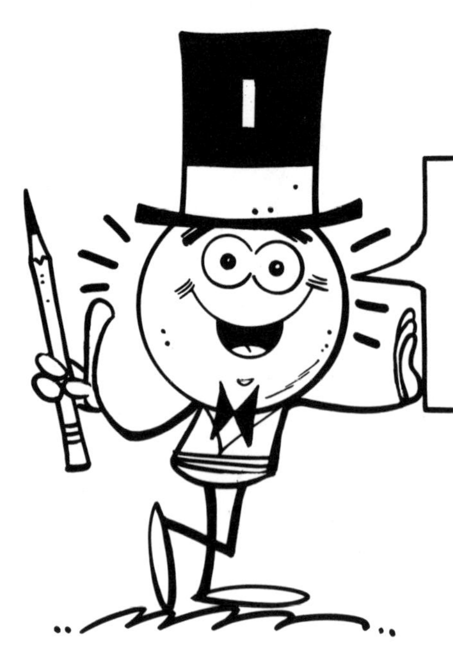

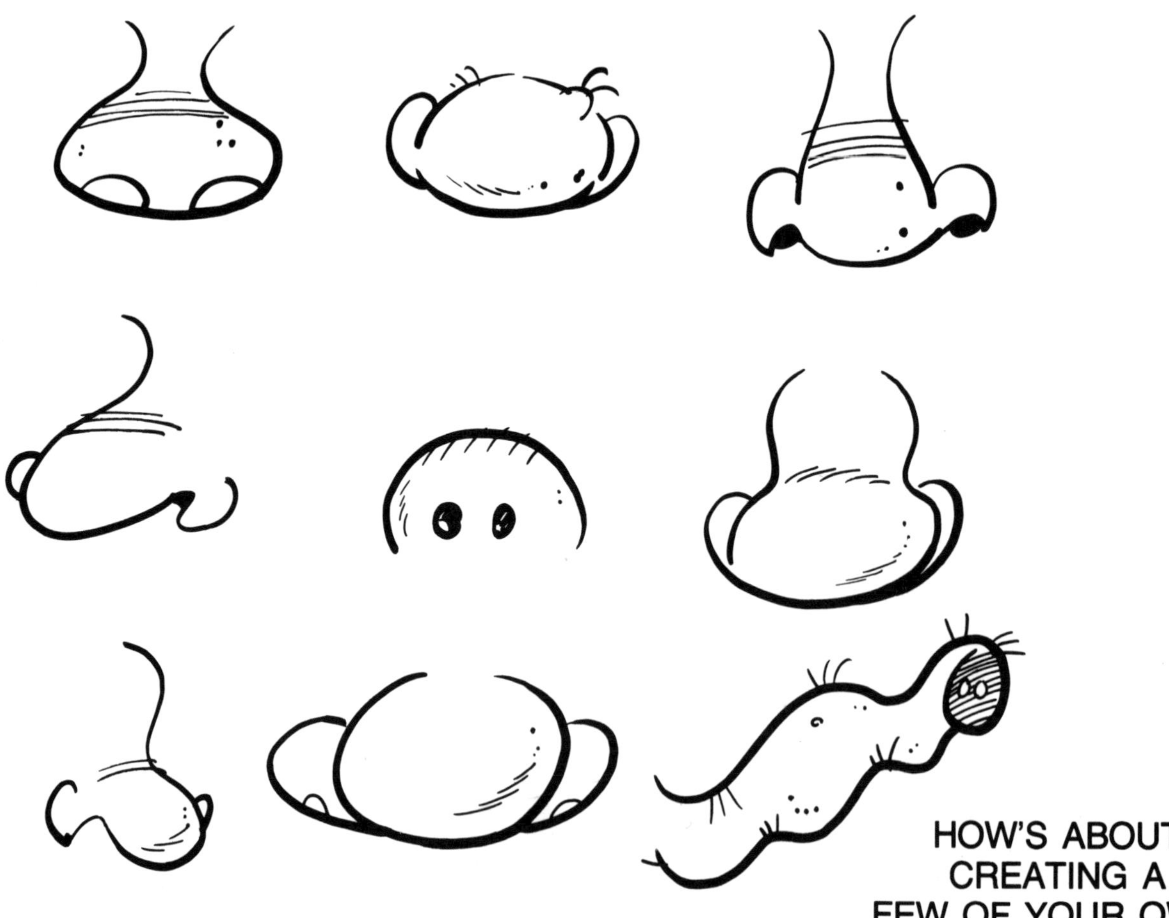

HOW'S ABOUT
CREATING A
FEW OF YOUR OWN?

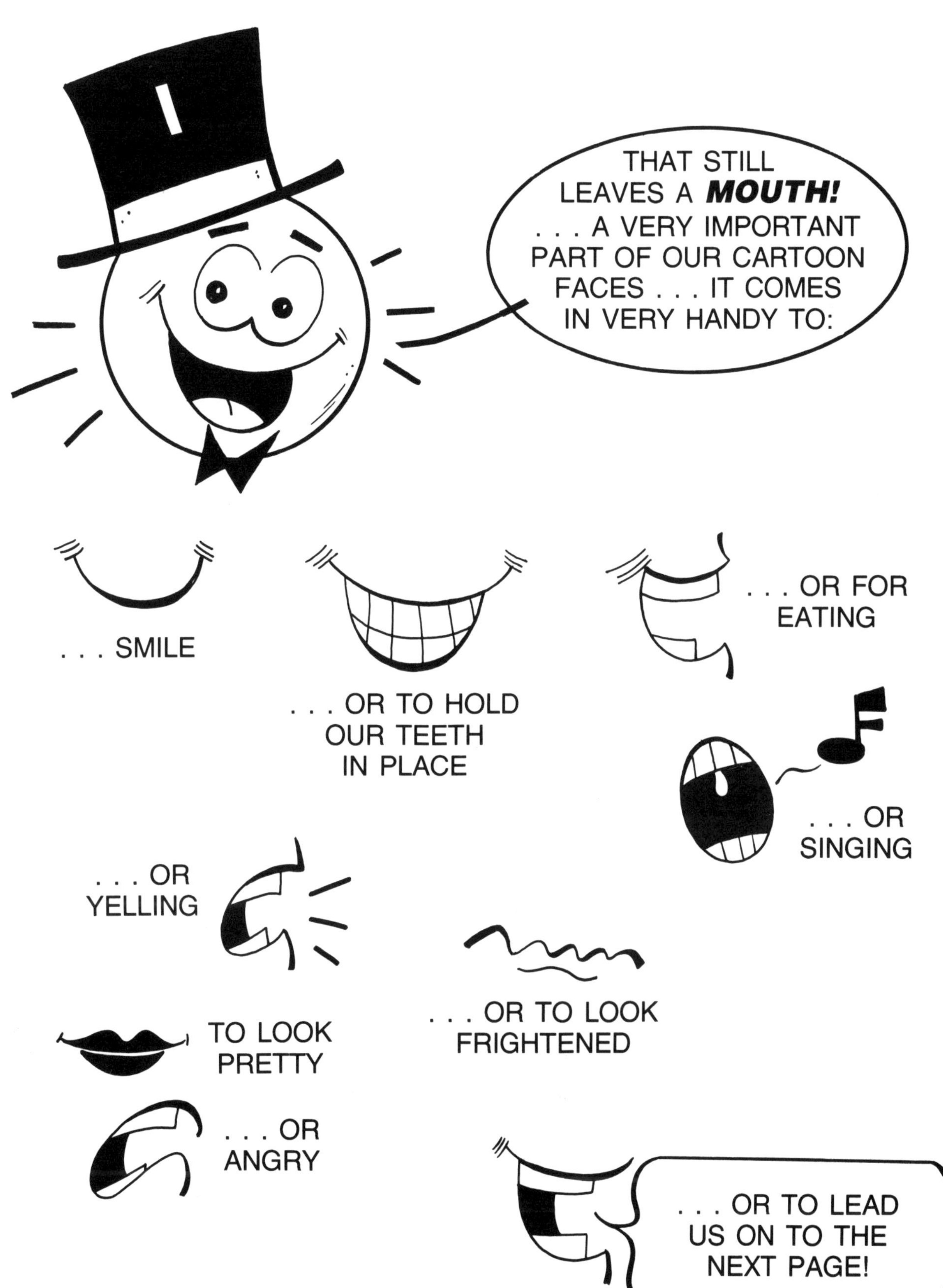
THAT STILL LEAVES A ***MOUTH!*** . . . A VERY IMPORTANT PART OF OUR CARTOON FACES . . . IT COMES IN VERY HANDY TO:
. . . SMILE
. . . OR TO HOLD OUR TEETH IN PLACE
. . . OR FOR EATING
. . . OR SINGING
. . . OR YELLING
. . . OR TO LOOK FRIGHTENED
TO LOOK PRETTY
. . . OR ANGRY
. . . OR TO LEAD US ON TO THE NEXT PAGE!

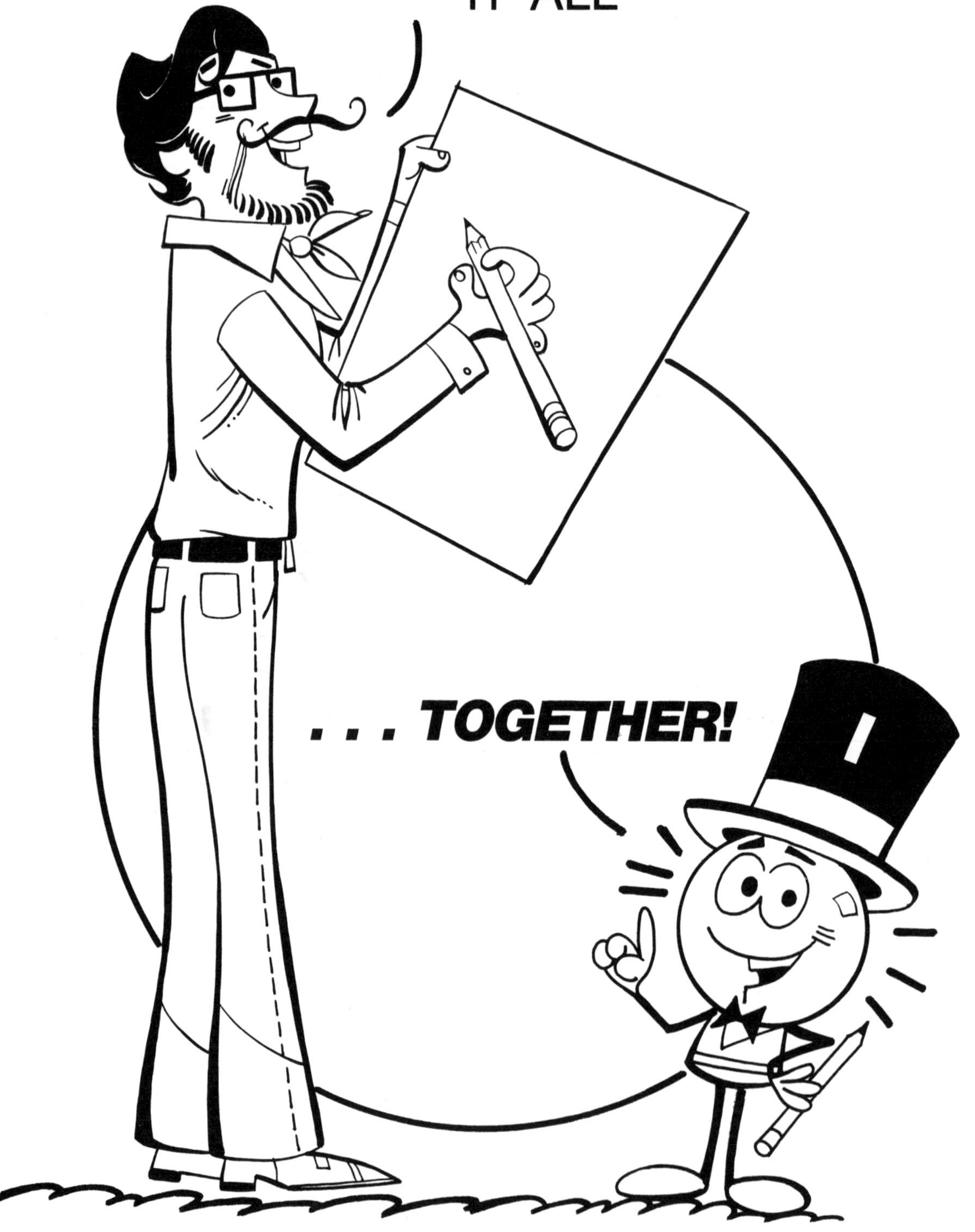
NOW. . . LET'S PUT
IT ALL
. . . TOGETHER!

REMEMBER THOSE HEAD SHAPES A FEW PAGES BACK, WELL, IF WE ADD ON A VARIETY OF FEATURES THEY MIGHT LOOK SOMETHING LIKE THIS:

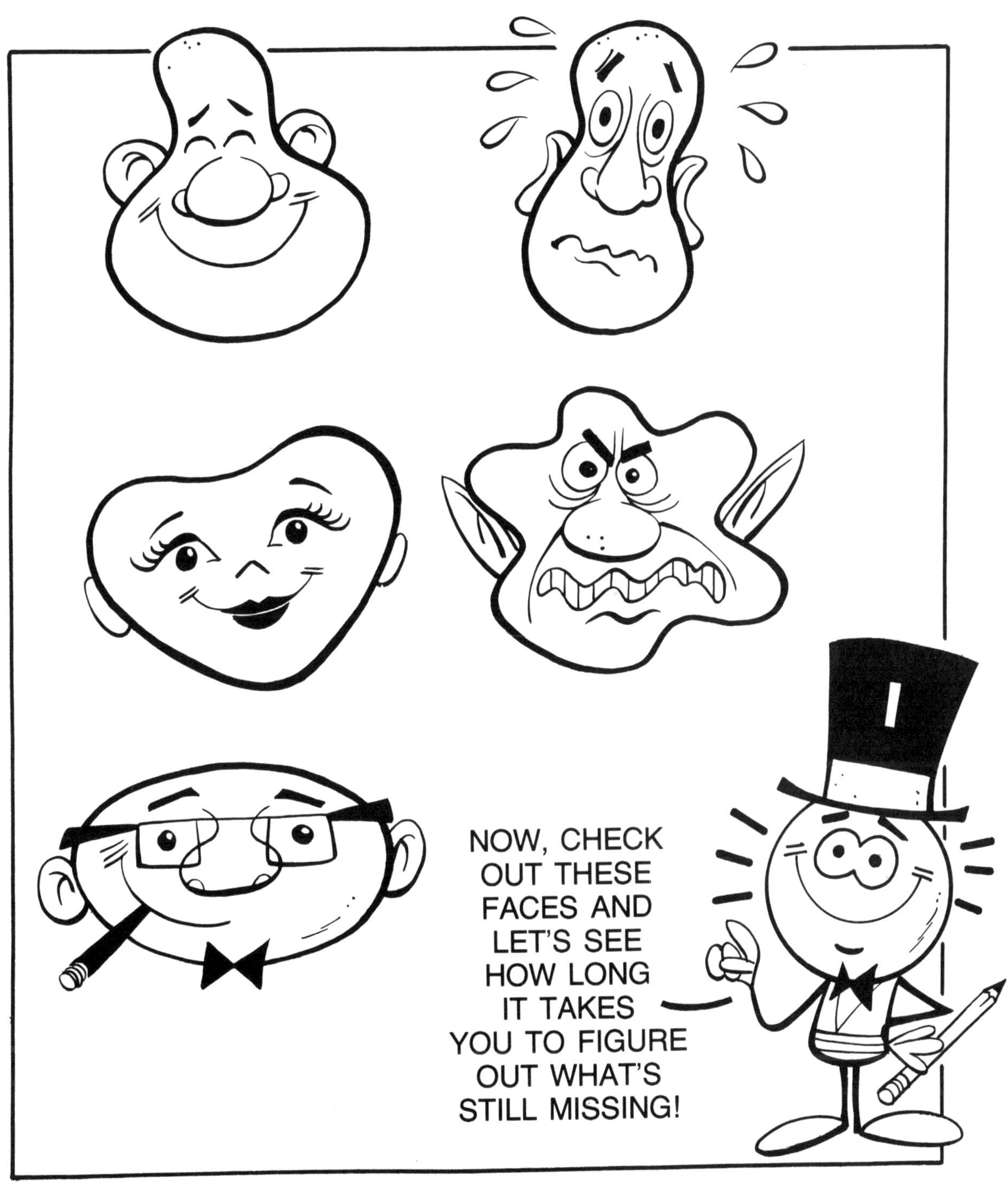

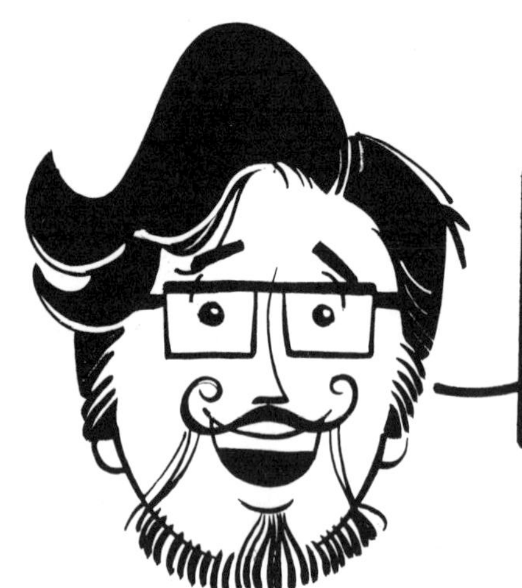

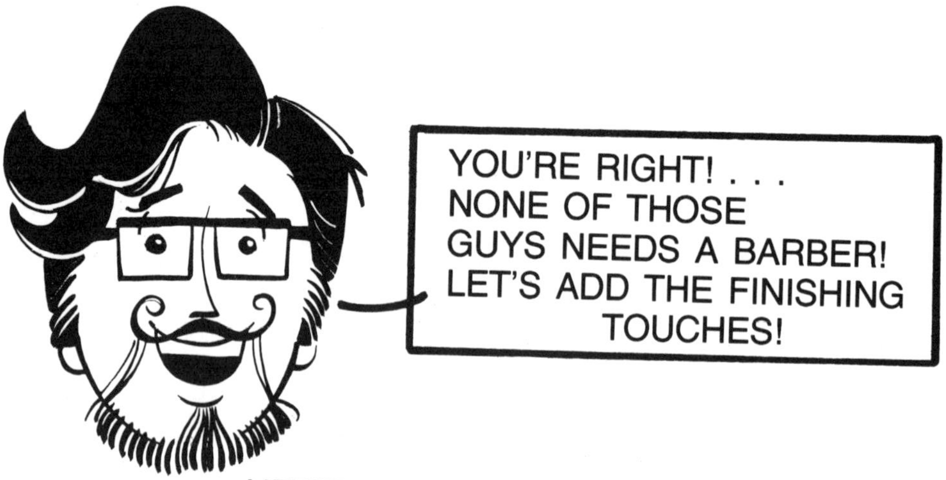

HERE ARE SOME HAIRDOS TO INSPIRE YOU!

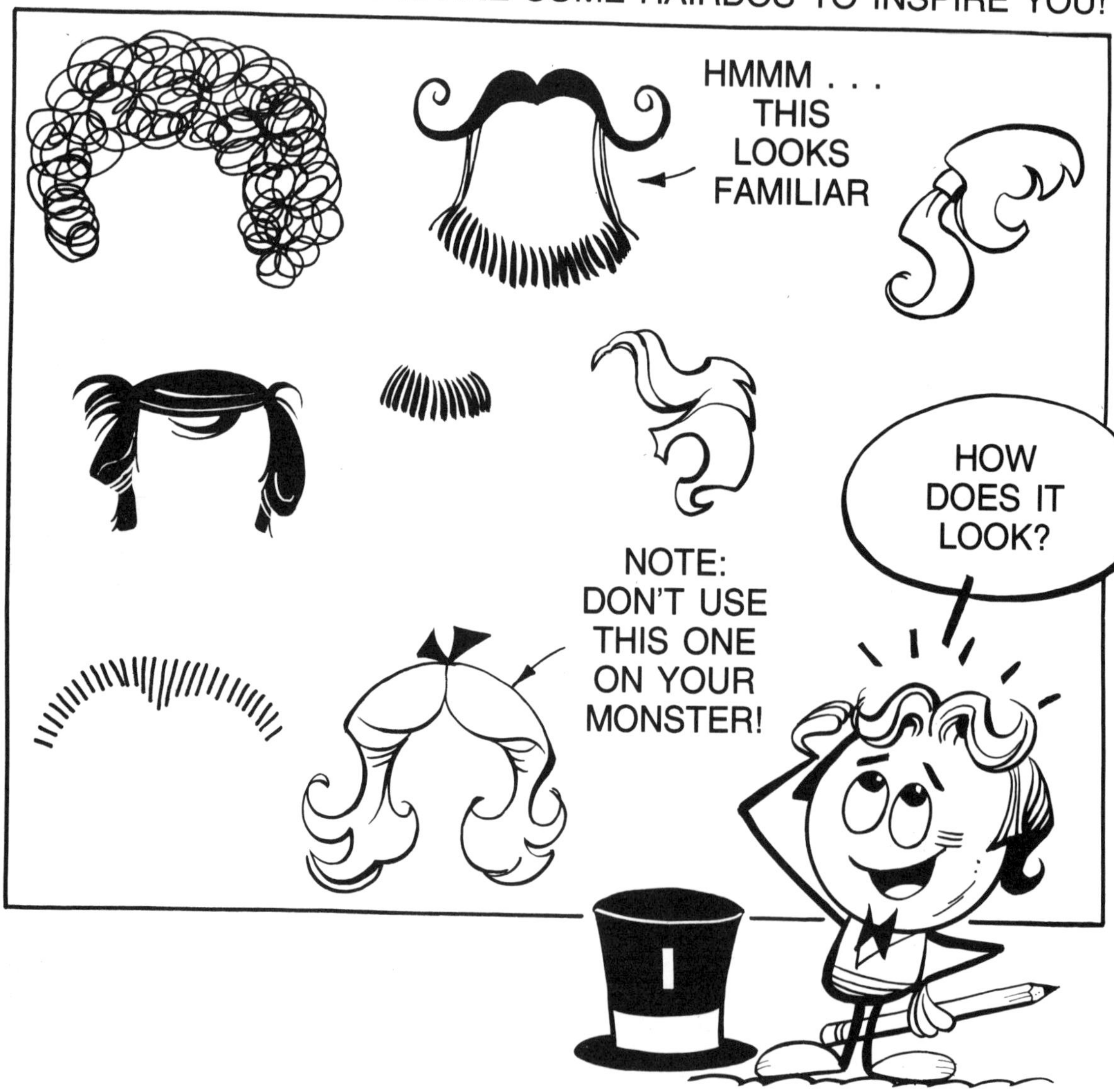

HMMM . . .
THIS
LOOKS
FAMILIAR

HOW
DOES IT
LOOK?

NOTE:
DON'T USE
THIS ONE
ON YOUR
MONSTER!

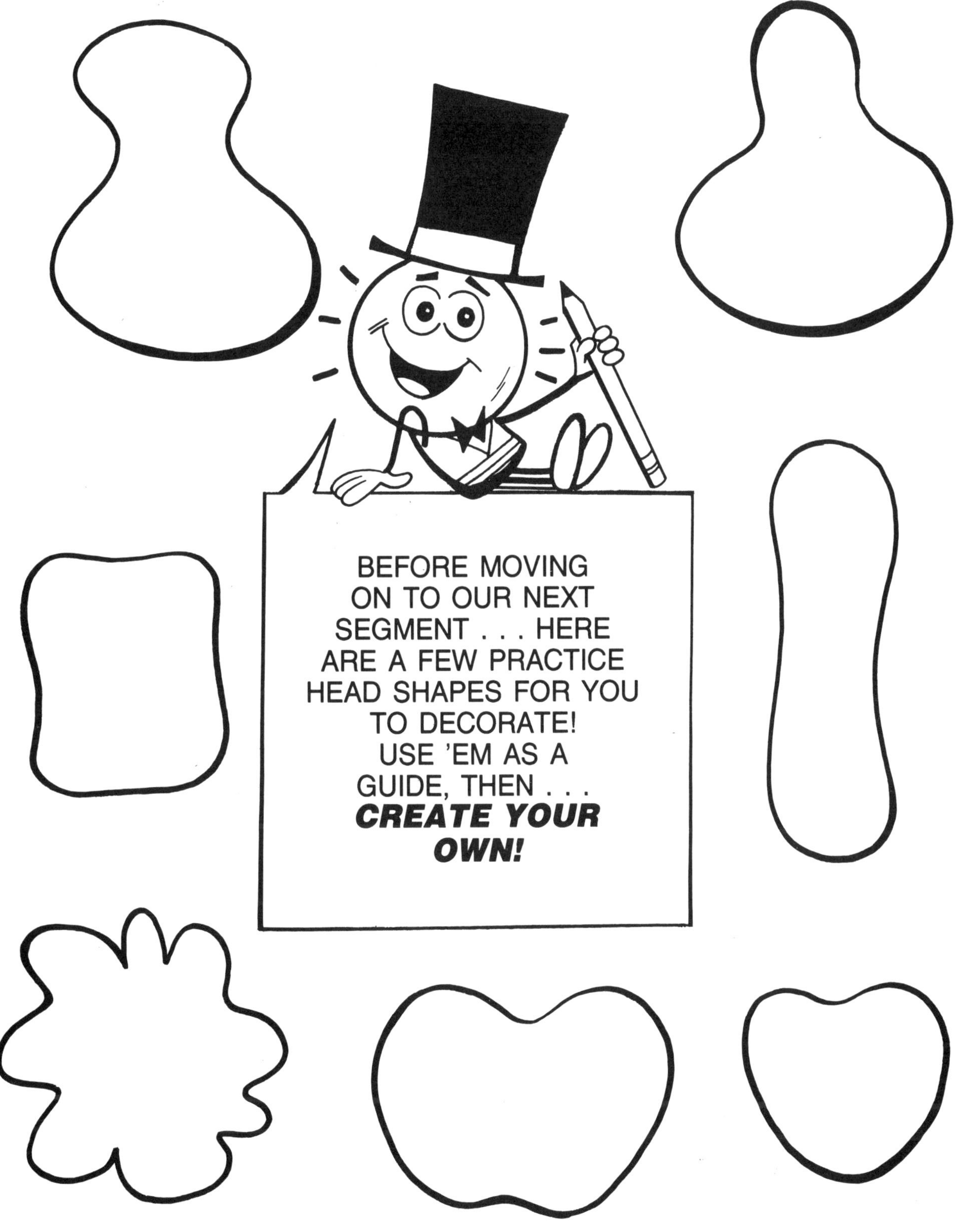
BEFORE MOVING
ON TO OUR NEXT
SEGMENT . . . HERE
ARE A FEW PRACTICE
HEAD SHAPES FOR YOU
TO DECORATE!
USE 'EM AS A
GUIDE, THEN . . .
CREATE YOUR
OWN!

WELL . . . WE NOW
KNOW HOW TO DRAW
HEADS AND FACES
. . . CAN YOU GUESS
WHAT'S NEXT?

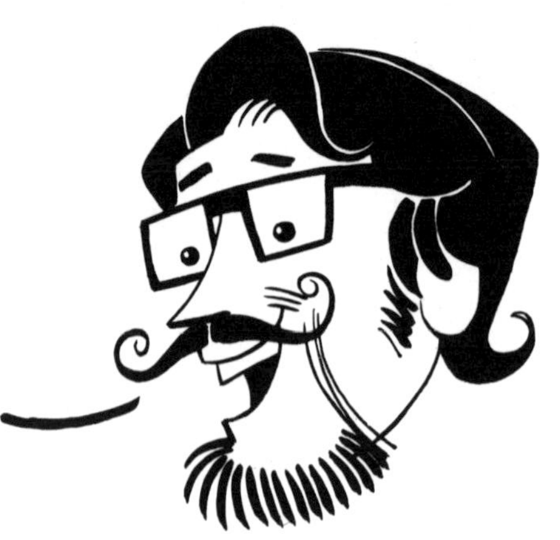

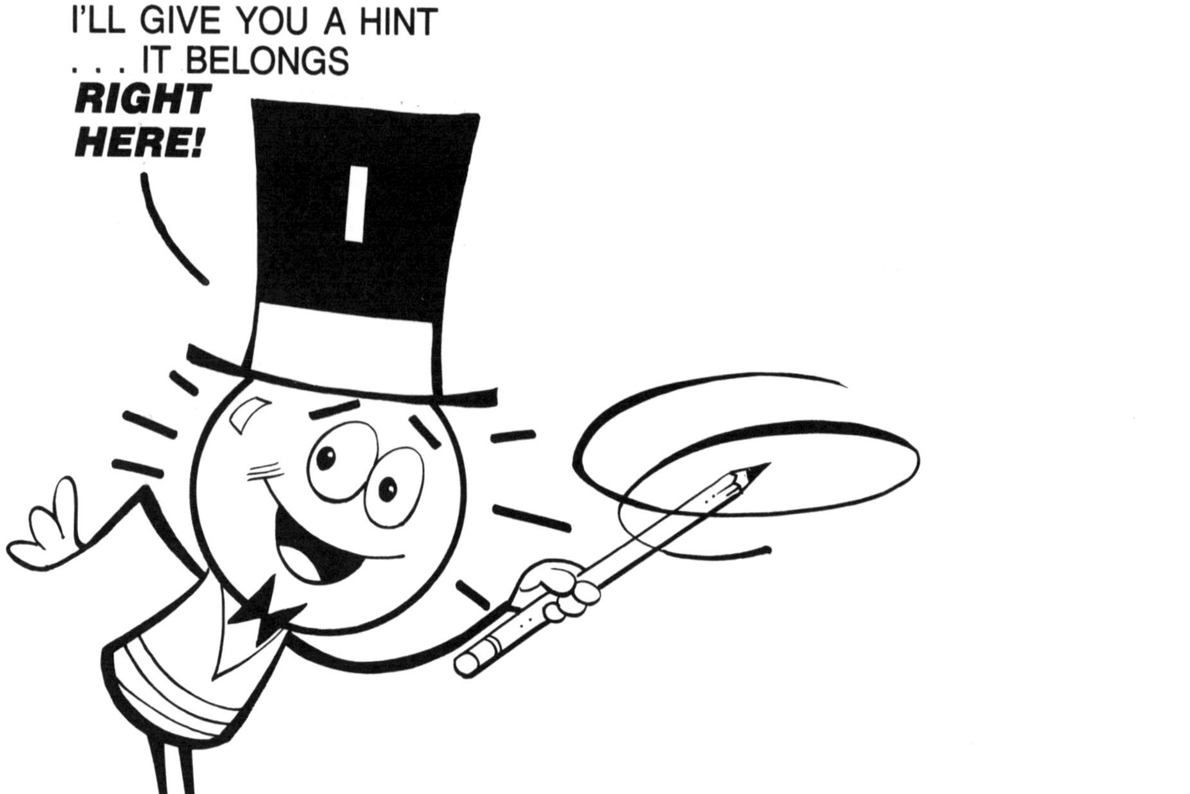

I'LL GIVE YOU A HINT
. . . IT BELONGS
RIGHT HERE!

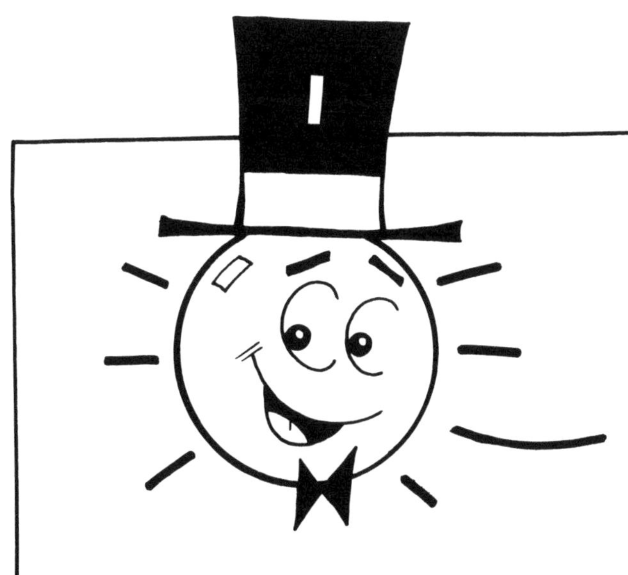

A PERFECT PLACE
FOR YOU TO REST
YOUR CARTOON HEAD IS
ON A ***CARTOON BODY.***
BODIES CAN BE CONSTRUCTED
JUST LIKE OUR HEADS,
ONLY . . . MAKE 'EM
LARGER!

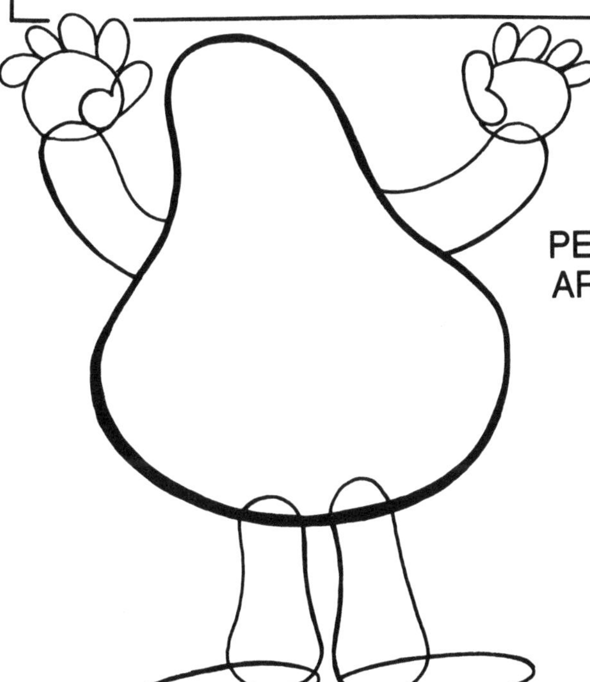

PEAR SHAPES
ARE O.K. FOR
CERTAIN
TYPES.

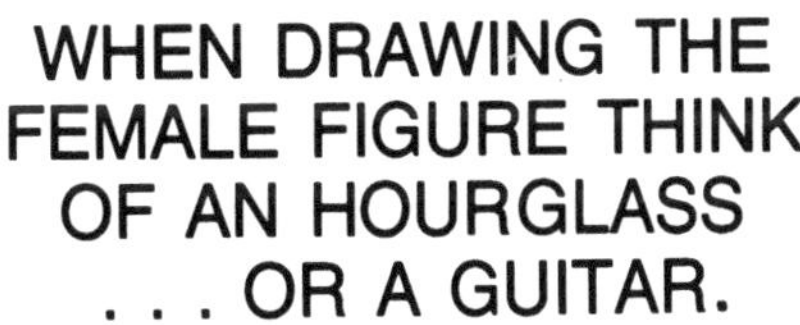

WHEN DRAWING THE
FEMALE FIGURE THINK
OF AN HOURGLASS
. . . OR A GUITAR.

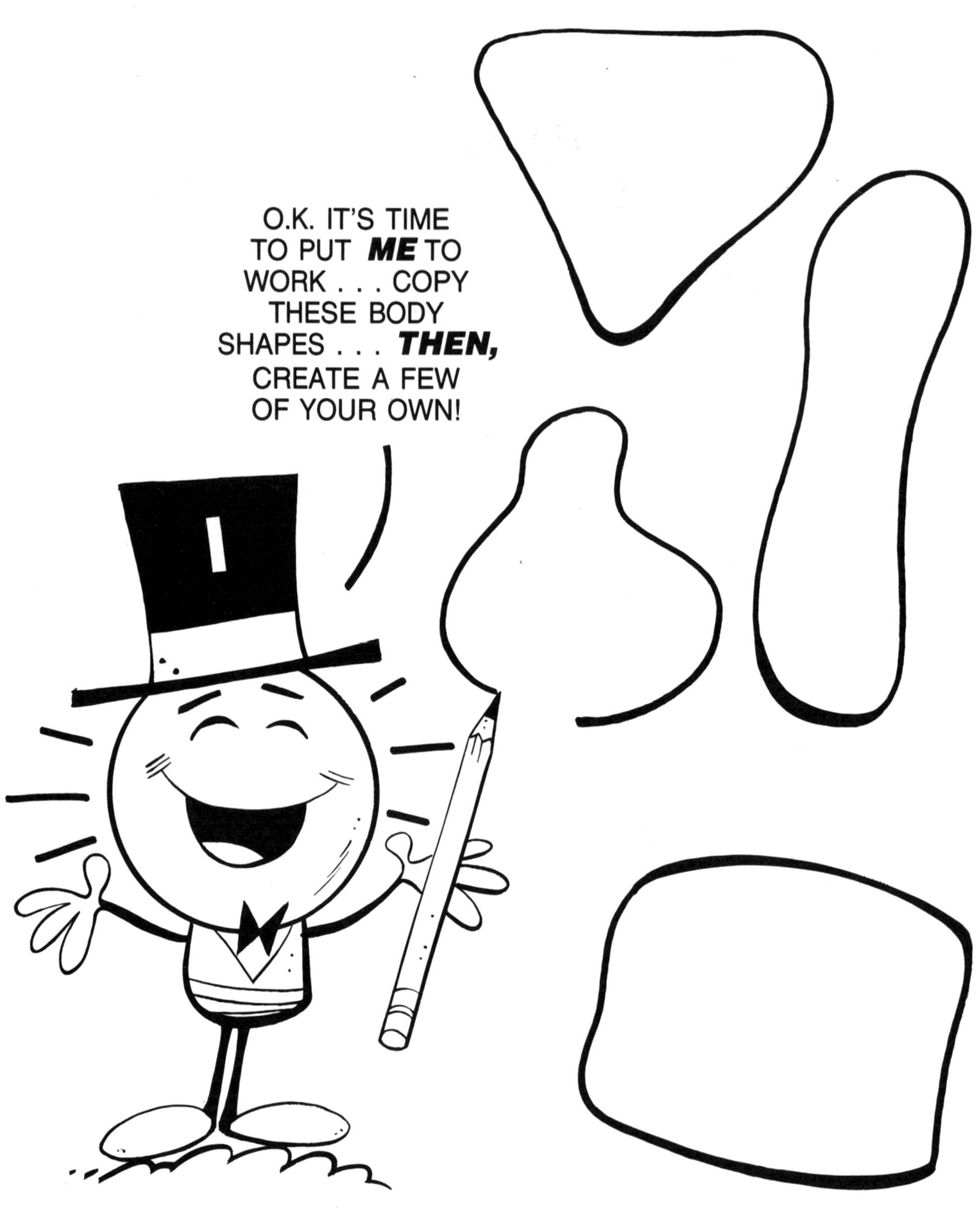
O.K. IT'S TIME
TO PUT ***ME*** TO
WORK . . . COPY
THESE BODY
SHAPES . . . ***THEN,***
CREATE A FEW
OF YOUR OWN!

I HOPE YOU FEEL CONFIDENT ENOUGH TO PUT ***ME*** TOGETHER . . .
'CAUSE BEING IN ***THIS*** CONDITION SURE CAN GIVE A GUY THAT EMPTY FEELING!

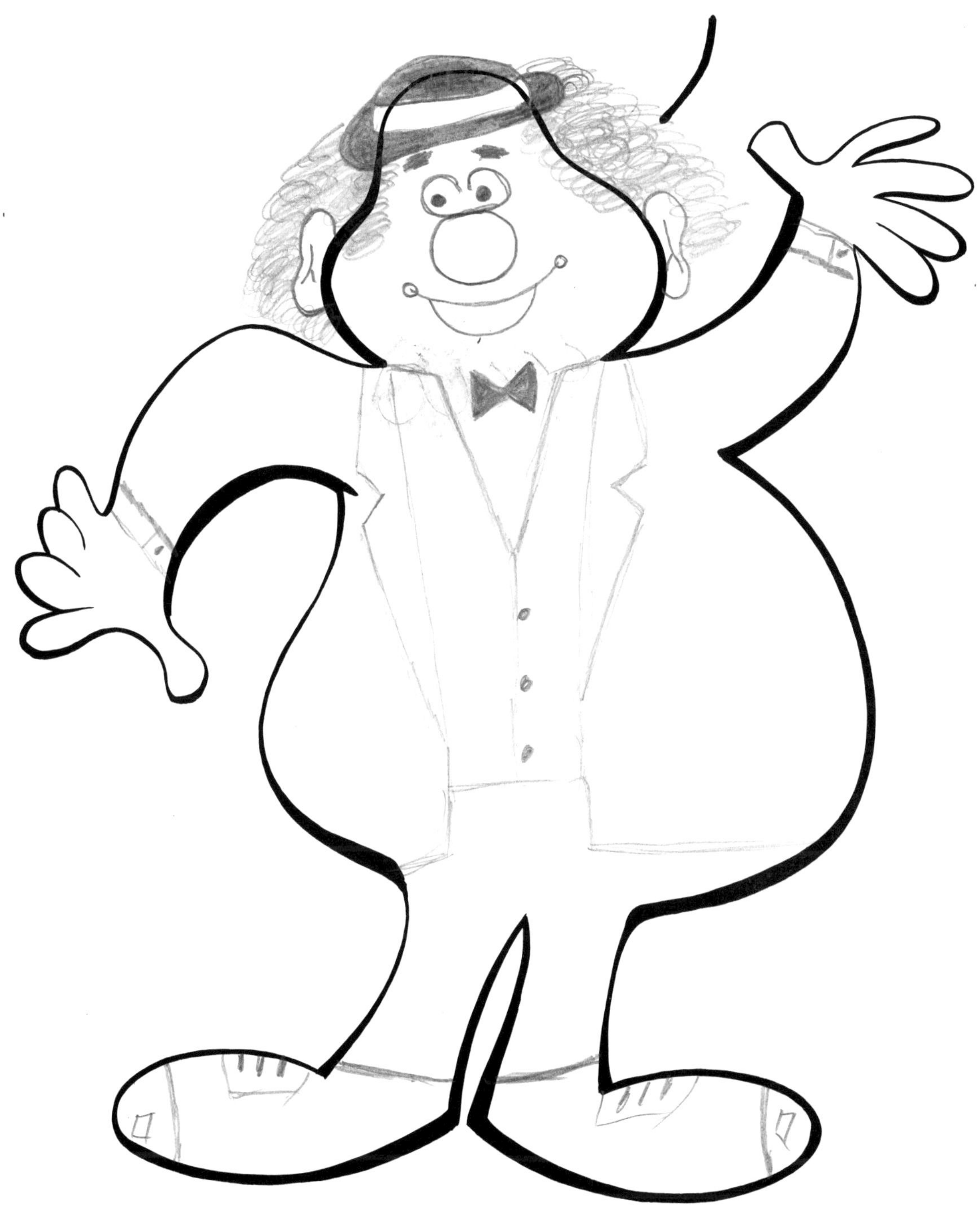

WAS IT FUN FILLING IN THE FEATURES?
I HOPE SO . . . BECAUSE . . .

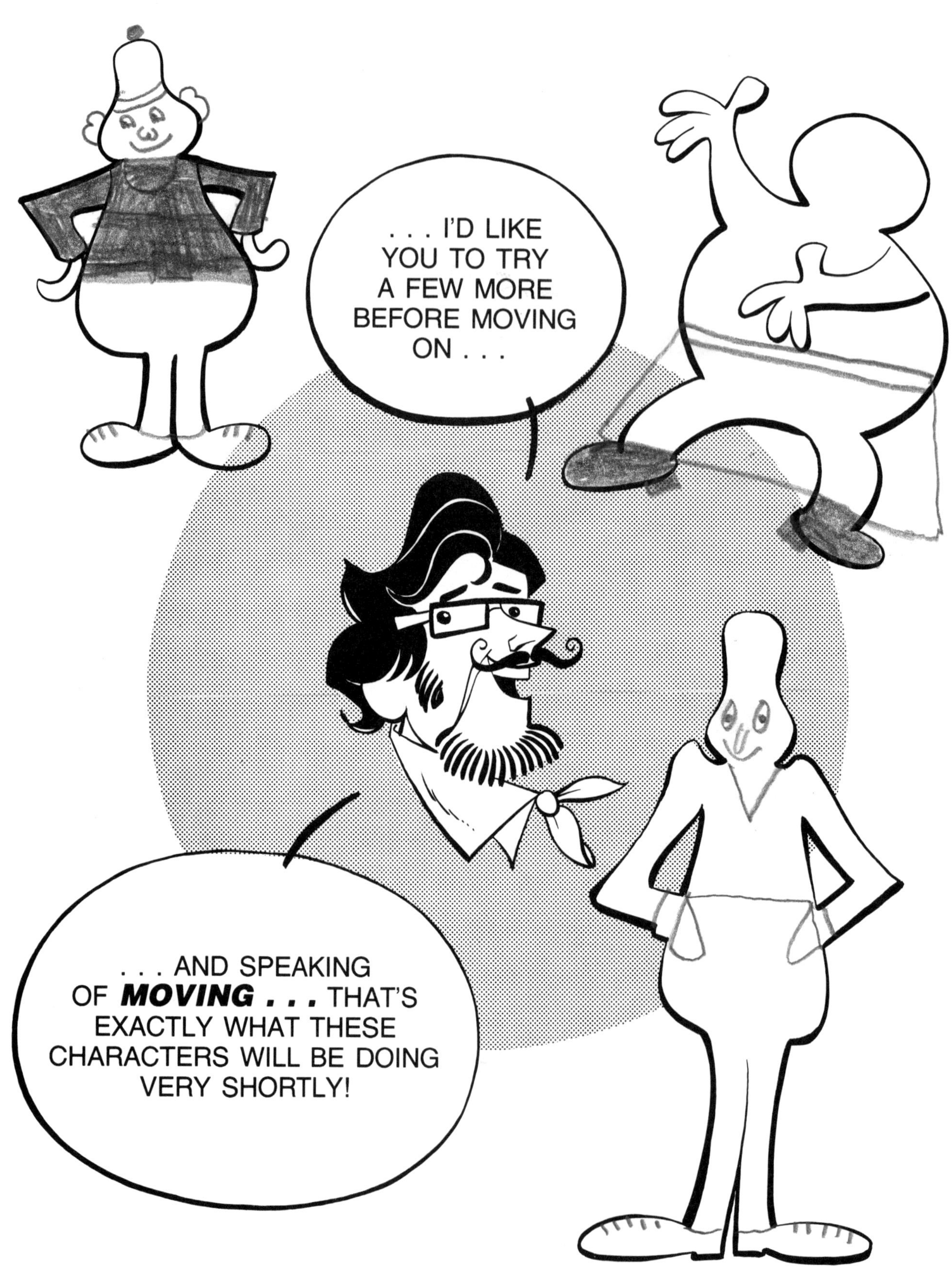
. . . I'D LIKE YOU TO TRY A FEW MORE BEFORE MOVING ON . . .
. . . AND SPEAKING OF ***MOVING . . .*** THAT'S EXACTLY WHAT THESE CHARACTERS WILL BE DOING VERY SHORTLY!

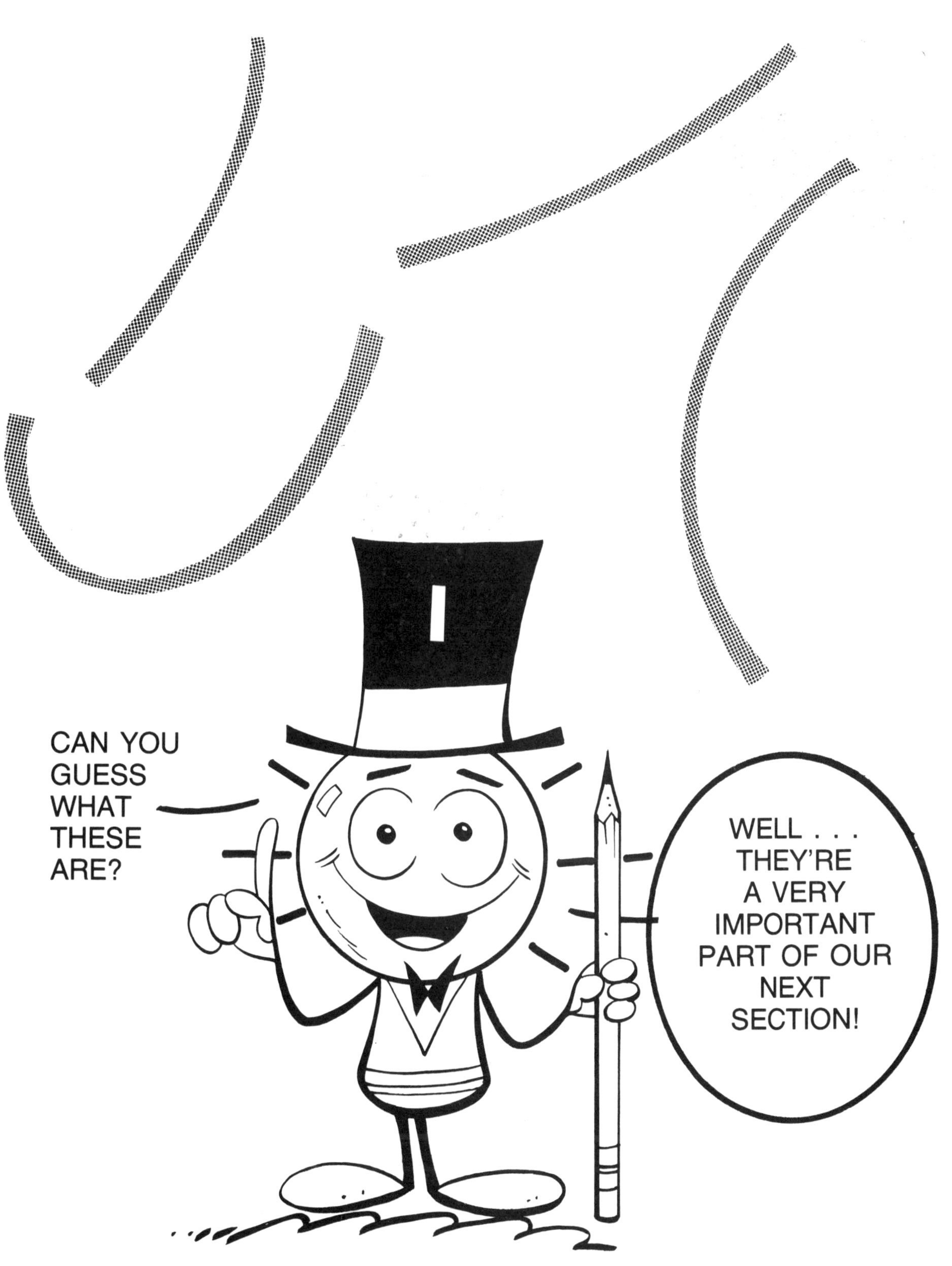
CAN YOU GUESS WHAT THESE ARE?
WELL . . . THEY'RE A VERY IMPORTANT PART OF OUR NEXT SECTION!

THEY'RE CALLED ***ACTION LINES*** AND THEY HELP OUR CARTOON CHARACTERS TO DO ALL SORTS OF THINGS!

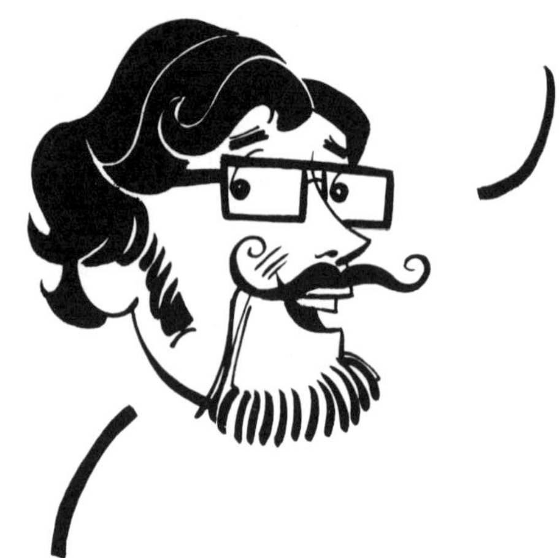

ACTION LINES HELP TO ESTABLISH THE MANY POSES OUR CARTOONS WILL ASSUME. AFTER ALL, VERY FEW OF US SIMPLY STAND AROUND ALL DAY . . . ***WE*** DO THINGS . . . AND SO SHOULD ***THEY!***

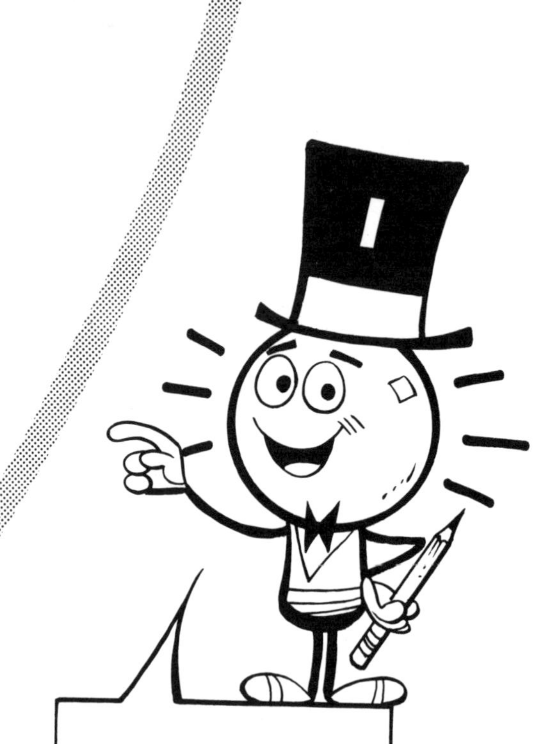

TAKE ***THIS*** LINE, FOR INSTANCE . . . WOULD YOU BELIEVE IT'S THE BASIS FOR TAKING OUR CARTOONS FOR A WALK? HERE'S HOW IT'S DONE!

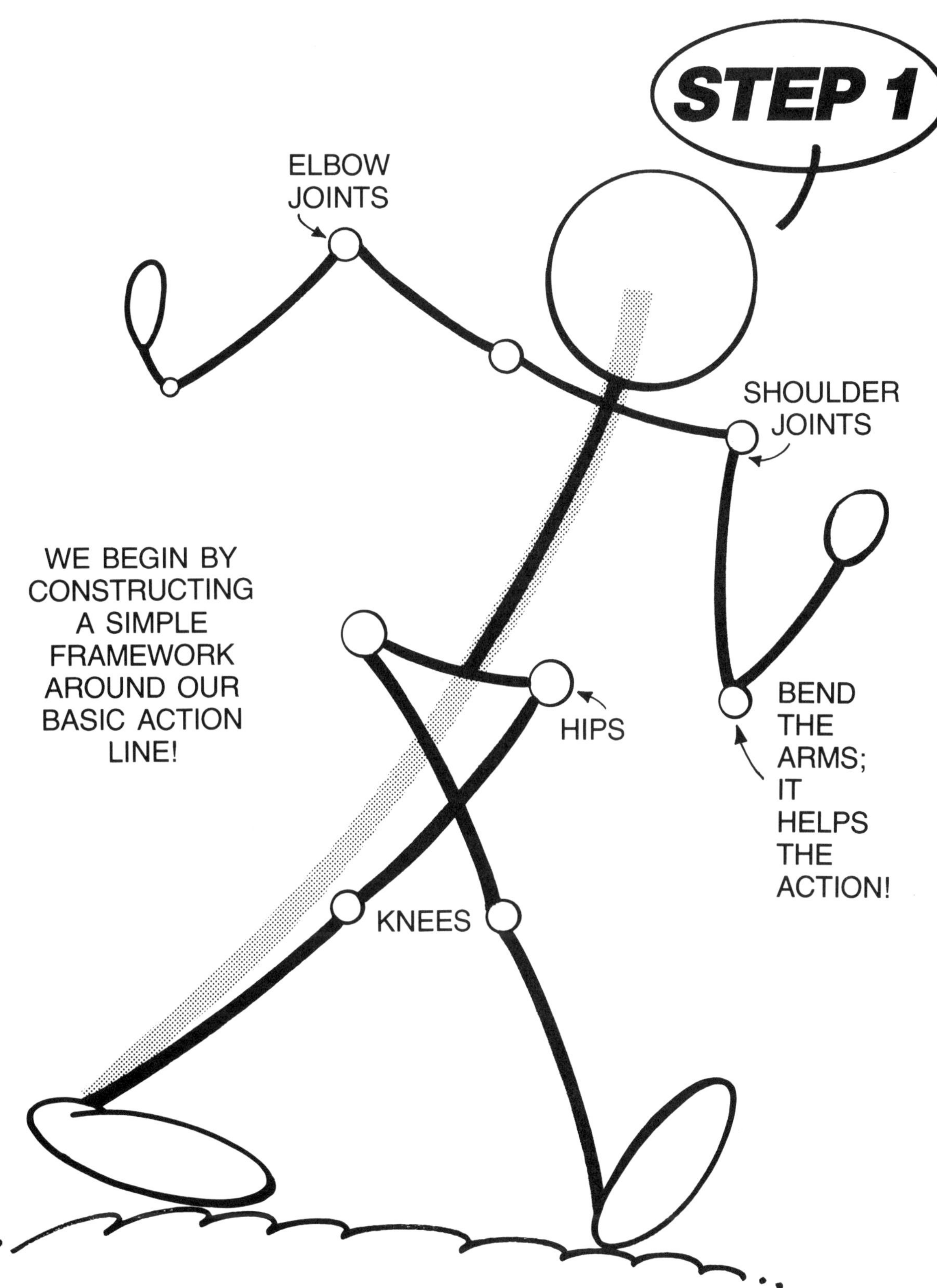

A GOOD WAY TO DRAW IS TO WATCH AND OBSERVE FIRST HOW WE DO THINGS . . . THEN WE DO SOMETHING VERY IMPORTANT IN CARTOONING . . . ***WE EXAGGERATE*** WHAT WE SEE!

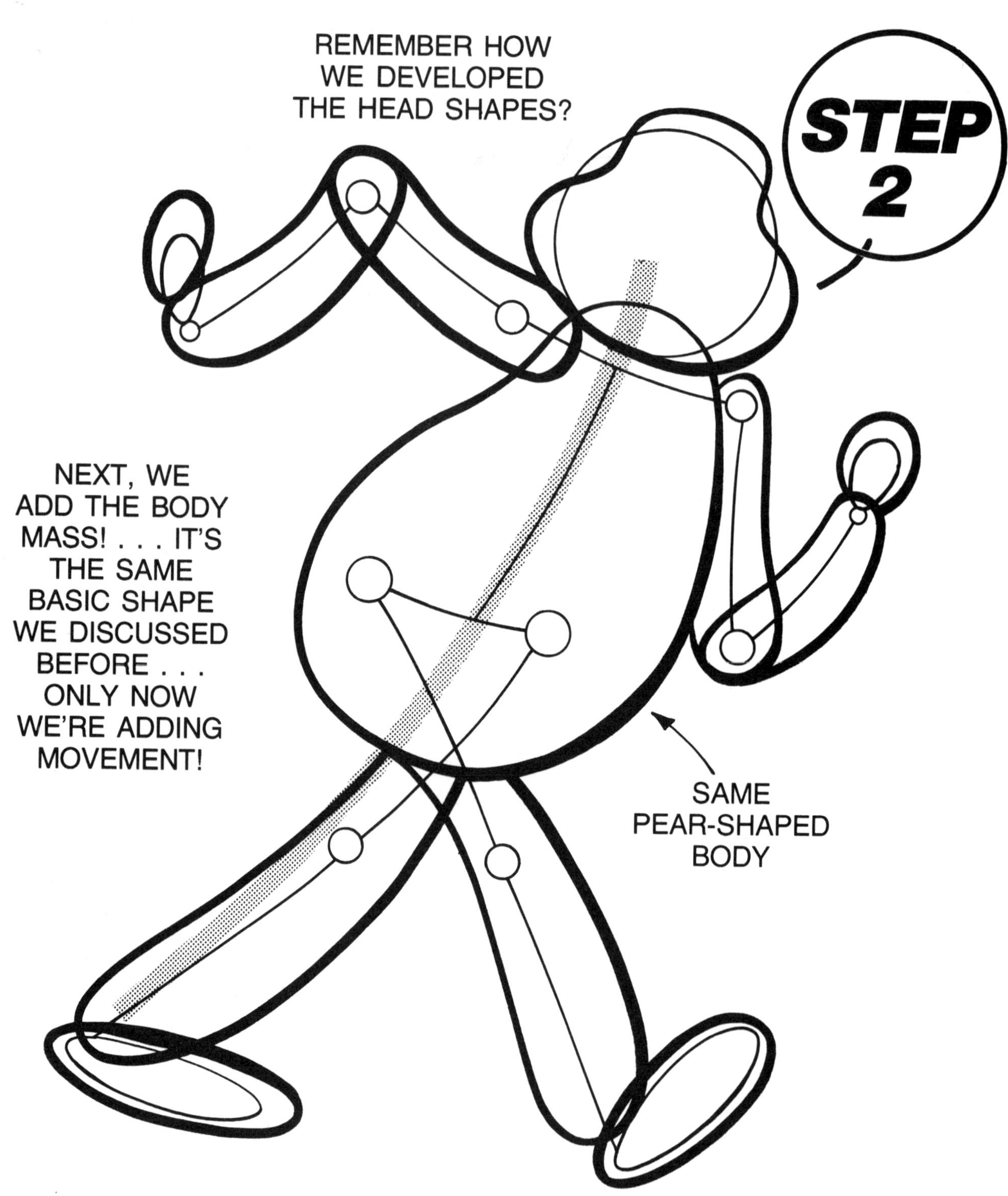
REMEMBER HOW
WE DEVELOPED
THE HEAD SHAPES?
STEP
2
NEXT, WE
ADD THE BODY
MASS! . . . IT'S
THE SAME
BASIC SHAPE
WE DISCUSSED
BEFORE . . .
ONLY NOW
WE'RE ADDING
MOVEMENT!
SAME
PEAR-SHAPED
BODY

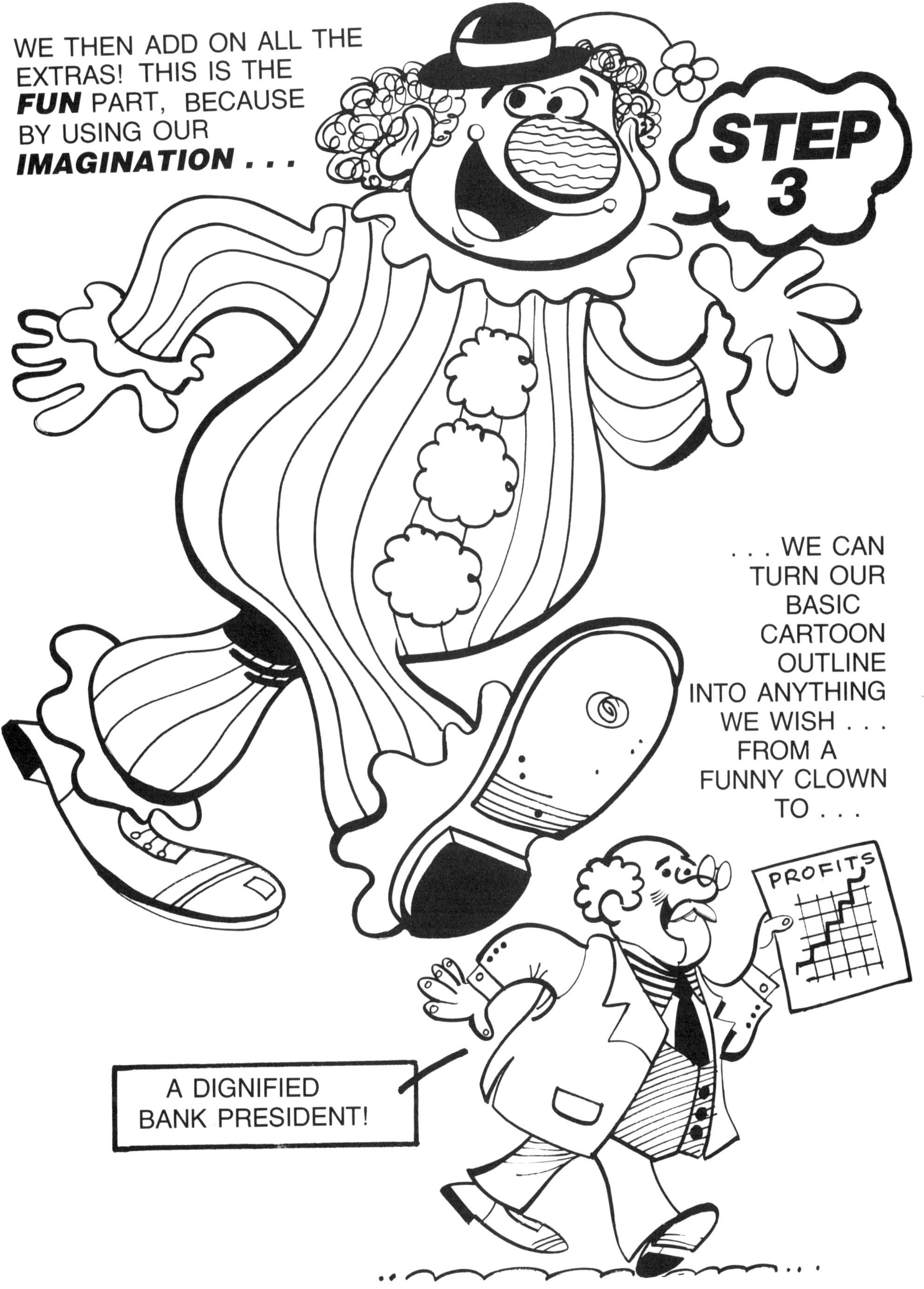
WE THEN ADD ON ALL THE EXTRAS! THIS IS THE **FUN** PART, BECAUSE BY USING OUR ***IMAGINATION . . .***
STEP 3
. . . WE CAN TURN OUR BASIC CARTOON OUTLINE INTO ANYTHING WE WISH . . . FROM A FUNNY CLOWN TO . . .
PROFITS
A DIGNIFIED BANK PRESIDENT!

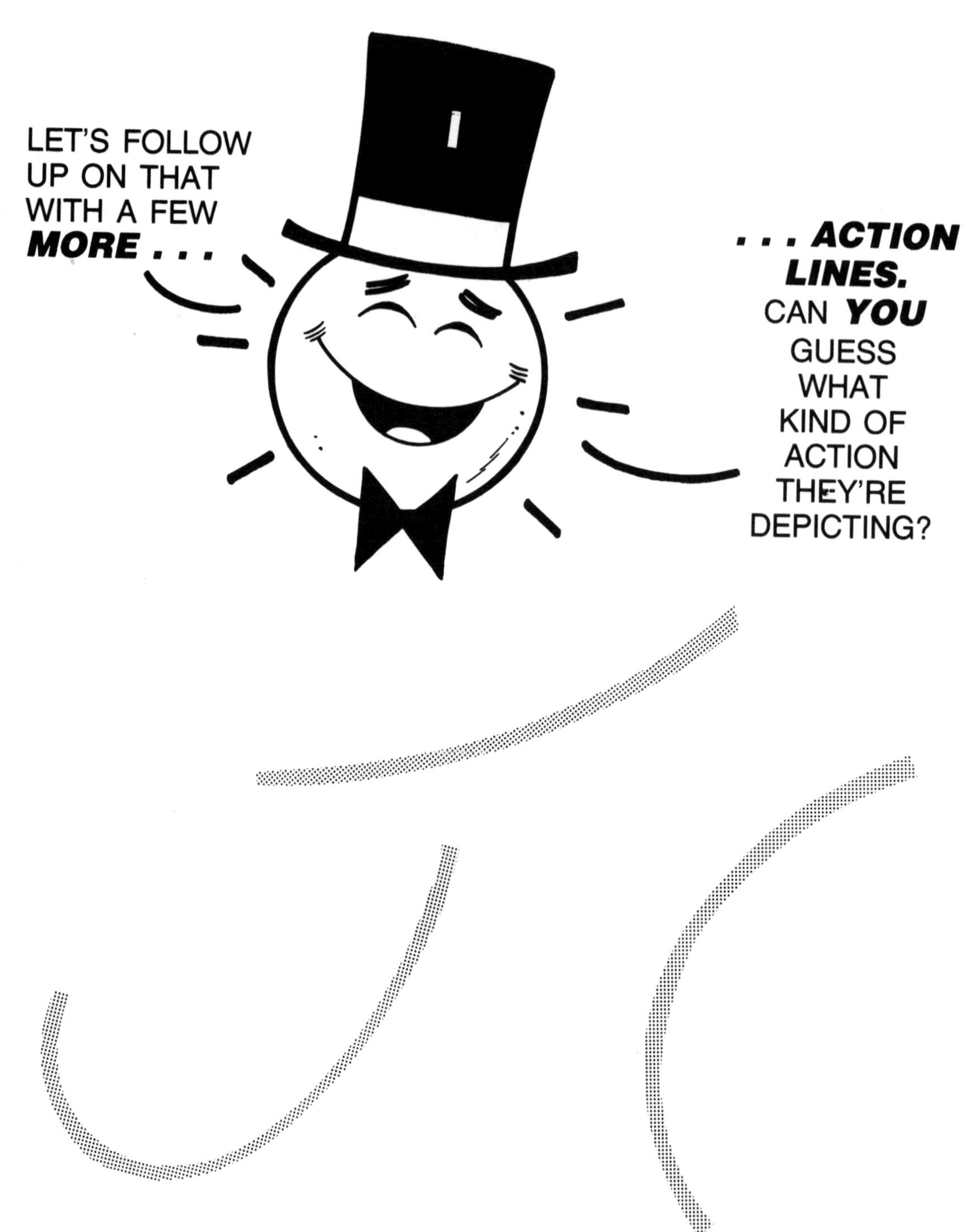

BEFORE PEEKING AT THE NEXT PAGE . . . HOW'S ABOUT TRYING TO CONSTRUCT A FEW OF ***YOUR OWN*** CARTOONS AROUND THESE LINES! THEN . . . COMPARE YOURS WITH THE FOLLOWING . . .

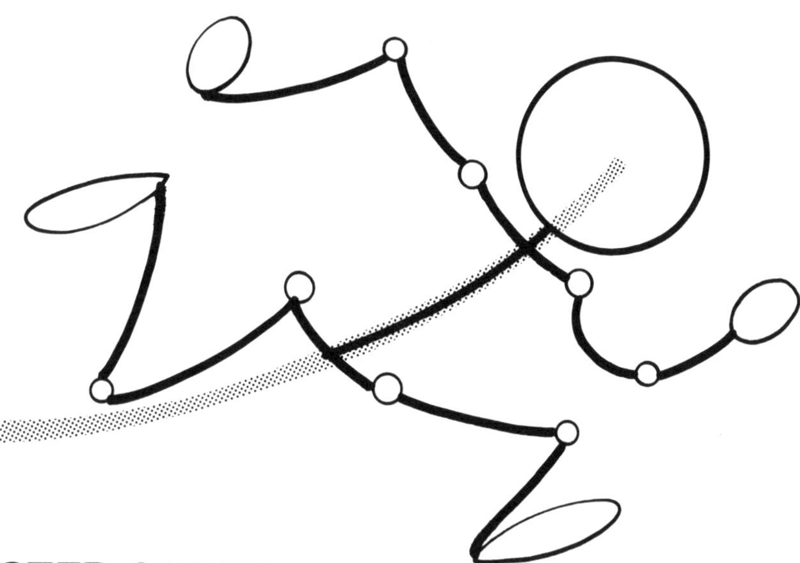

HERE'S ***STEP 1*** AGAIN. NOW YOU SHOULD BE ABLE TO TELL WHAT THESE GUYS ARE UP TO.

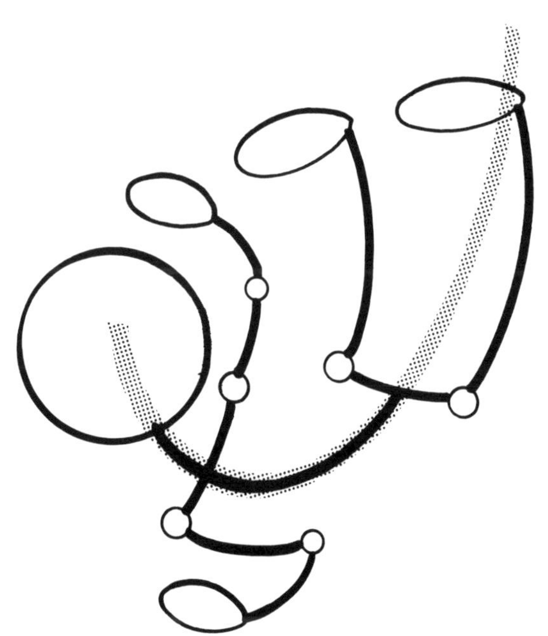

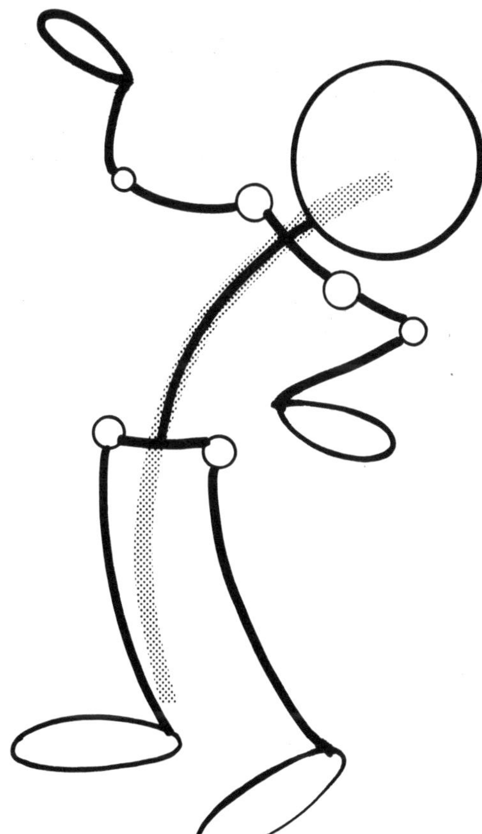

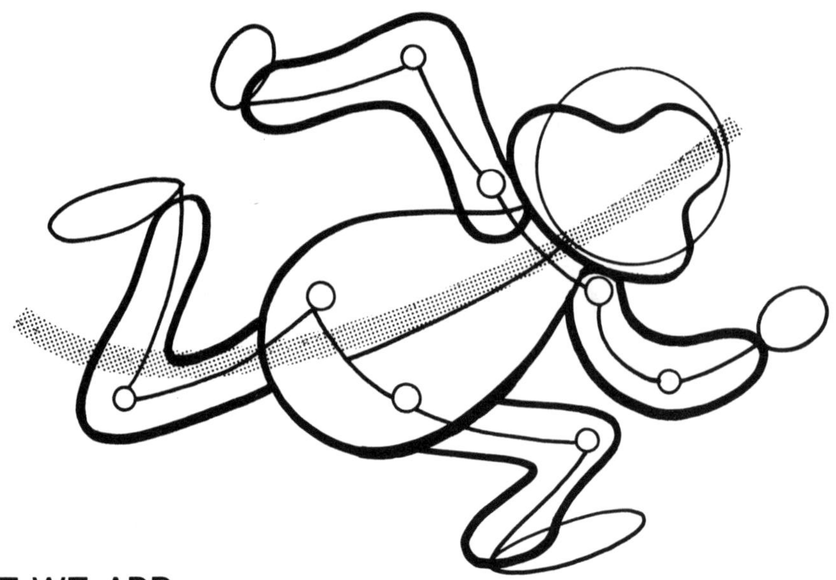

NEXT WE ADD THE NECESSARY SHAPES TO FILL OUT THE FORM.

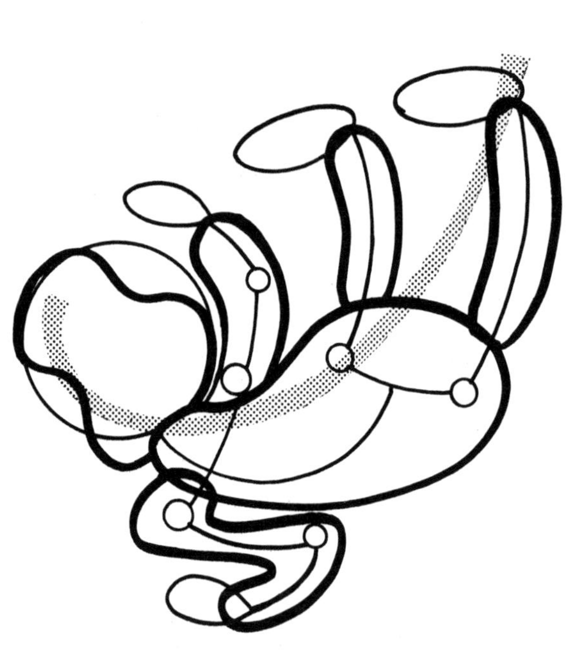

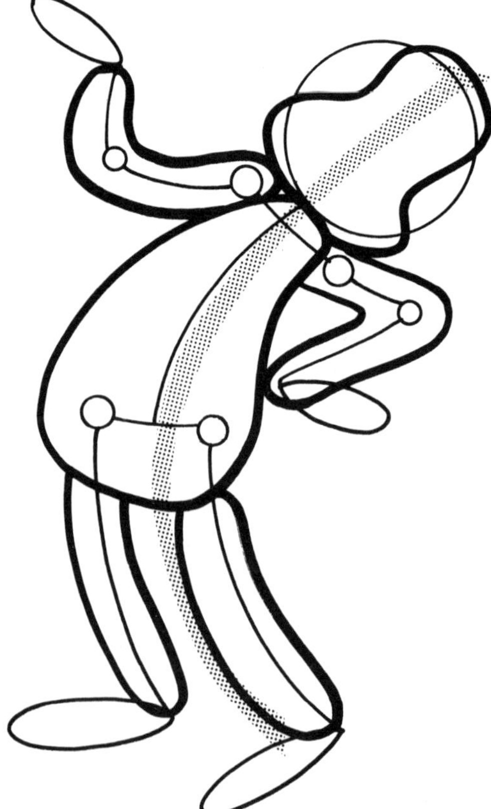

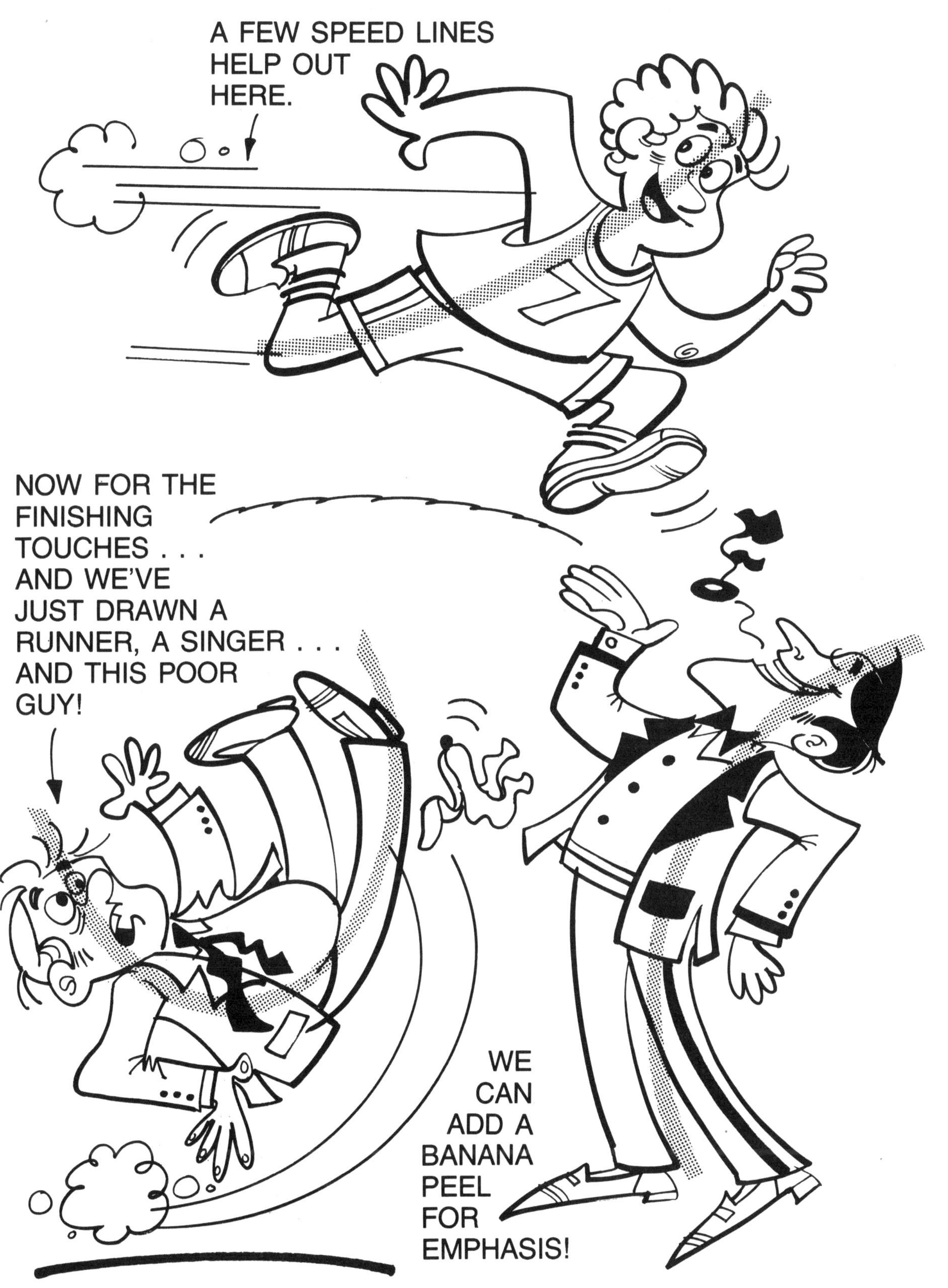
A FEW SPEED LINES HELP OUT HERE.
NOW FOR THE FINISHING TOUCHES . . . AND WE'VE JUST DRAWN A RUNNER, A SINGER . . . AND THIS POOR GUY!
WE CAN ADD A BANANA PEEL FOR EMPHASIS!

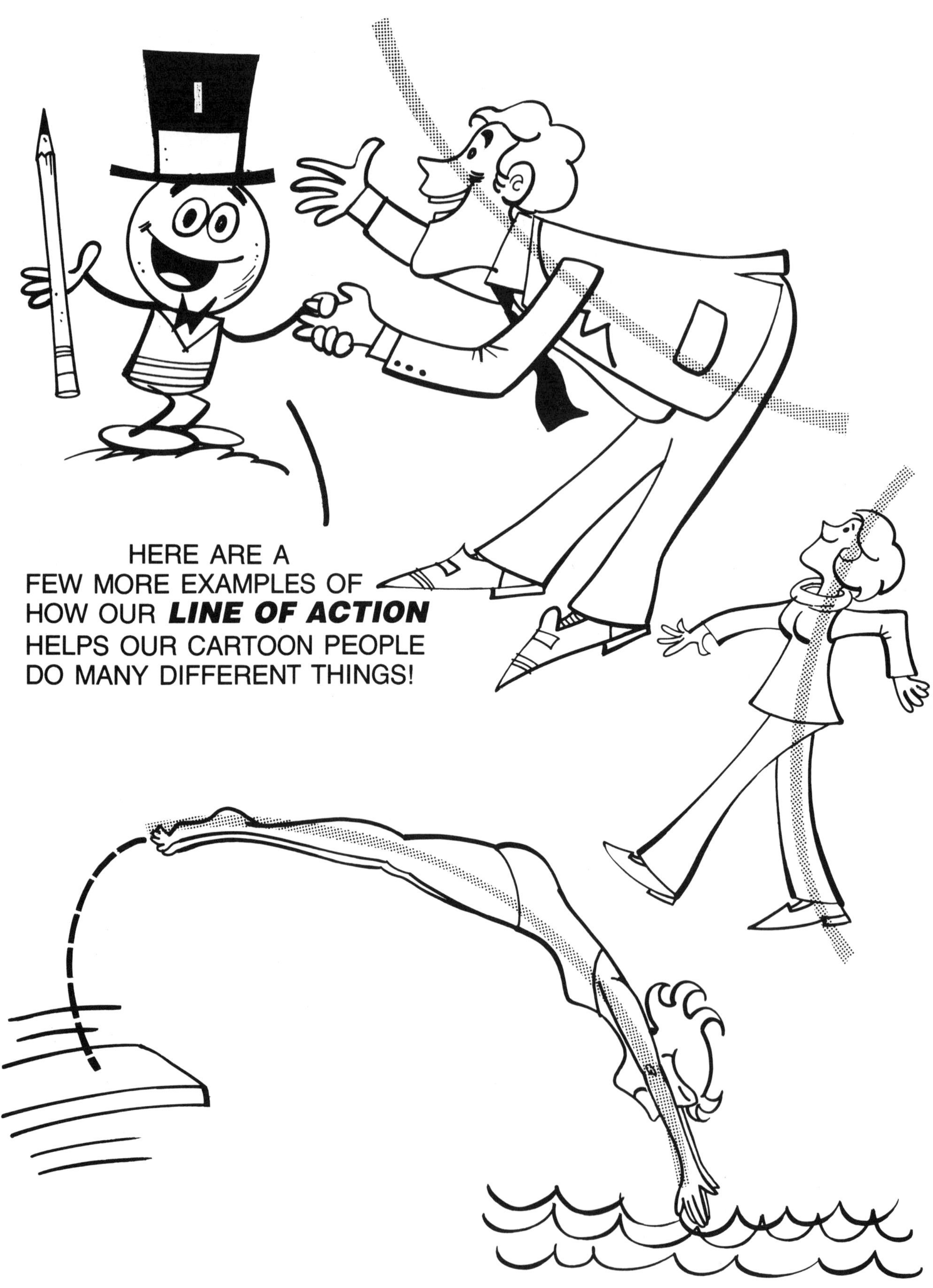
HERE ARE A
FEW MORE EXAMPLES OF
HOW OUR ***LINE OF ACTION***
HELPS OUR CARTOON PEOPLE
DO MANY DIFFERENT THINGS!

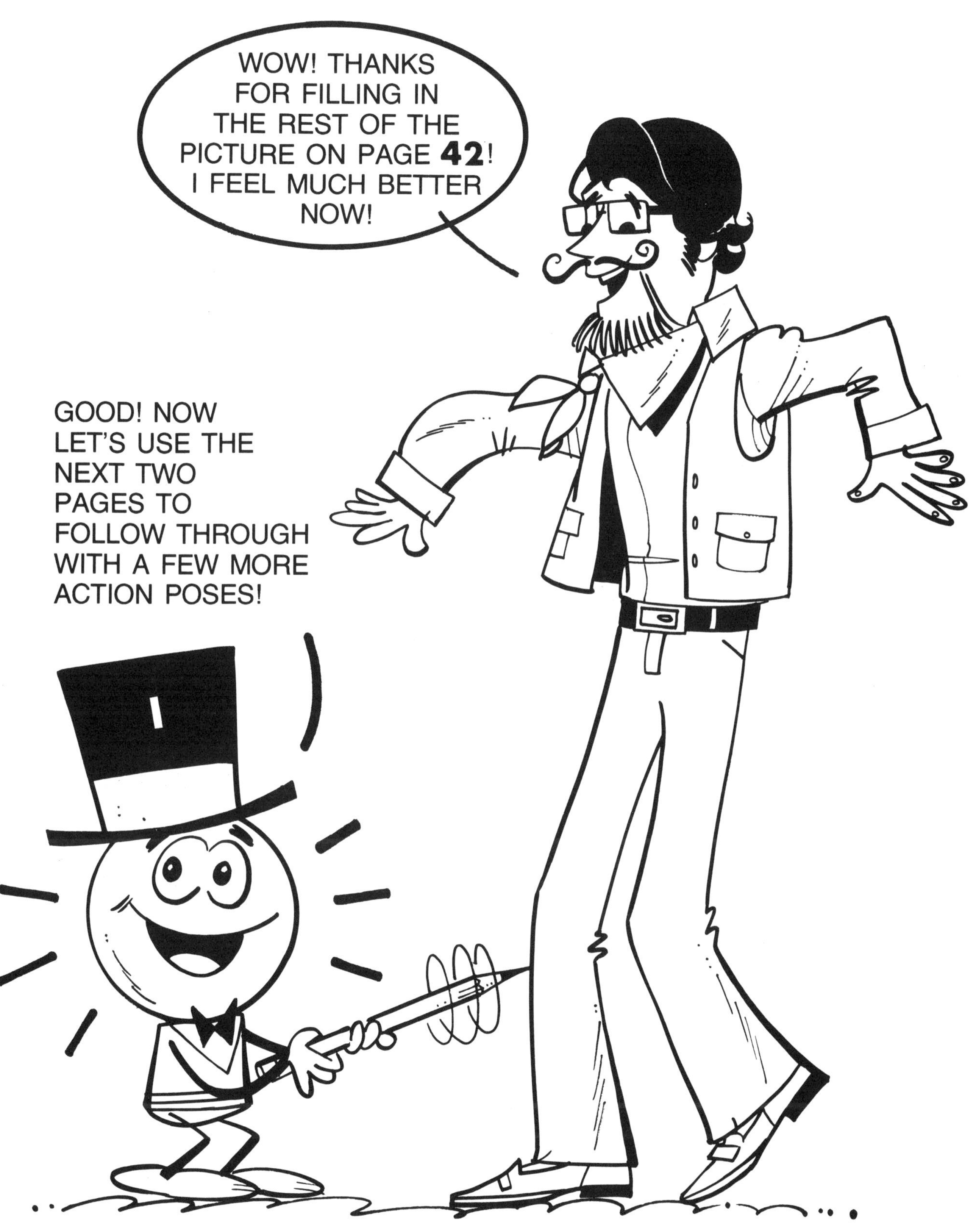
WOW! THANKS FOR FILLING IN THE REST OF THE PICTURE ON PAGE 42! I FEEL MUCH BETTER NOW!
GOOD! NOW LET'S USE THE NEXT TWO PAGES TO FOLLOW THROUGH WITH A FEW MORE ACTION POSES!

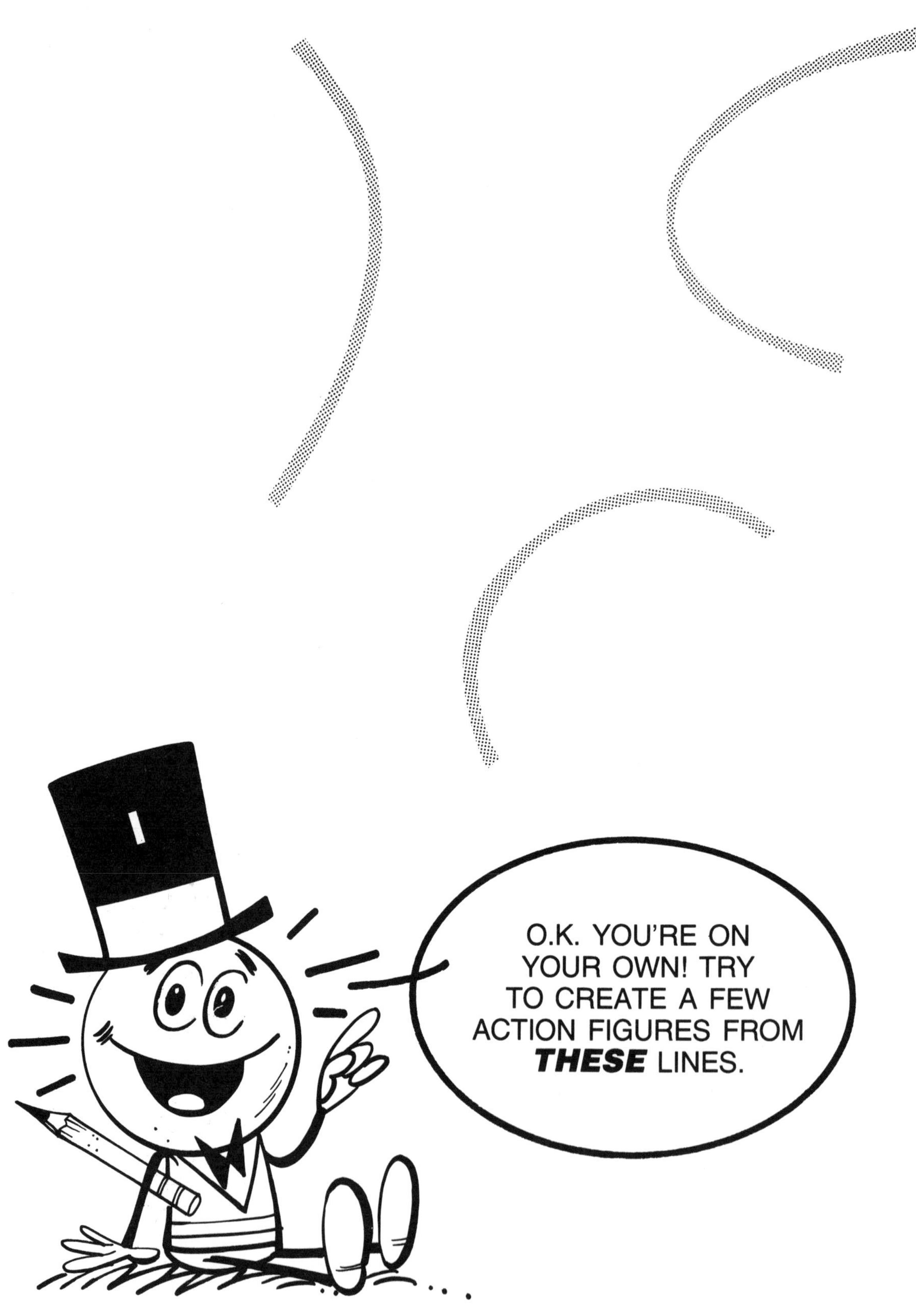
O.K. YOU'RE ON YOUR OWN! TRY TO CREATE A FEW ACTION FIGURES FROM ***THESE*** LINES.

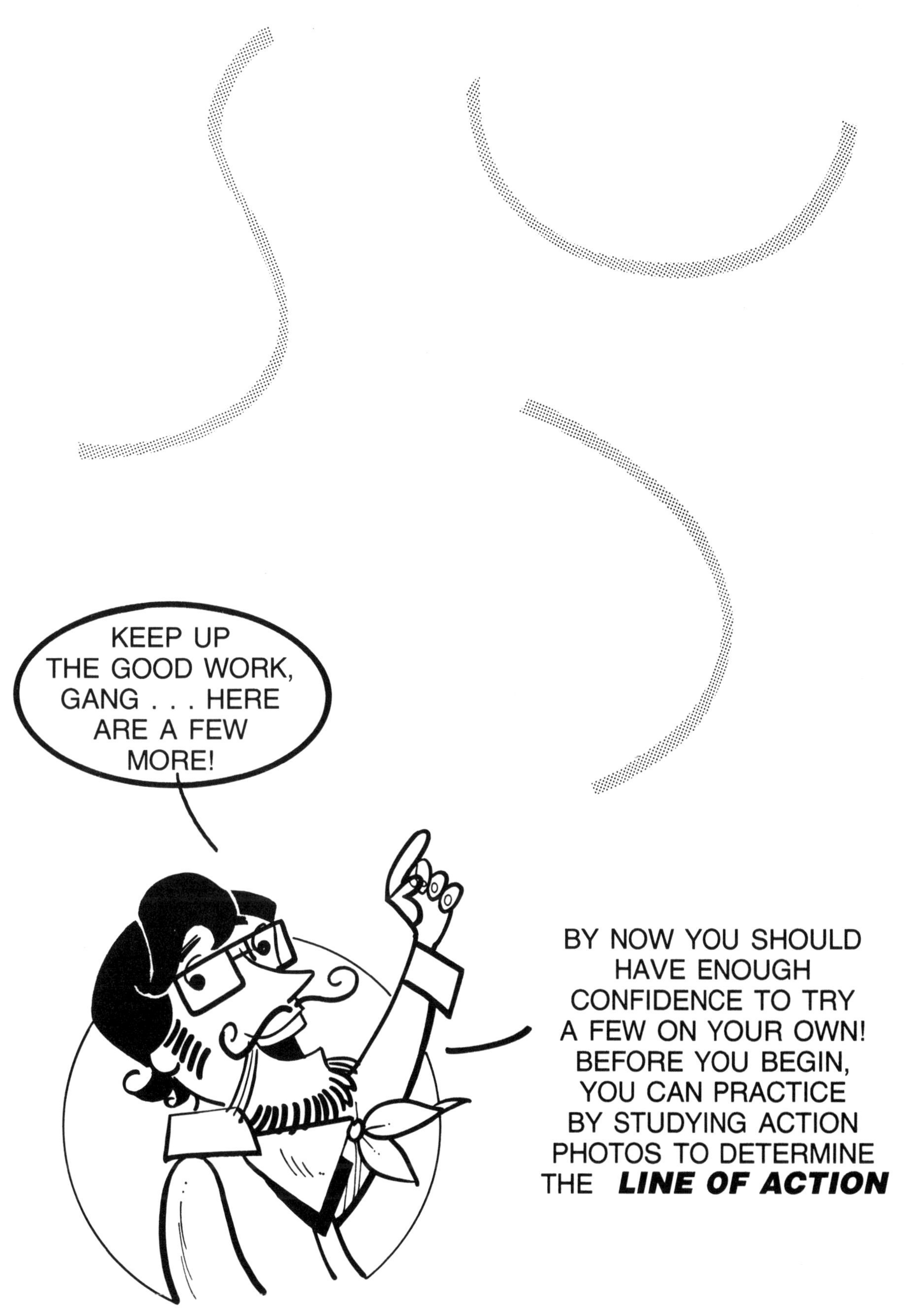

BY NOW YOU SHOULD HAVE ENOUGH CONFIDENCE TO TRY A FEW ON YOUR OWN! BEFORE YOU BEGIN, YOU CAN PRACTICE BY STUDYING ACTION PHOTOS TO DETERMINE THE ***LINE OF ACTION***

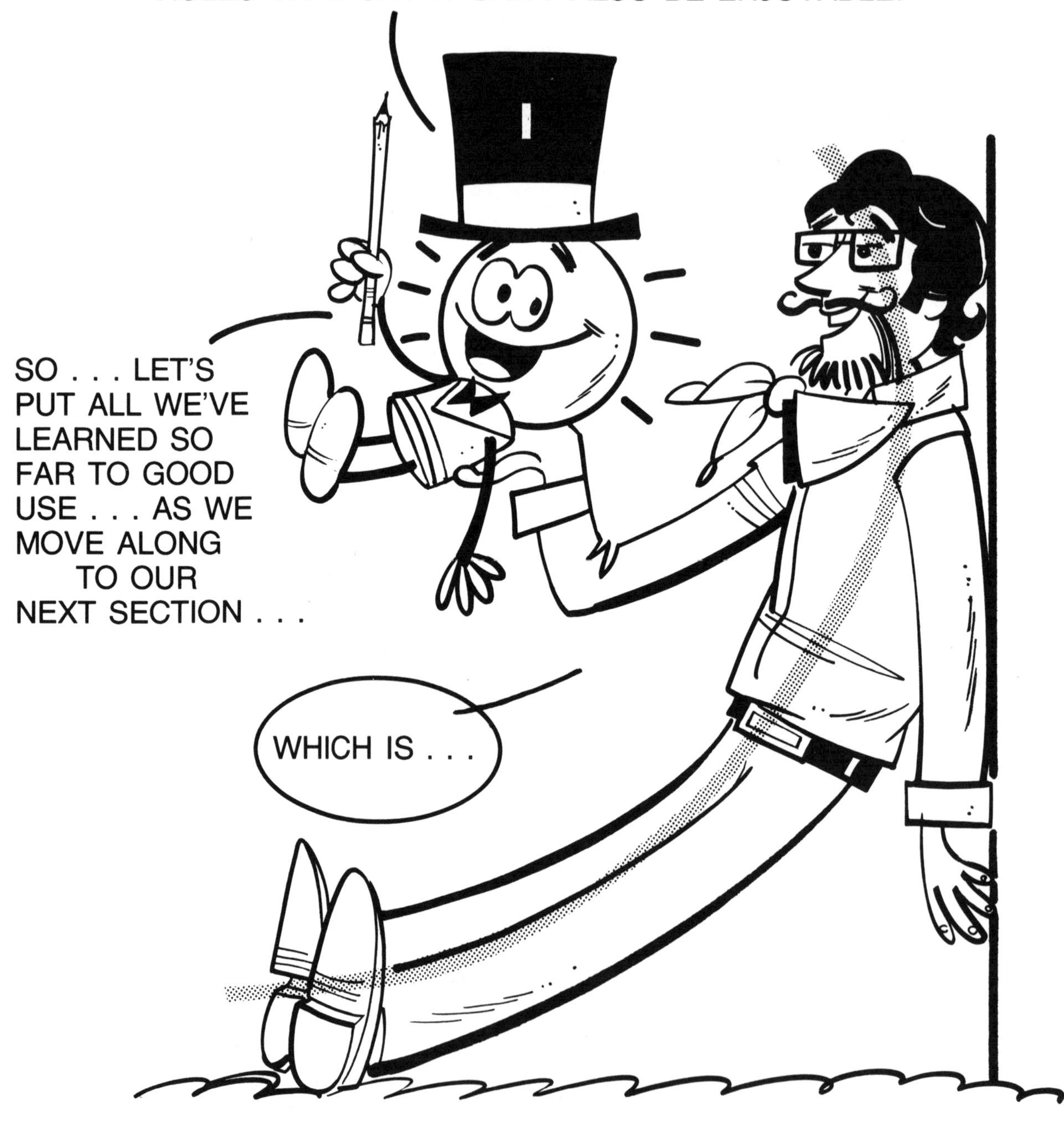
O.K. I HOPE YOU LIKED THAT EXERCISE. THE CREATIVE PROCESS CAN BE VERY REWARDING AND THERE ARE NO RULES THAT SAY IT CAN'T ALSO BE ENJOYABLE!
SO . . . LET'S PUT ALL WE'VE LEARNED SO FAR TO GOOD USE . . . AS WE MOVE ALONG TO OUR NEXT SECTION . . .
WHICH IS . . .

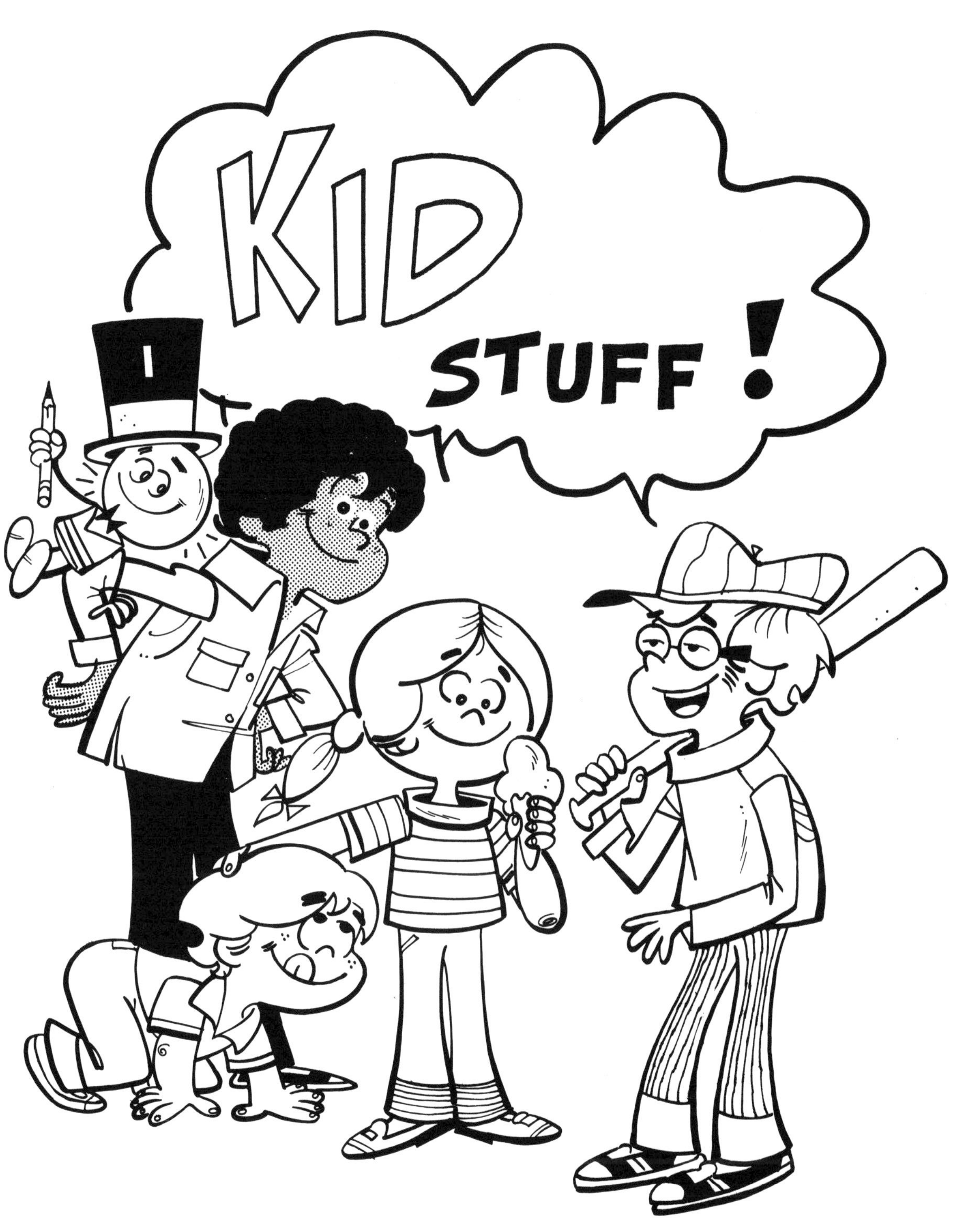
KID
STUFF!

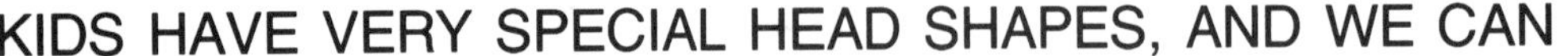

KIDS HAVE VERY SPECIAL HEAD SHAPES, AND WE CAN CONSTRUCT THESE SHAPES STARTING WITH OUR OLD FRIEND, THE CIRCLE . . . AND THEN ADD AN OVAL FOR THE CHIN AREA

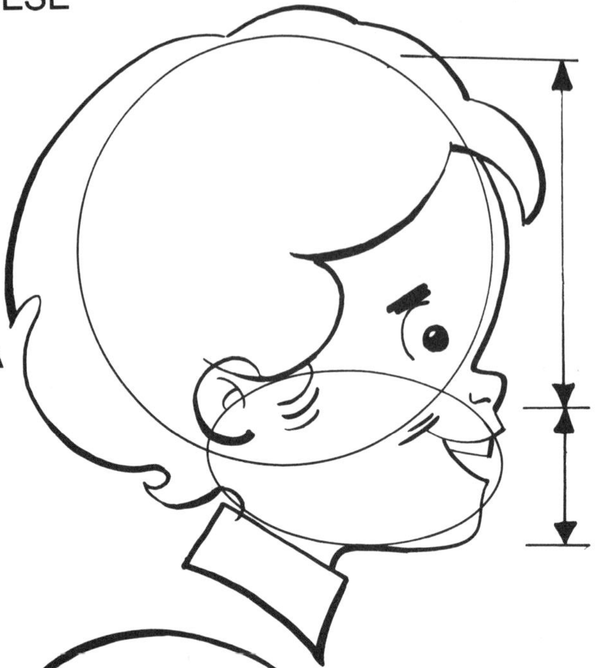

WHEN DRAWING CHILDREN'S HEAD SHAPES, NOTICE THE HEIGHT OF THE FOREHEAD . . . IN RELATION TO THE LOWER PART OF THE HEAD!

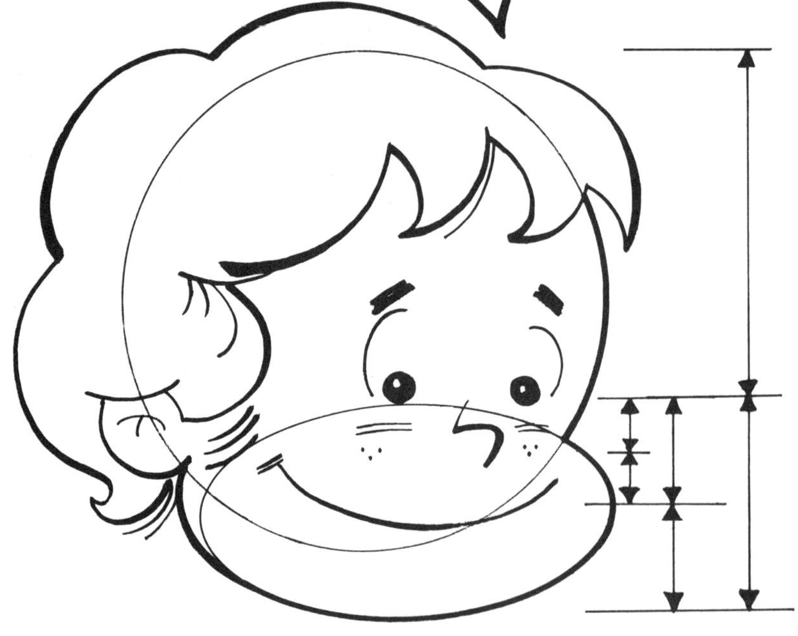

NOTICE, EVEN THOUGH WE'VE ALTERED THE CONSTRUCTION FROM OUR BASIC CIRCLE SHAPE, THIS LITTLE FELLOW'S FEATURES ARE PLACED IN THE SAME POSITION AS ON OUR CIRCLE.

A YOUNGSTER'S BODY SIZE, DEPENDING ON AGE, SHOULD BE 3½ TO 5 HEADS IN HEIGHT . . . AND OUR OLD FRIEND THE CIRCLE AND THE PEAR SHAPE WILL CONSTITUTE THE BASIC CONSTRUCTION.

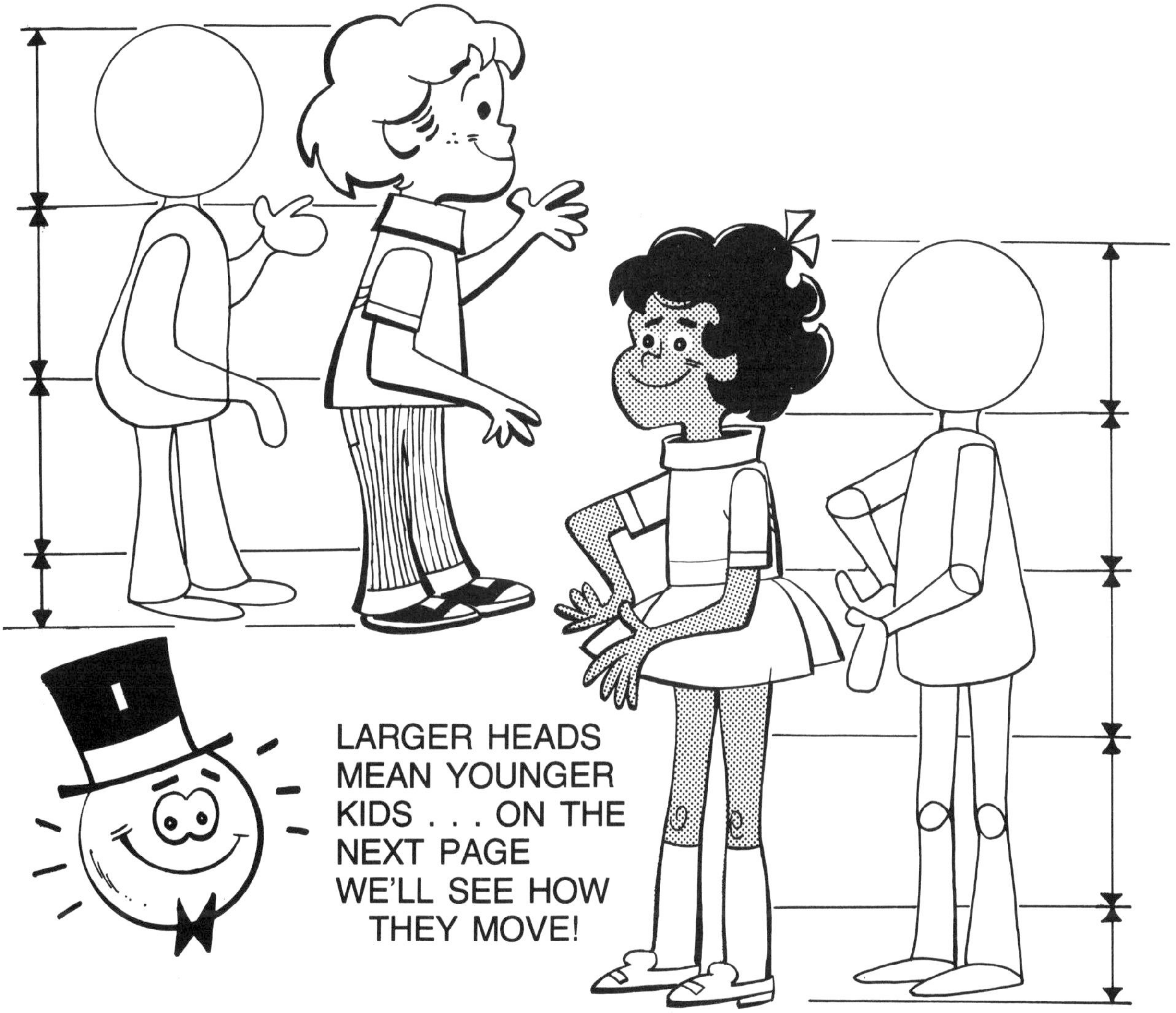

LARGER HEADS MEAN YOUNGER KIDS . . . ON THE NEXT PAGE WE'LL SEE HOW THEY MOVE!

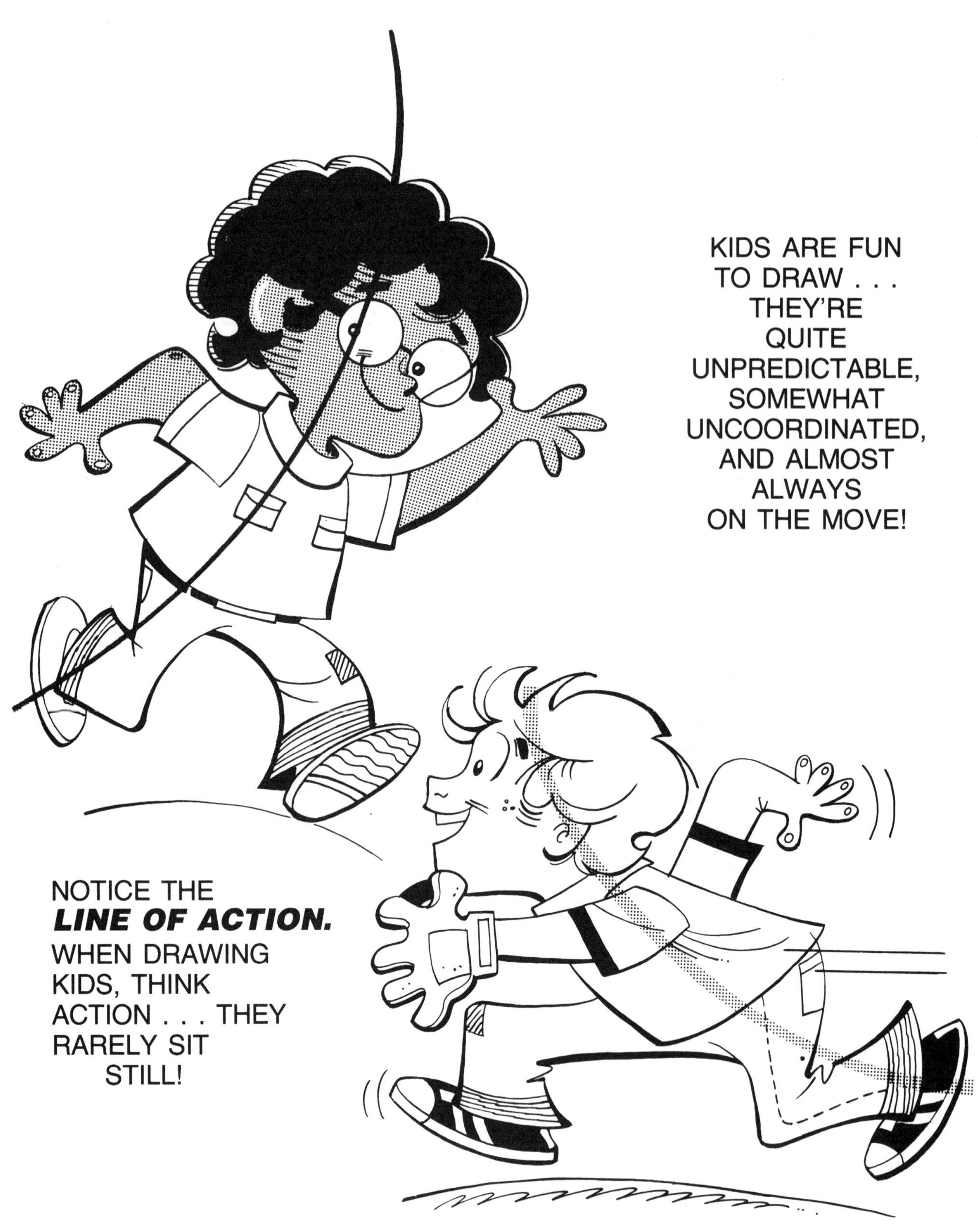

ANOTHER INTERESTING THING ABOUT KIDS IS . . .

. . . THEY GROW!

5
4
3
2
1
LITTLE CARTOON GUYS LIKE THIS USUALLY START OUT ABOUT 2 HEADS HIGH!

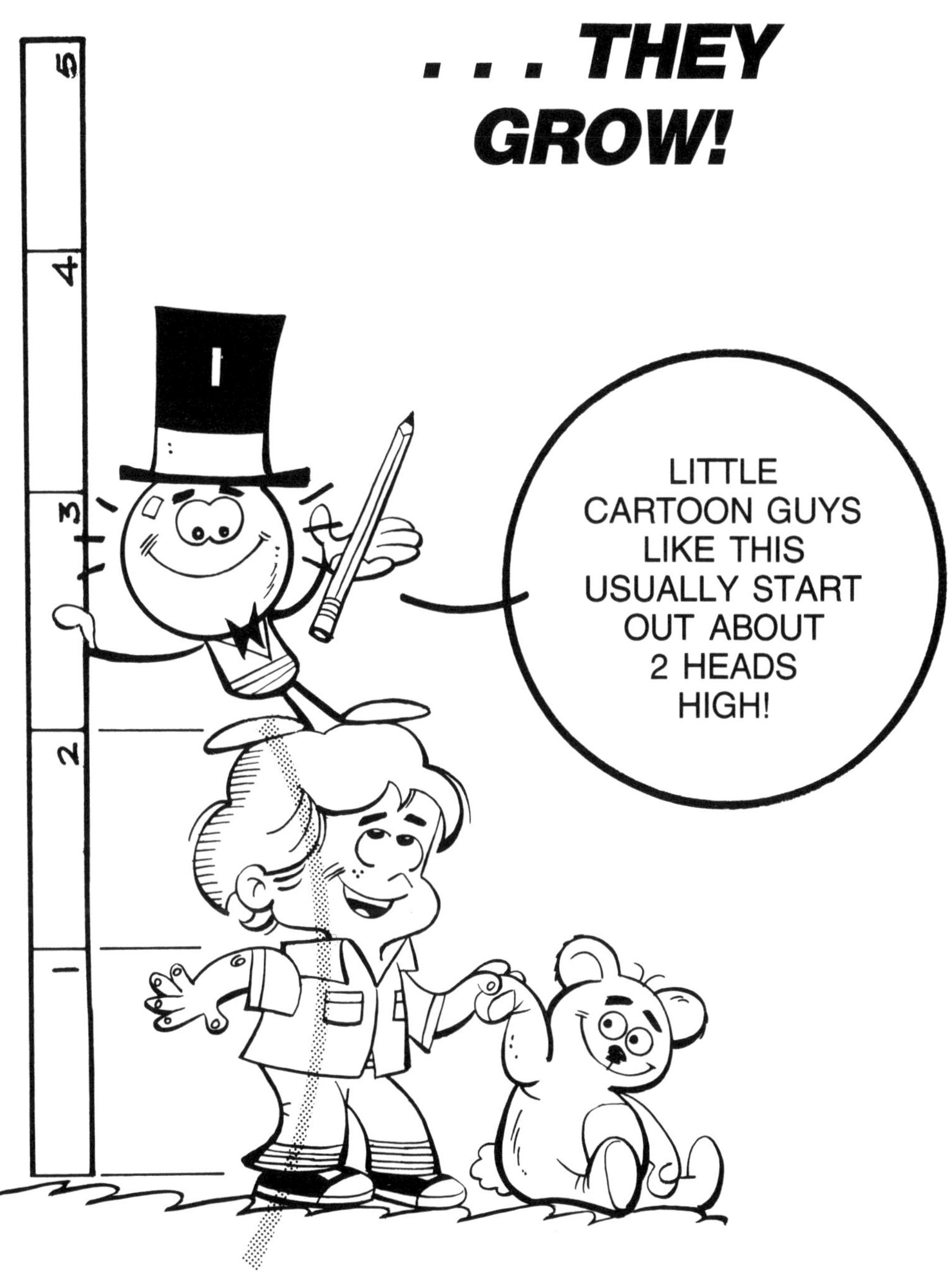

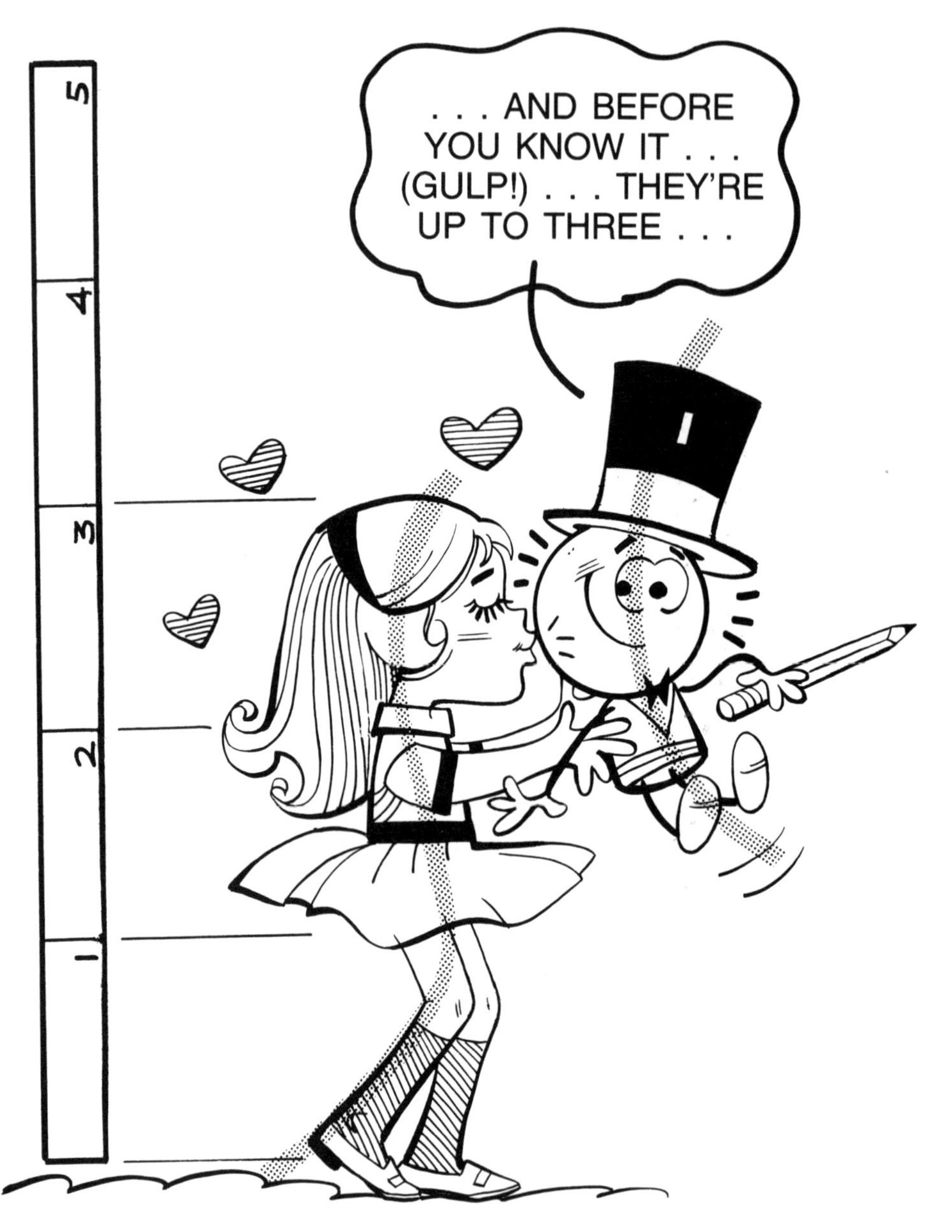
. . . AND BEFORE
YOU KNOW IT . . .
(GULP!) . . . THEY'RE
UP TO THREE . . .
5
4
3
2
1

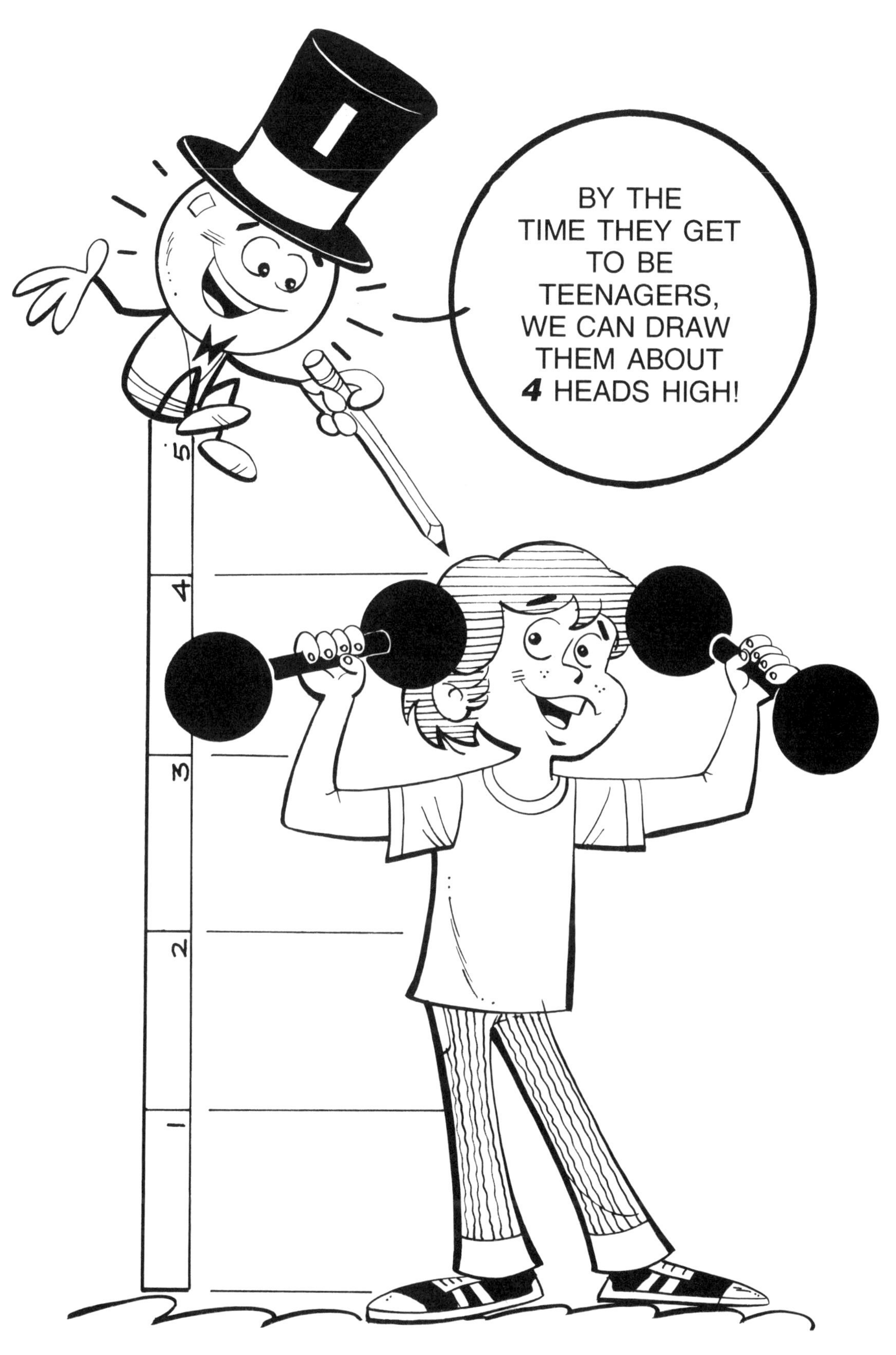
BY THE TIME THEY GET TO BE TEENAGERS, WE CAN DRAW THEM ABOUT **4** HEADS HIGH!
5
4
3
2
1

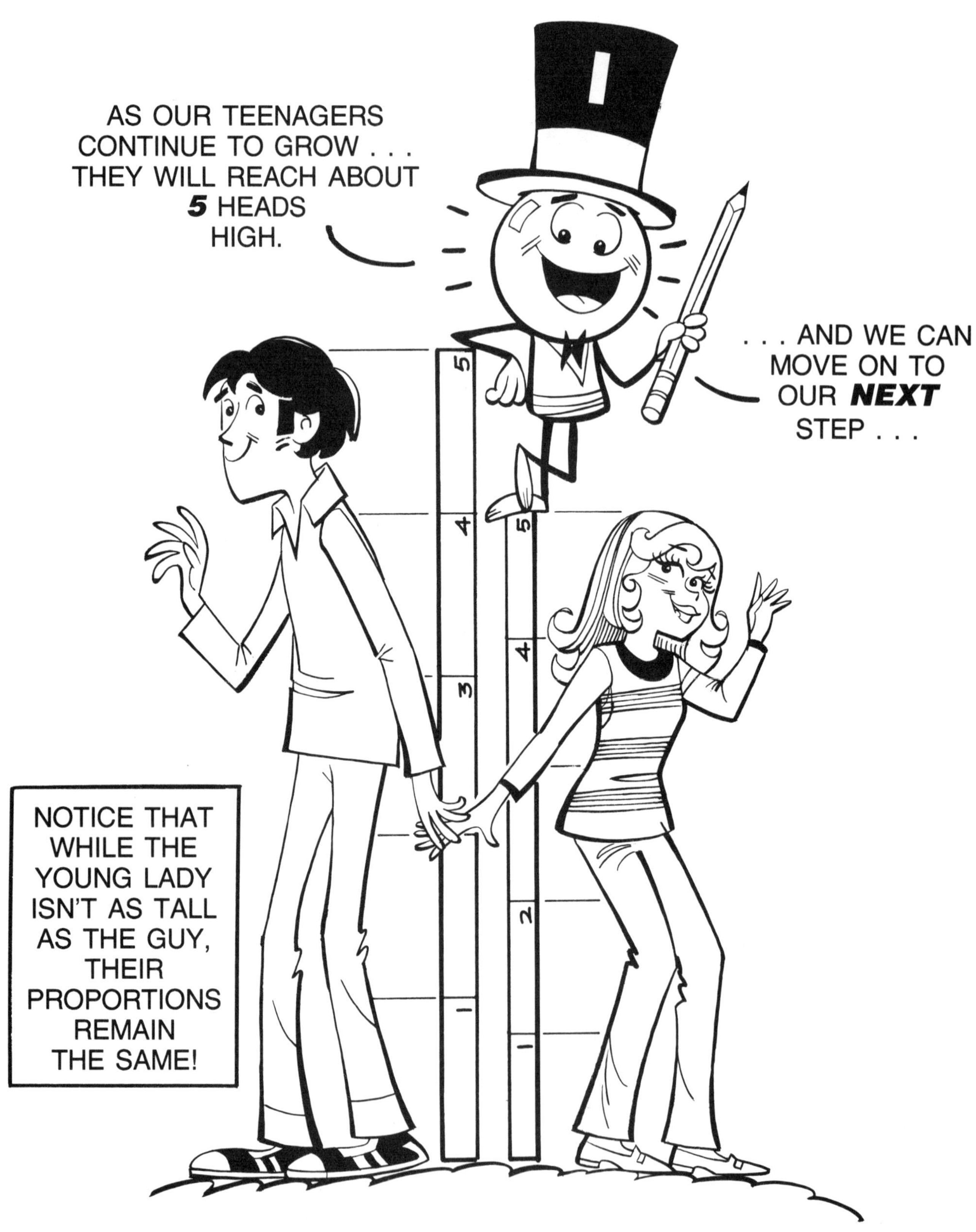
AS OUR TEENAGERS CONTINUE TO GROW . . . THEY WILL REACH ABOUT **5** HEADS HIGH.
. . . AND WE CAN MOVE ON TO OUR **NEXT** STEP . . .
NOTICE THAT WHILE THE YOUNG LADY ISN'T AS TALL AS THE GUY, THEIR PROPORTIONS REMAIN THE SAME!
5
4
3
1
5
4
2
1

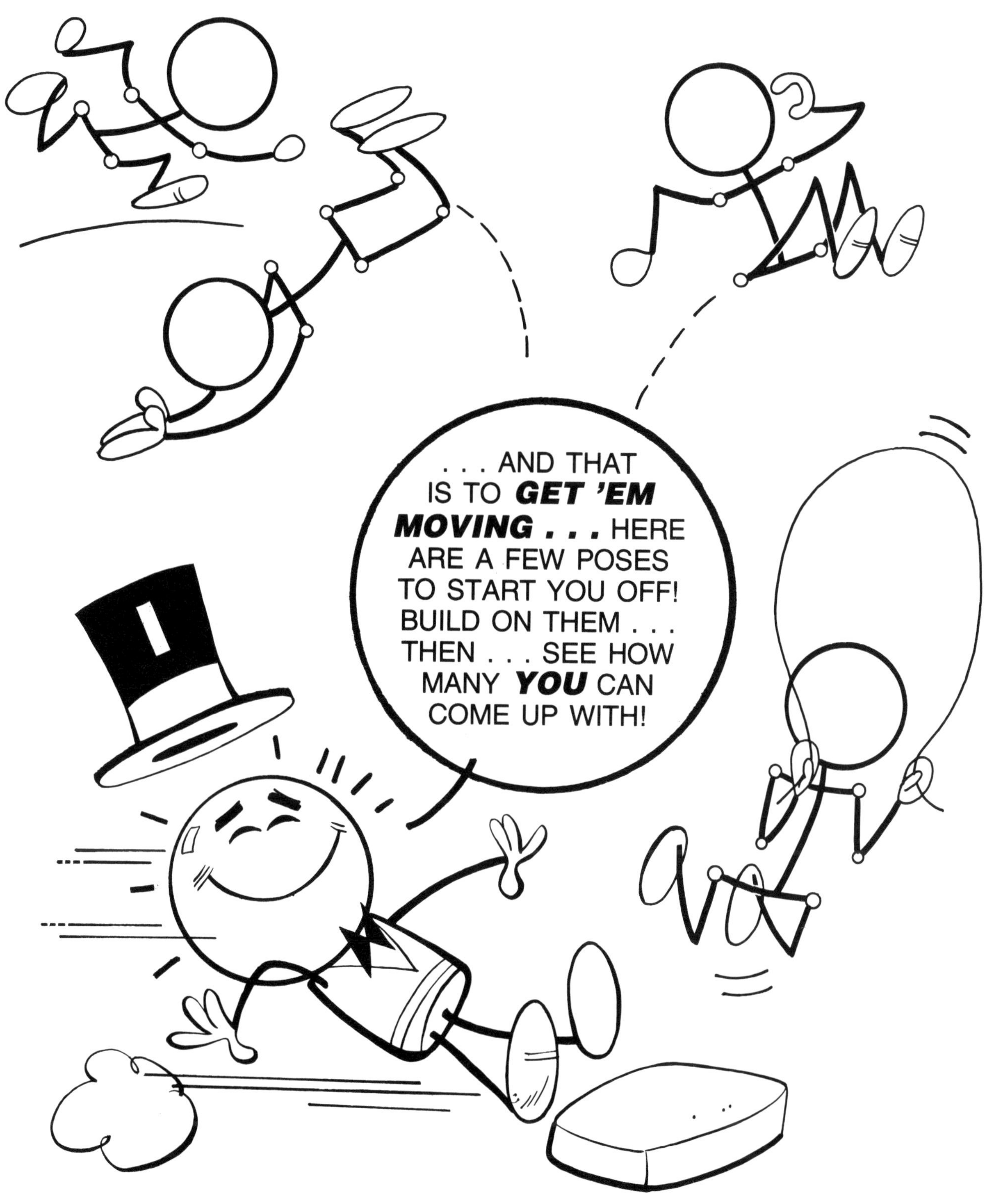
. . . AND THAT IS TO **GET 'EM MOVING . . .** HERE ARE A FEW POSES TO START YOU OFF! BUILD ON THEM . . . THEN . . . SEE HOW MANY **YOU** CAN COME UP WITH!

AS OUR YOUNG MEN BECOME YOUNG ADULTS, THEY LOOK SOMETHING LIKE THIS . . .
KEEP THEM ABOUT 5½ HEADS HIGH. (UNLESS YOU FEEL LIKE DRAWING A BASKETBALL PLAYER!)

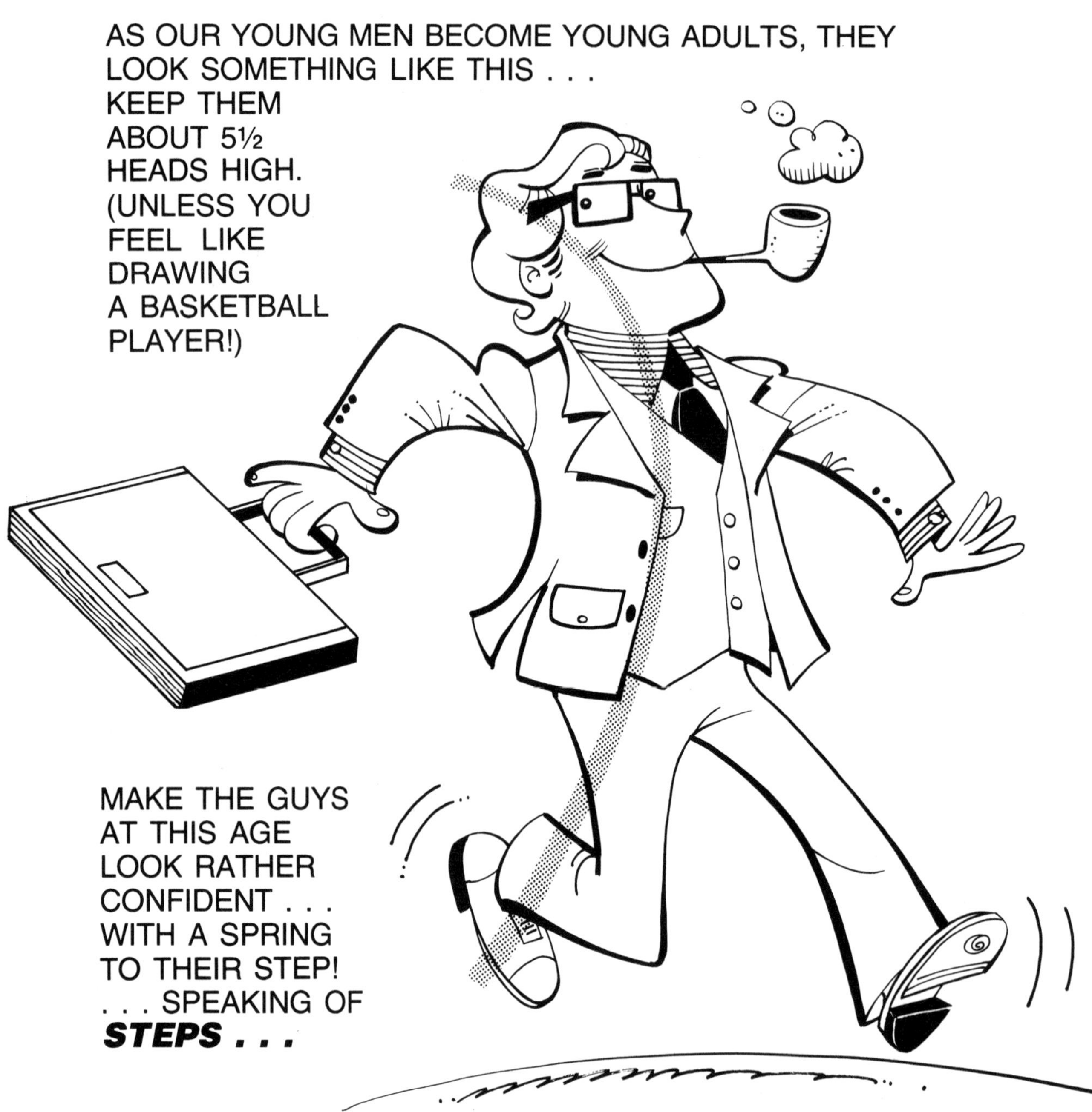

MAKE THE GUYS AT THIS AGE LOOK RATHER CONFIDENT . . . WITH A SPRING TO THEIR STEP! . . . SPEAKING OF ***STEPS . . .***

. . . HOW ABOUT WORKING BACKWARDS WITH THIS GUY? TRY TO WORK OUT THE NECESSARY STEPS TO PRODUCE THIS FINISHED DRAWING!

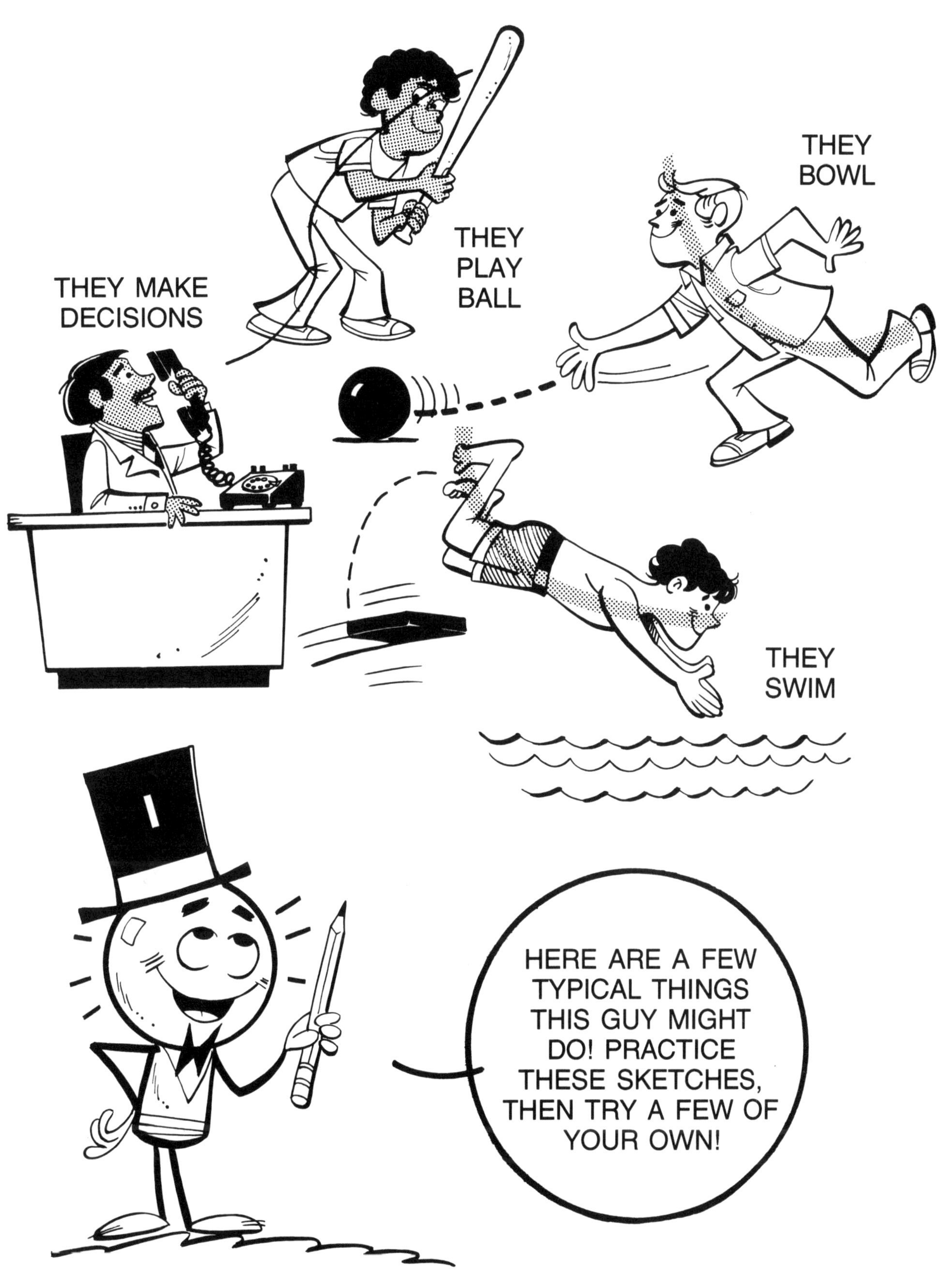
THEY MAKE DECISIONS
THEY PLAY BALL
THEY BOWL
THEY SWIM
HERE ARE A FEW TYPICAL THINGS THIS GUY MIGHT DO! PRACTICE THESE SKETCHES, THEN TRY A FEW OF YOUR OWN!

AS OUR YOUNG MAN MATURES INTO MIDDLE AGE, HIS APPEARANCE WILL CHANGE SOMEWHAT!

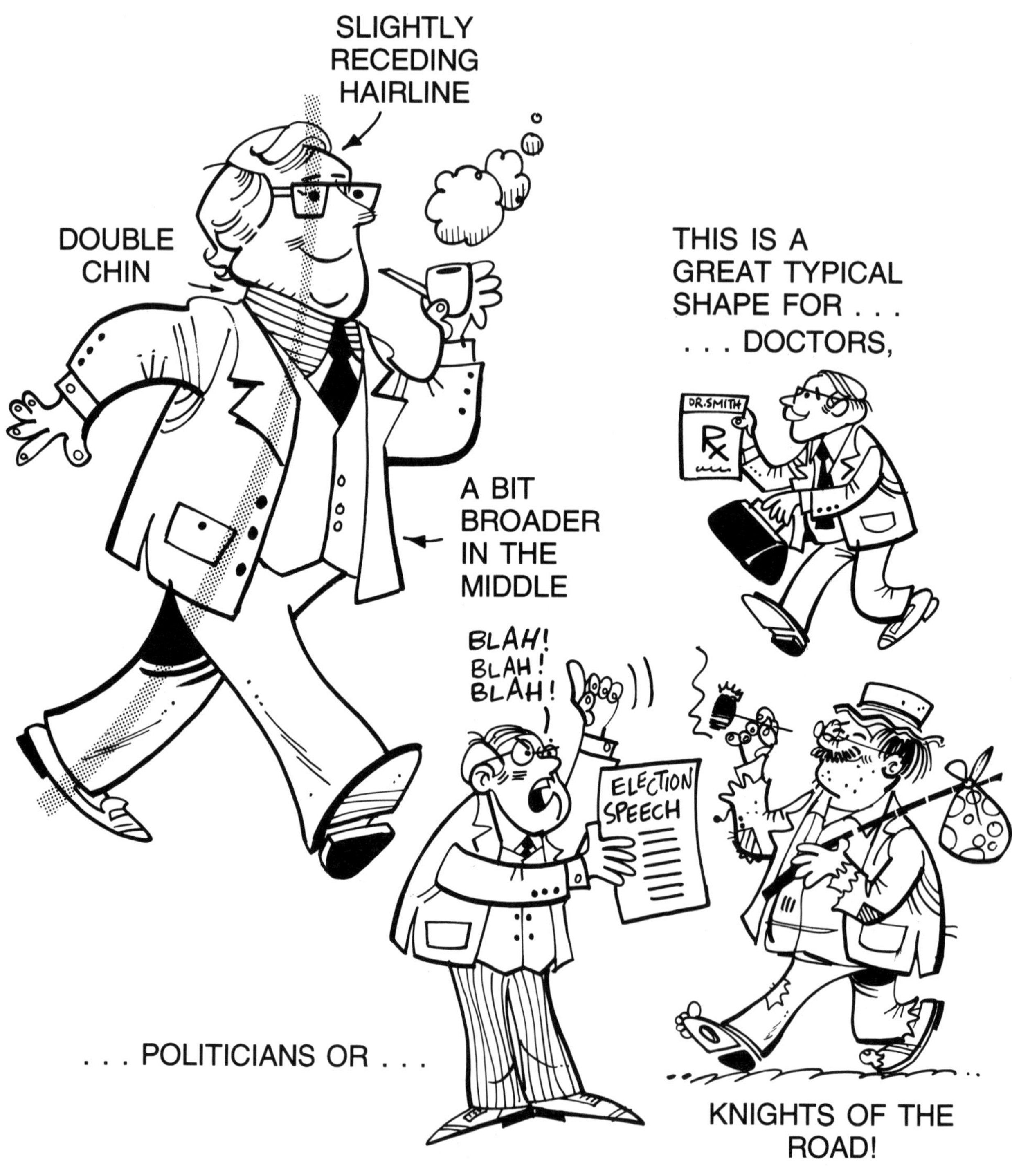

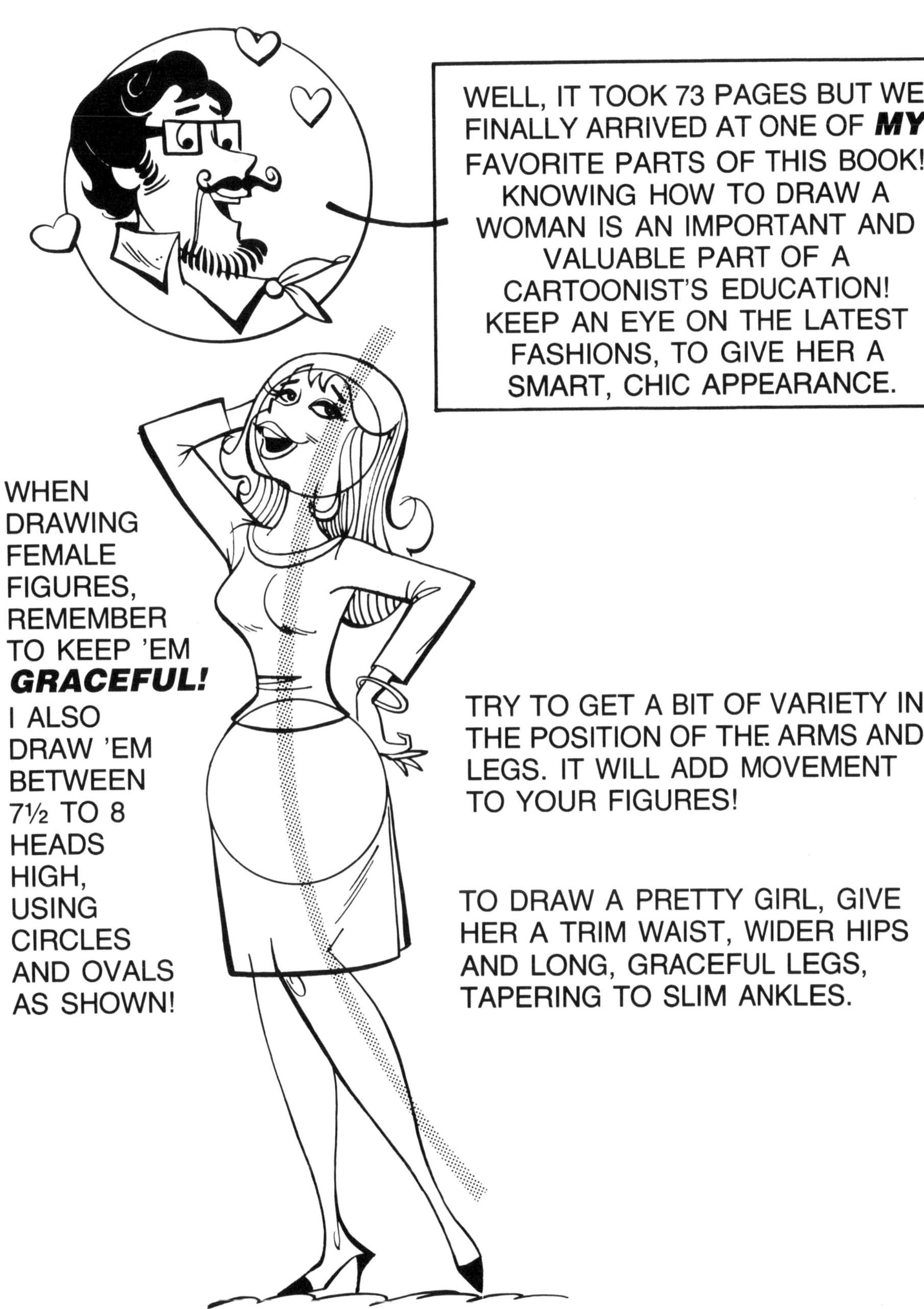
WELL, IT TOOK 73 PAGES BUT WE FINALLY ARRIVED AT ONE OF ***MY*** FAVORITE PARTS OF THIS BOOK! KNOWING HOW TO DRAW A WOMAN IS AN IMPORTANT AND VALUABLE PART OF A CARTOONIST'S EDUCATION! KEEP AN EYE ON THE LATEST FASHIONS, TO GIVE HER A SMART, CHIC APPEARANCE.
WHEN DRAWING FEMALE FIGURES, REMEMBER TO KEEP 'EM ***GRACEFUL!*** I ALSO DRAW 'EM BETWEEN 7½ TO 8 HEADS HIGH, USING CIRCLES AND OVALS AS SHOWN!
TRY TO GET A BIT OF VARIETY IN THE POSITION OF THE ARMS AND LEGS. IT WILL ADD MOVEMENT TO YOUR FIGURES!
TO DRAW A PRETTY GIRL, GIVE HER A TRIM WAIST, WIDER HIPS AND LONG, GRACEFUL LEGS, TAPERING TO SLIM ANKLES.

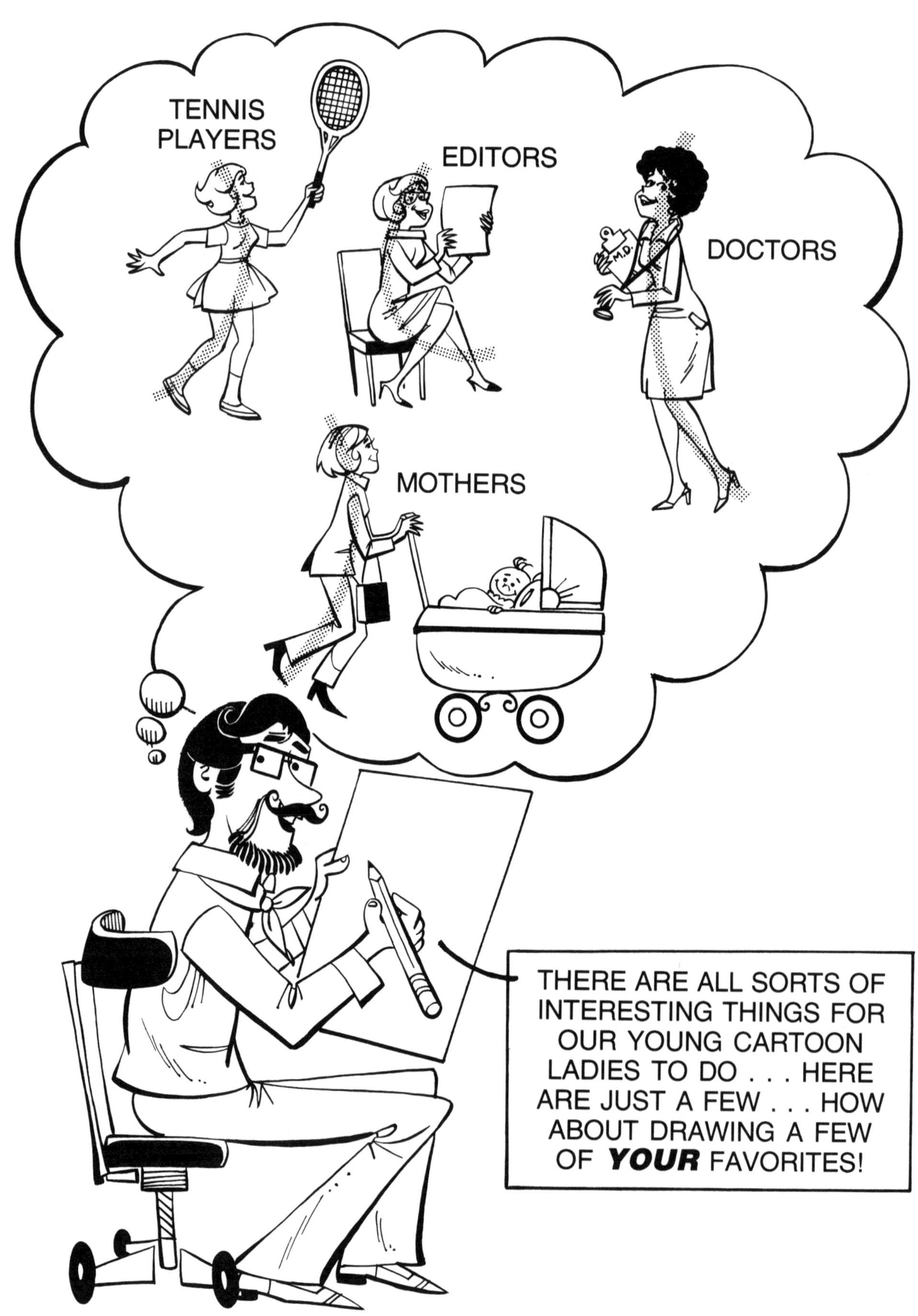
TENNIS PLAYERS
EDITORS
DOCTORS
M.D.
MOTHERS
THERE ARE ALL SORTS OF INTERESTING THINGS FOR OUR YOUNG CARTOON LADIES TO DO . . . HERE ARE JUST A FEW . . . HOW ABOUT DRAWING A FEW OF ***YOUR*** FAVORITES!

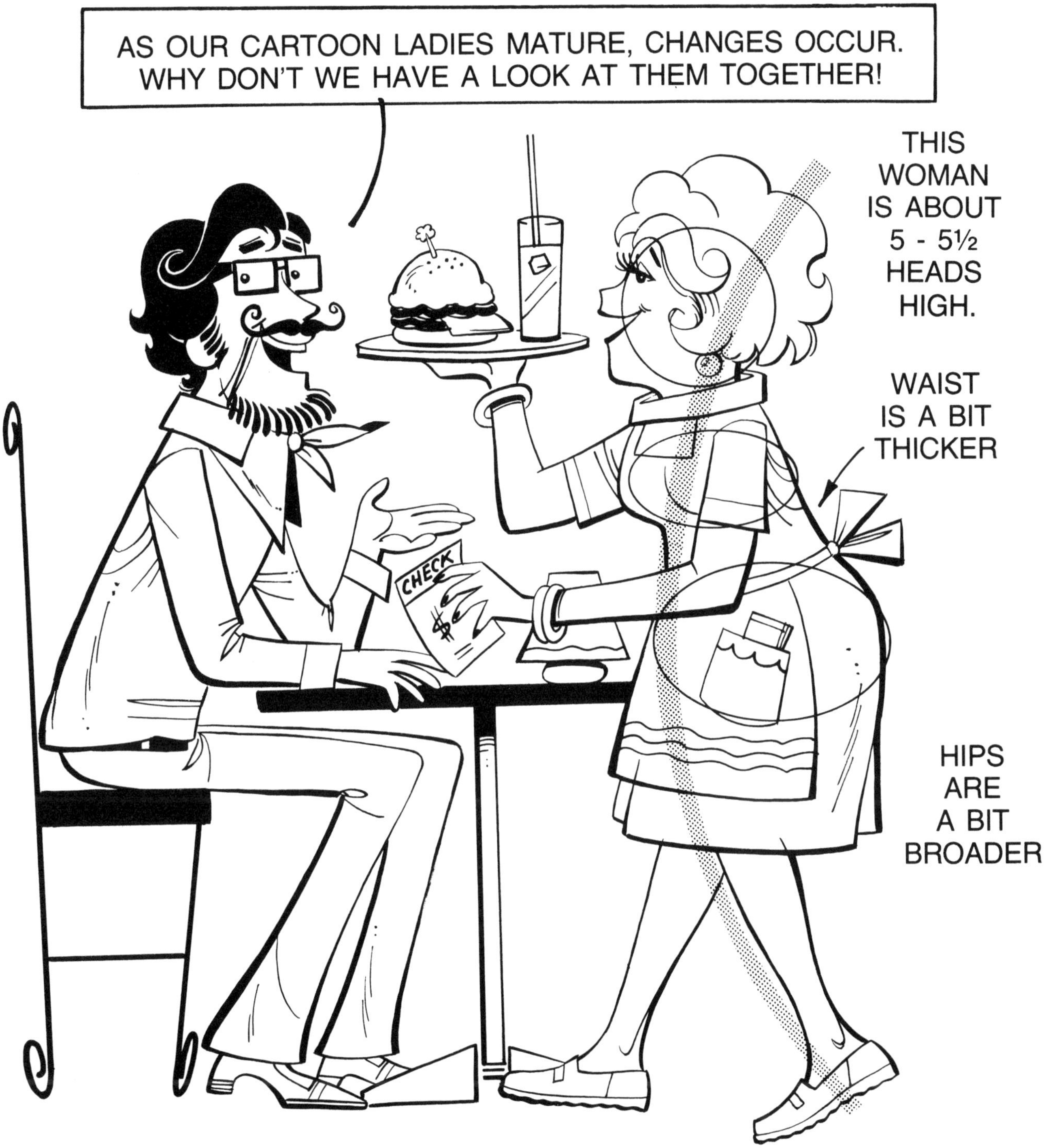

AS OUR CARTOON LADIES MATURE, CHANGES OCCUR.
WHY DON'T WE HAVE A LOOK AT THEM TOGETHER!

THIS WOMAN IS ABOUT 5 - 5½ HEADS HIGH.

WAIST IS A BIT THICKER

CHECK

HIPS ARE A BIT BROADER

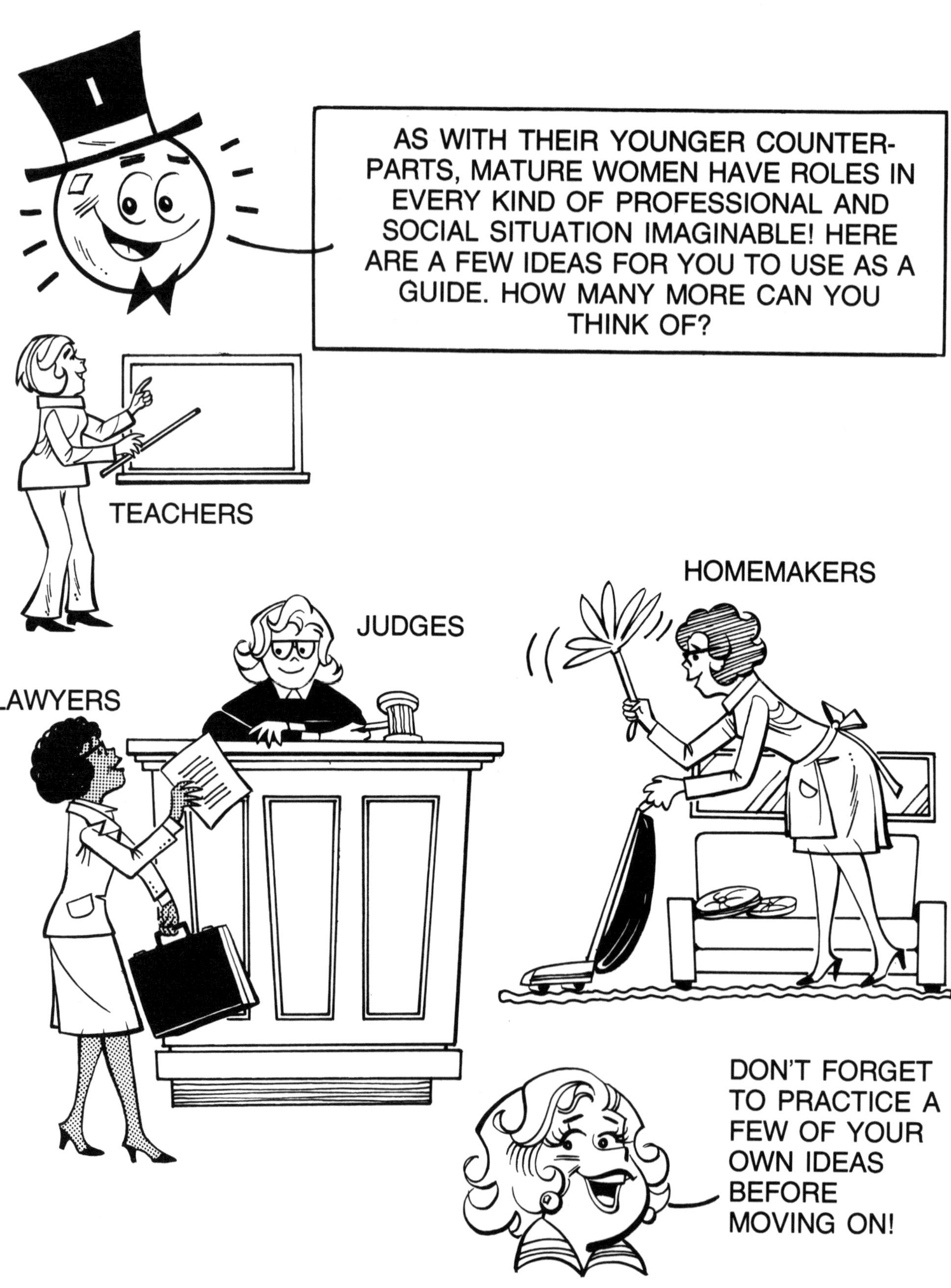
AS WITH THEIR YOUNGER COUNTER-PARTS, MATURE WOMEN HAVE ROLES IN EVERY KIND OF PROFESSIONAL AND SOCIAL SITUATION IMAGINABLE! HERE ARE A FEW IDEAS FOR YOU TO USE AS A GUIDE. HOW MANY MORE CAN YOU THINK OF?
TEACHERS
HOMEMAKERS
JUDGES
LAWYERS
DON'T FORGET TO PRACTICE A FEW OF YOUR OWN IDEAS BEFORE MOVING ON!

WHEW . . . THIS GUY IS HARD TO (PUFF) KEEP UP WITH! . . . BUT HE'S TYPICAL OF THE FELLOWS YOU WILL FIND ON THE NEXT FEW PAGES. THEY'RE A VERY (HUFF - PUFF) ACTIVE GROUP AND YOUR CARTOONS SHOULD DEPICT THEM IN ALL SORTS OF ACTIVITIES!

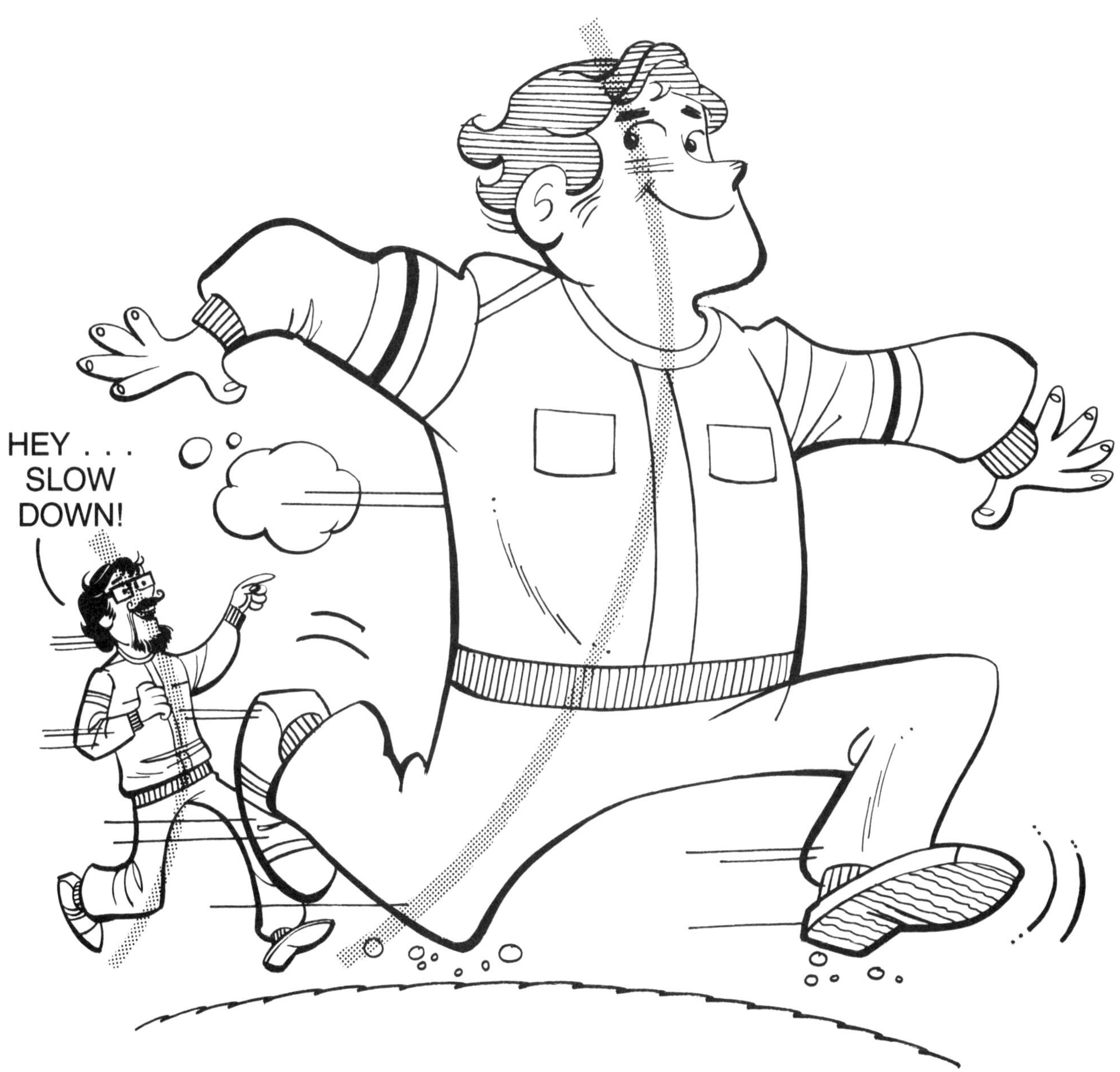

LET'S EXPLORE A FEW OF THESE VARIOUS ACTIVITIES . . . HOW'S ABOUT DRAWING ALONG WITH ME!

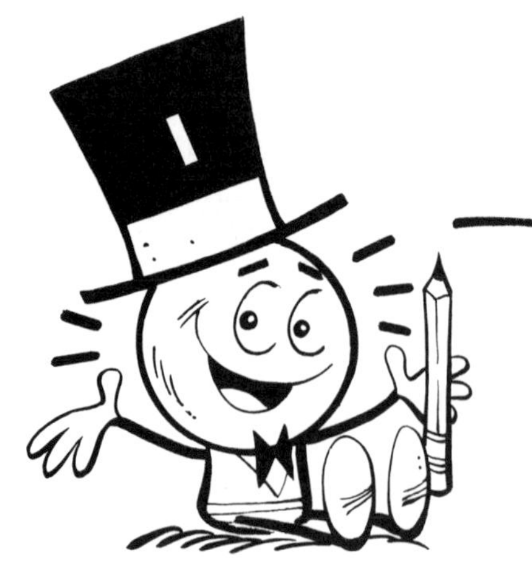

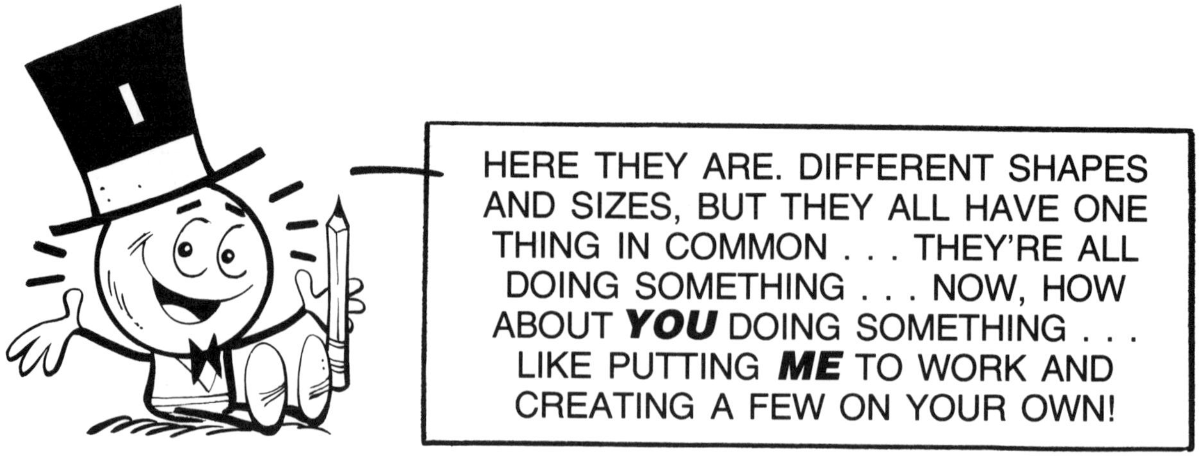

HERE THEY ARE. DIFFERENT SHAPES AND SIZES, BUT THEY ALL HAVE ONE THING IN COMMON . . . THEY'RE ALL DOING SOMETHING . . . NOW, HOW ABOUT ***YOU*** DOING SOMETHING . . . LIKE PUTTING ***ME*** TO WORK AND CREATING A FEW ON YOUR OWN!

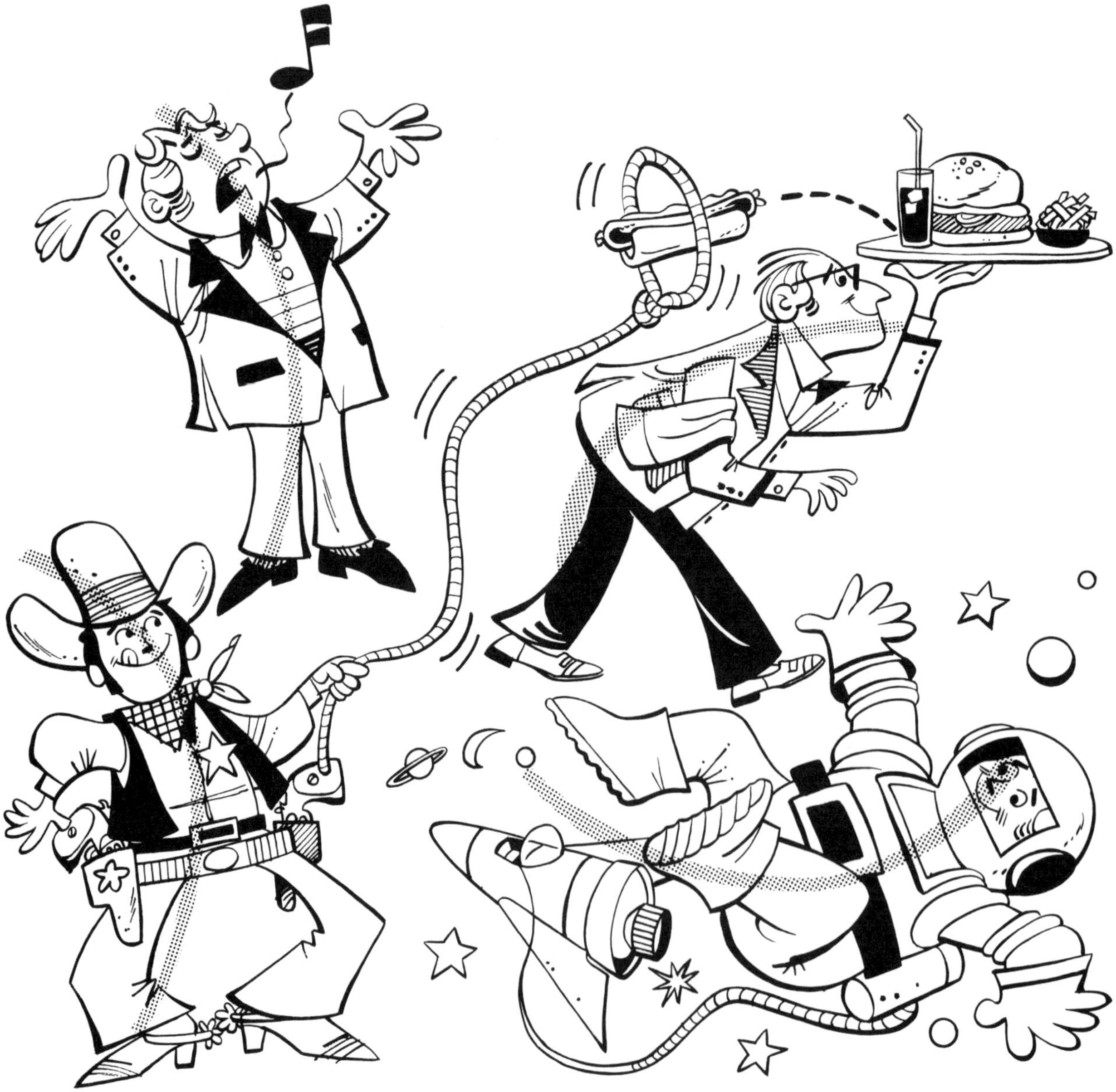

WHILE YOU'RE AT IT . . . HERE ARE A FEW
MORE TYPICAL THINGS OUR LADIES ARE INVOLVED IN.

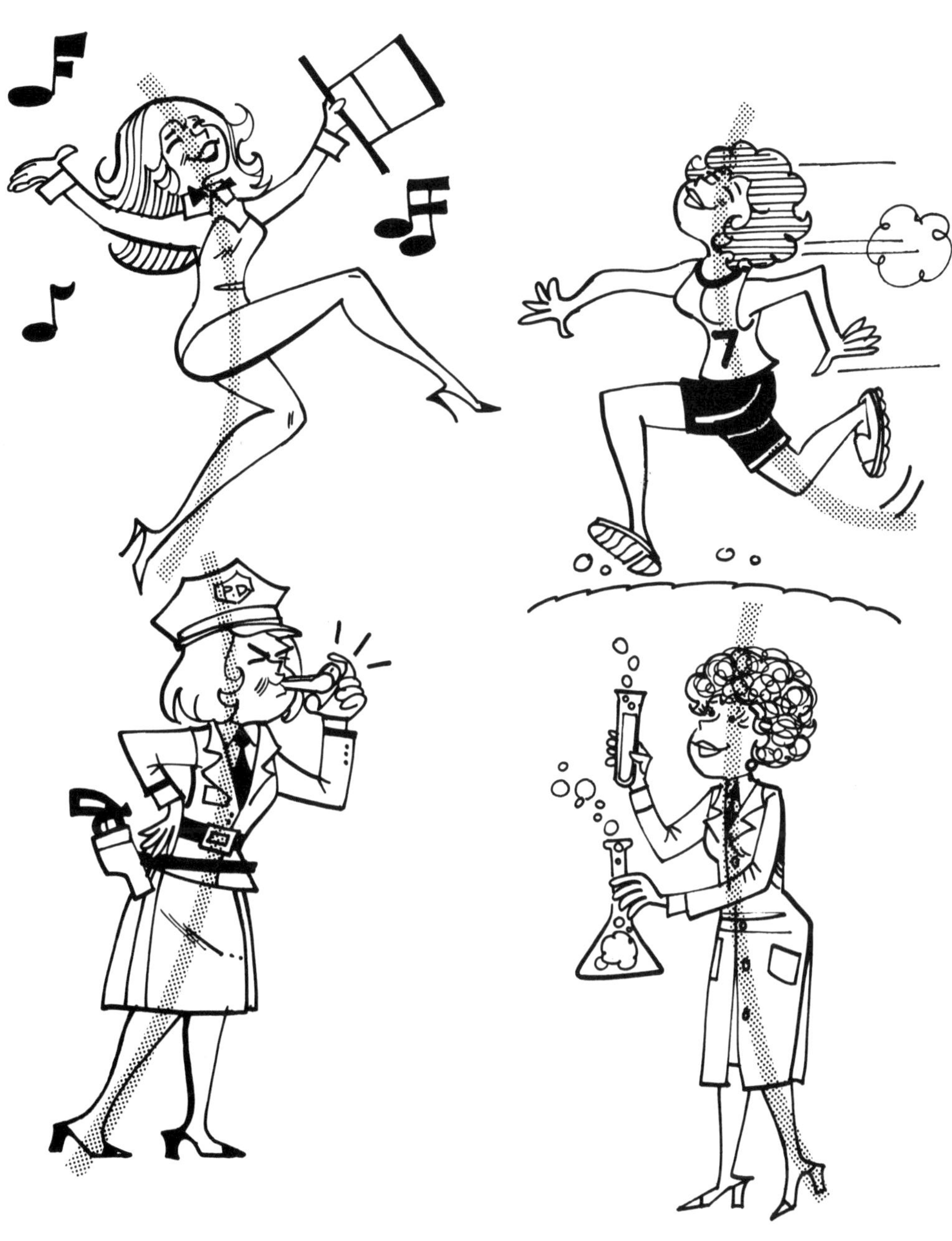

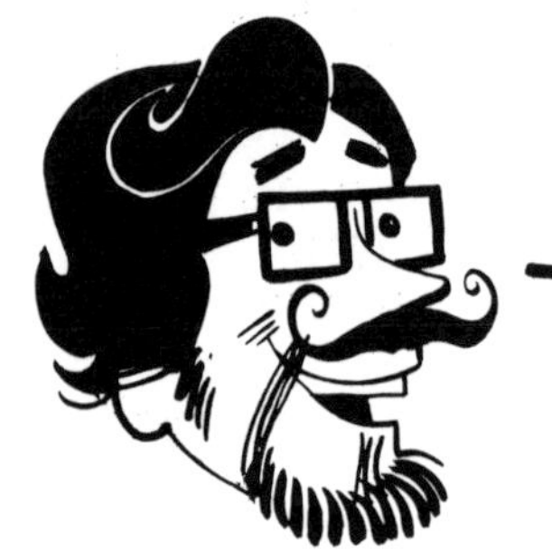
THERE IS STILL ANOTHER VERY IMPORTANT SEGMENT OF OUR POPULATION THAT WE MUST DIRECT OUR ATTENTION TO! . . . THEY HAVE A LOT OF ENERGY AND ARE INVOLVED IN ALL SORTS OF ACTIVITIES . . . AND THEY'RE CALLED. . .
SENIORS!
. . . AND YOU WILL FIND A FEW OF ***OUR*** ACTIVITIES ON THE NEXT PAGE!

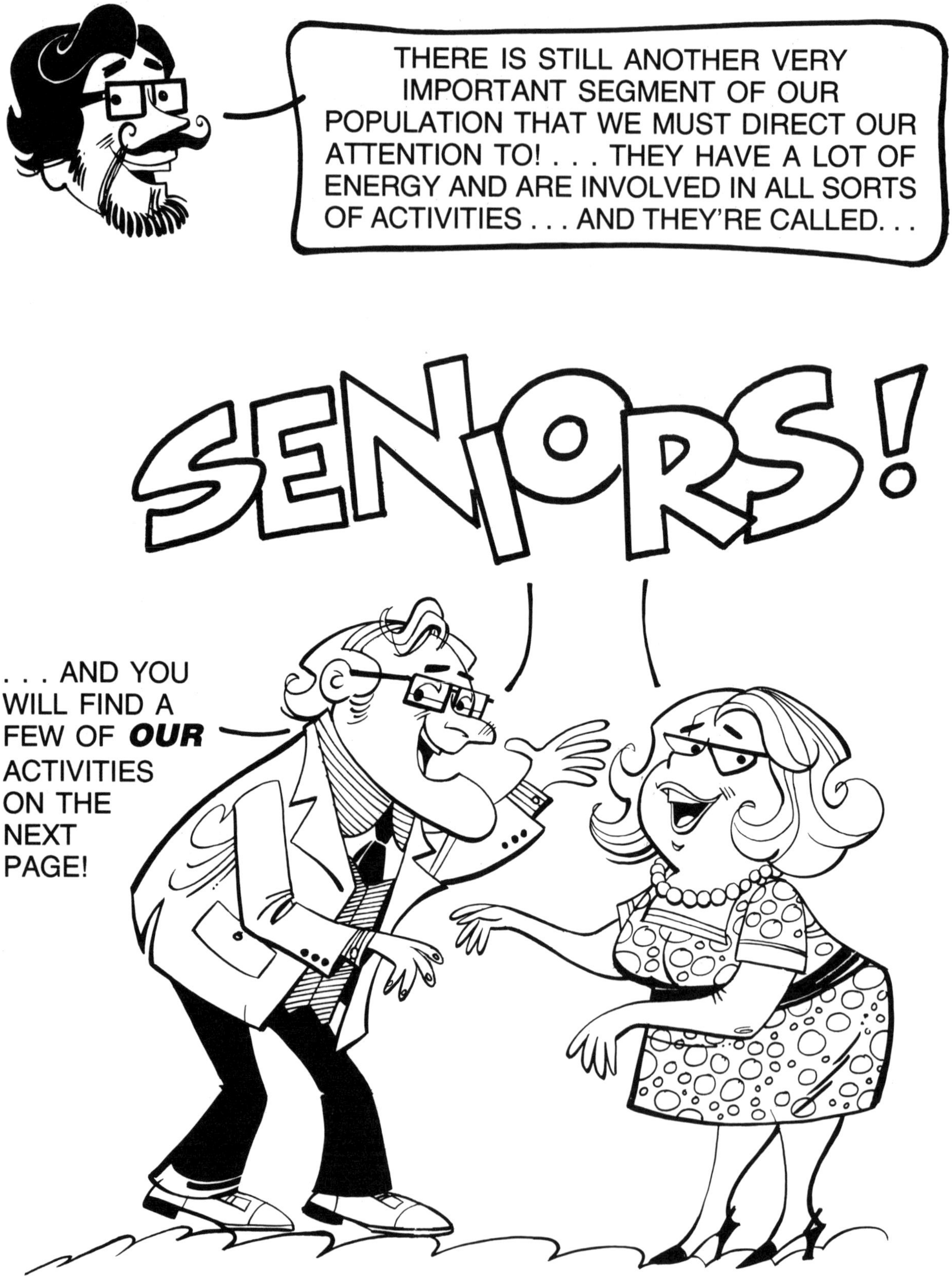

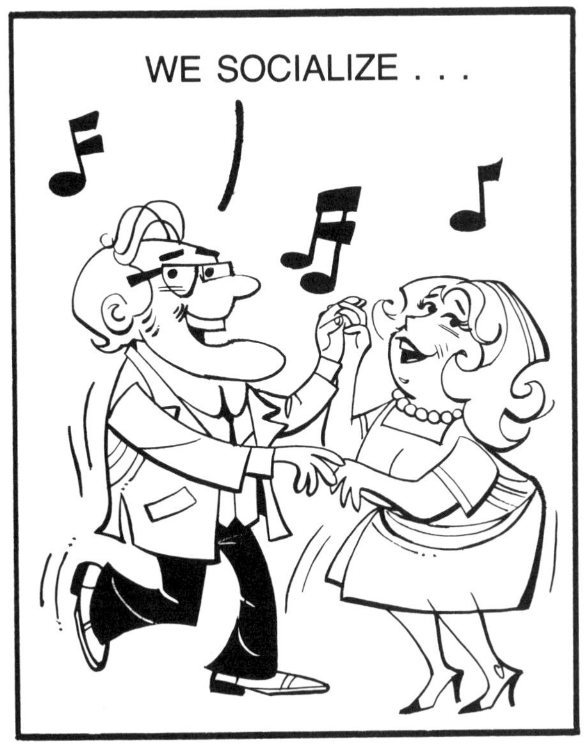

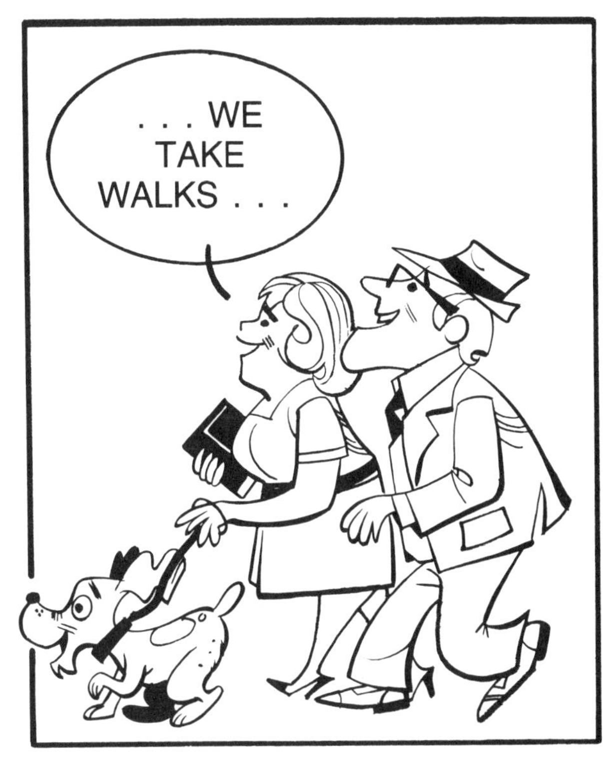

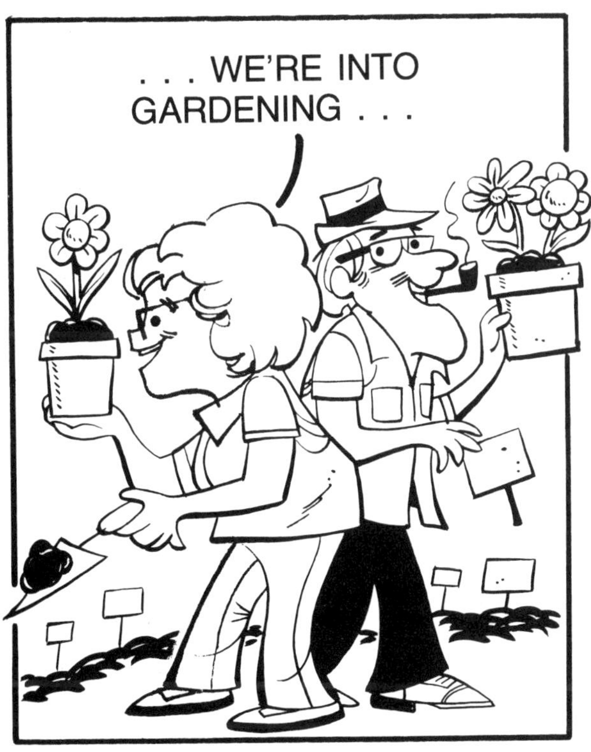

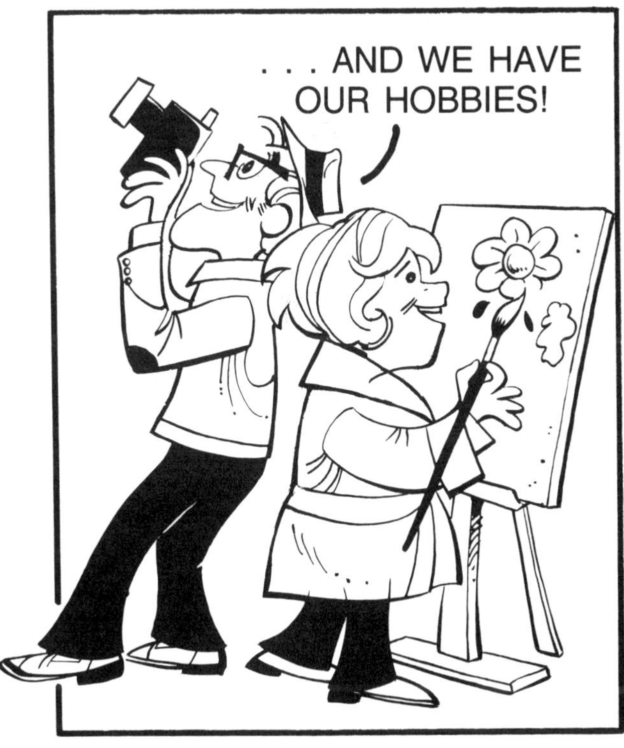

HERE'S A PROBLEM FOR YOU! . . . TRY AND FIND THE ***LINE OF ACTION*** IN THE ABOVE SKETCHES, THEN . . . BUILD UP YOUR OWN CARTOONS AROUND IT!

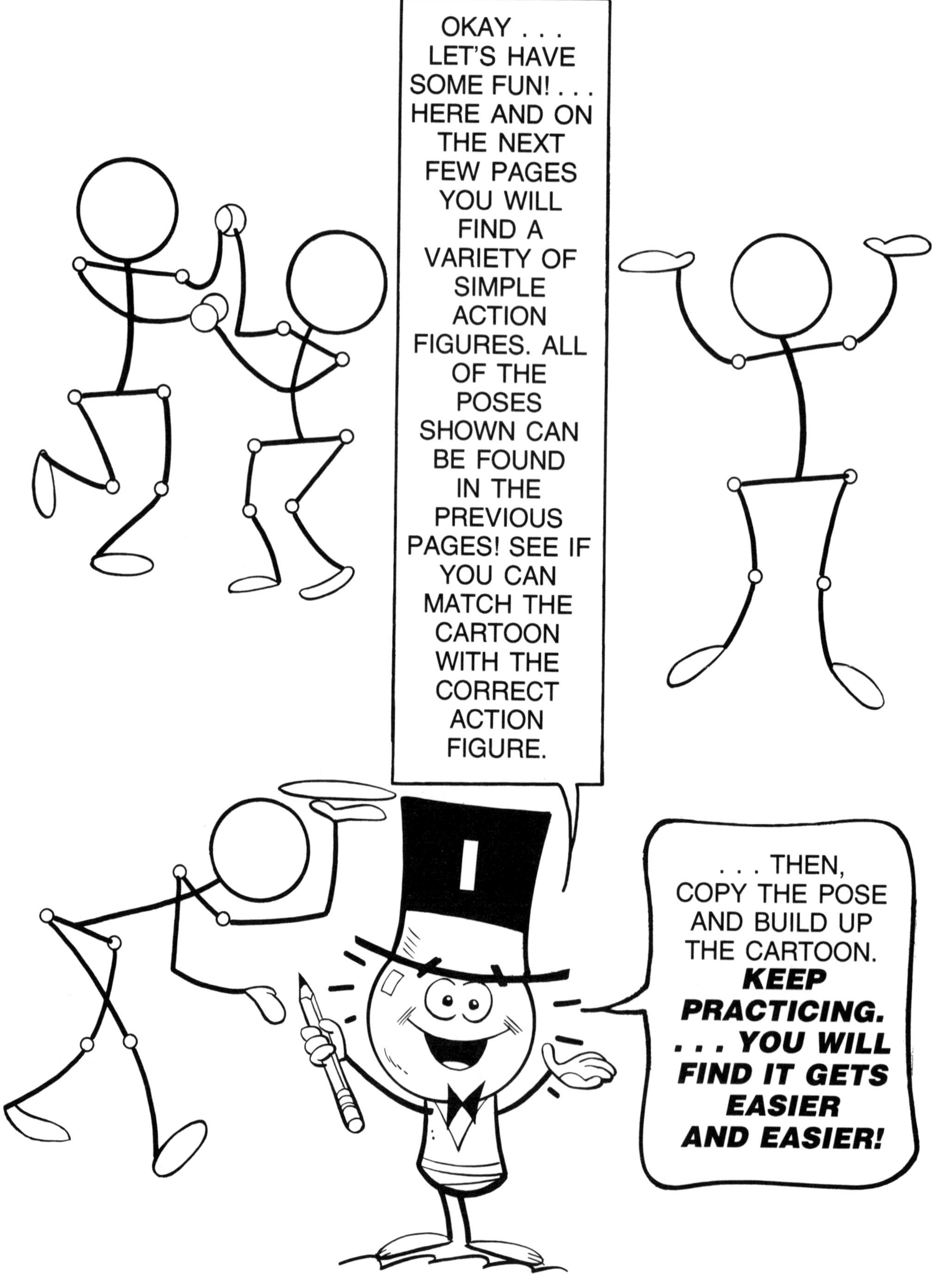
OKAY . . .
LET'S HAVE
SOME FUN! . . .
HERE AND ON
THE NEXT
FEW PAGES
YOU WILL
FIND A
VARIETY OF
SIMPLE
ACTION
FIGURES. ALL
OF THE
POSES
SHOWN CAN
BE FOUND
IN THE
PREVIOUS
PAGES! SEE IF
YOU CAN
MATCH THE
CARTOON
WITH THE
CORRECT
ACTION
FIGURE.
. . . THEN,
COPY THE POSE
AND BUILD UP
THE CARTOON.
KEEP
PRACTICING.
. . . YOU WILL
FIND IT GETS
EASIER
AND EASIER!

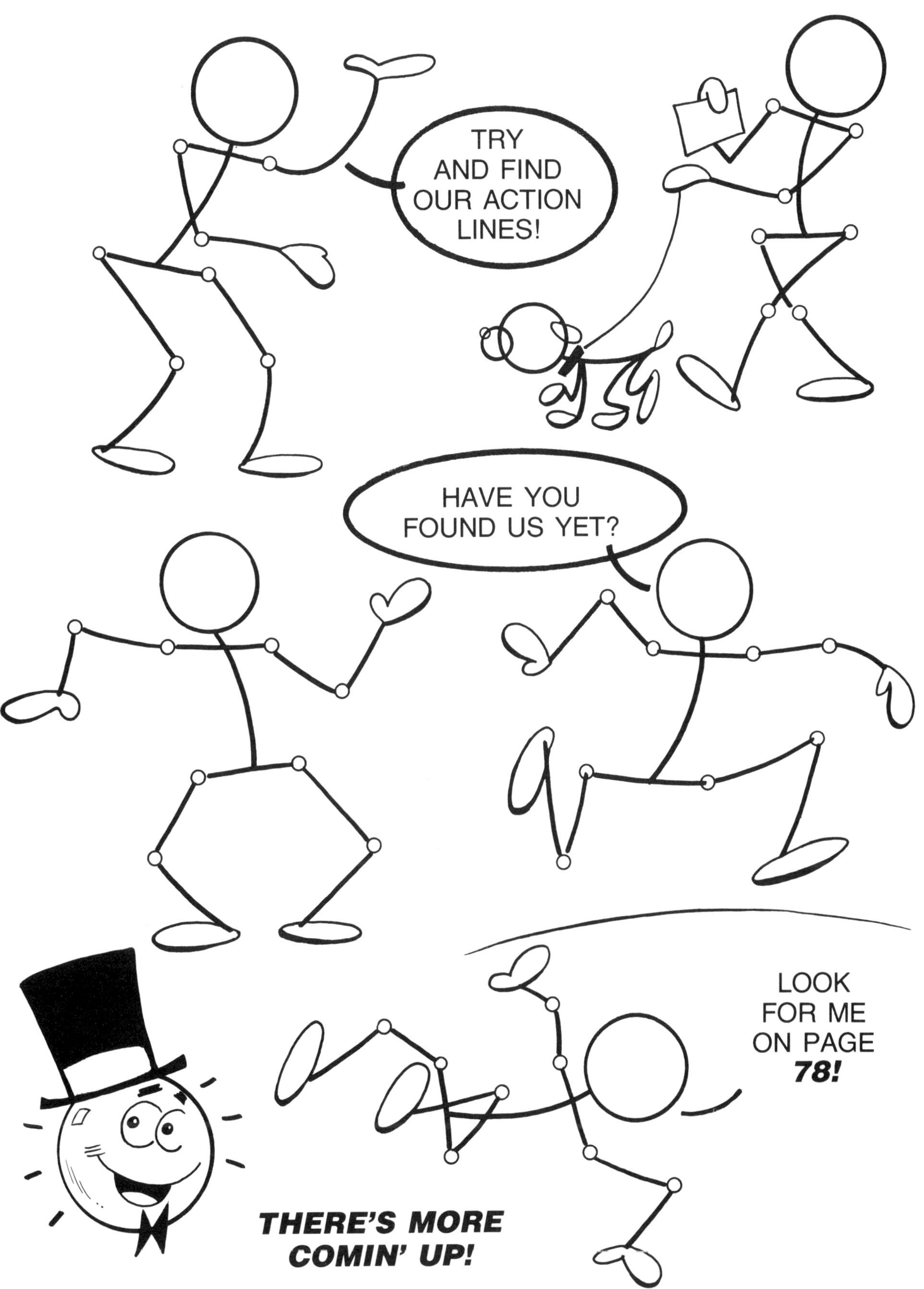
TRY AND FIND OUR ACTION LINES!
HAVE YOU FOUND US YET?
LOOK FOR ME ON PAGE 78!
THERE'S MORE COMIN' UP!

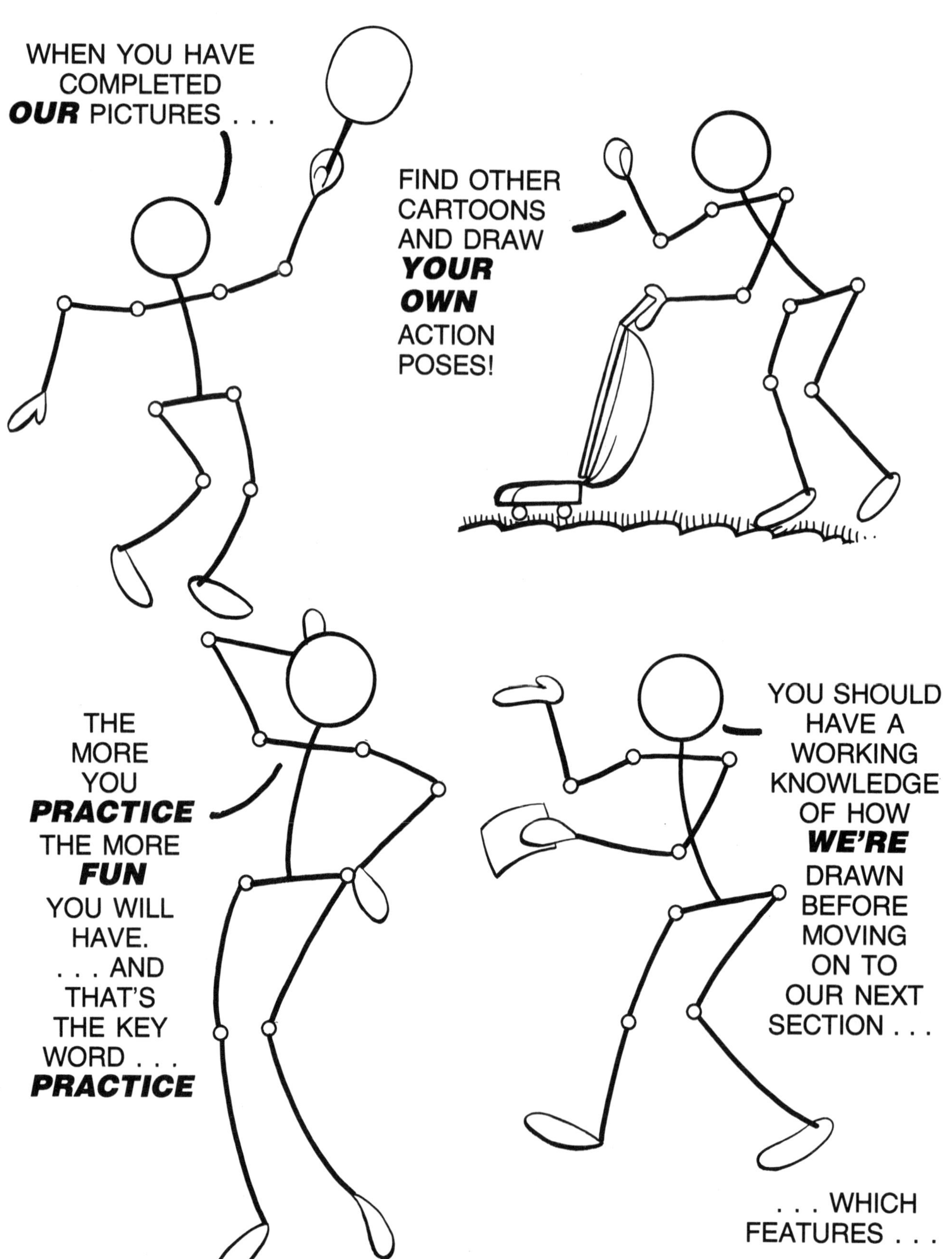

. . . WHICH
FEATURES . . .

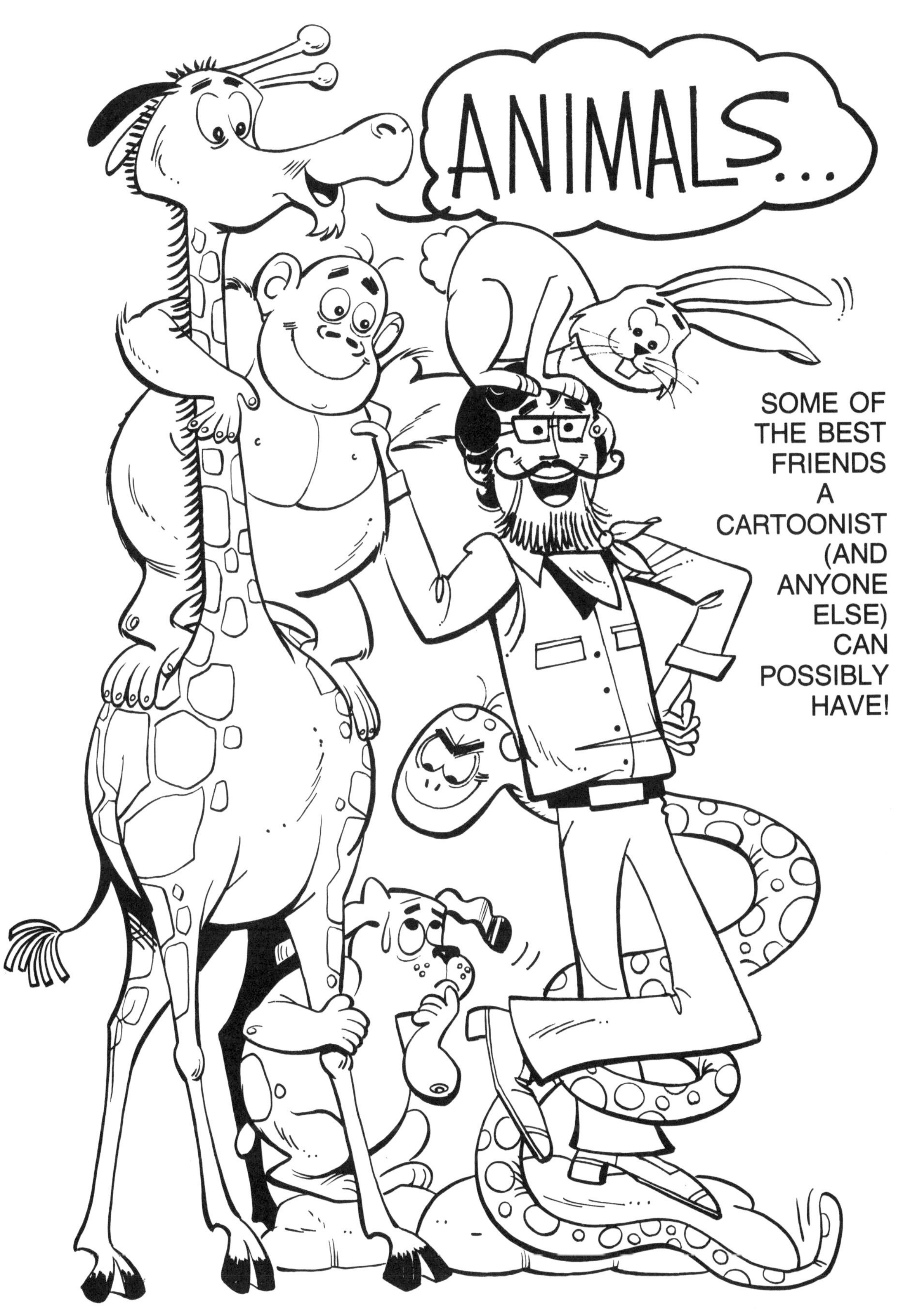
ANIMALS...
SOME OF THE BEST FRIENDS A CARTOONIST (AND ANYONE ELSE) CAN POSSIBLY HAVE!

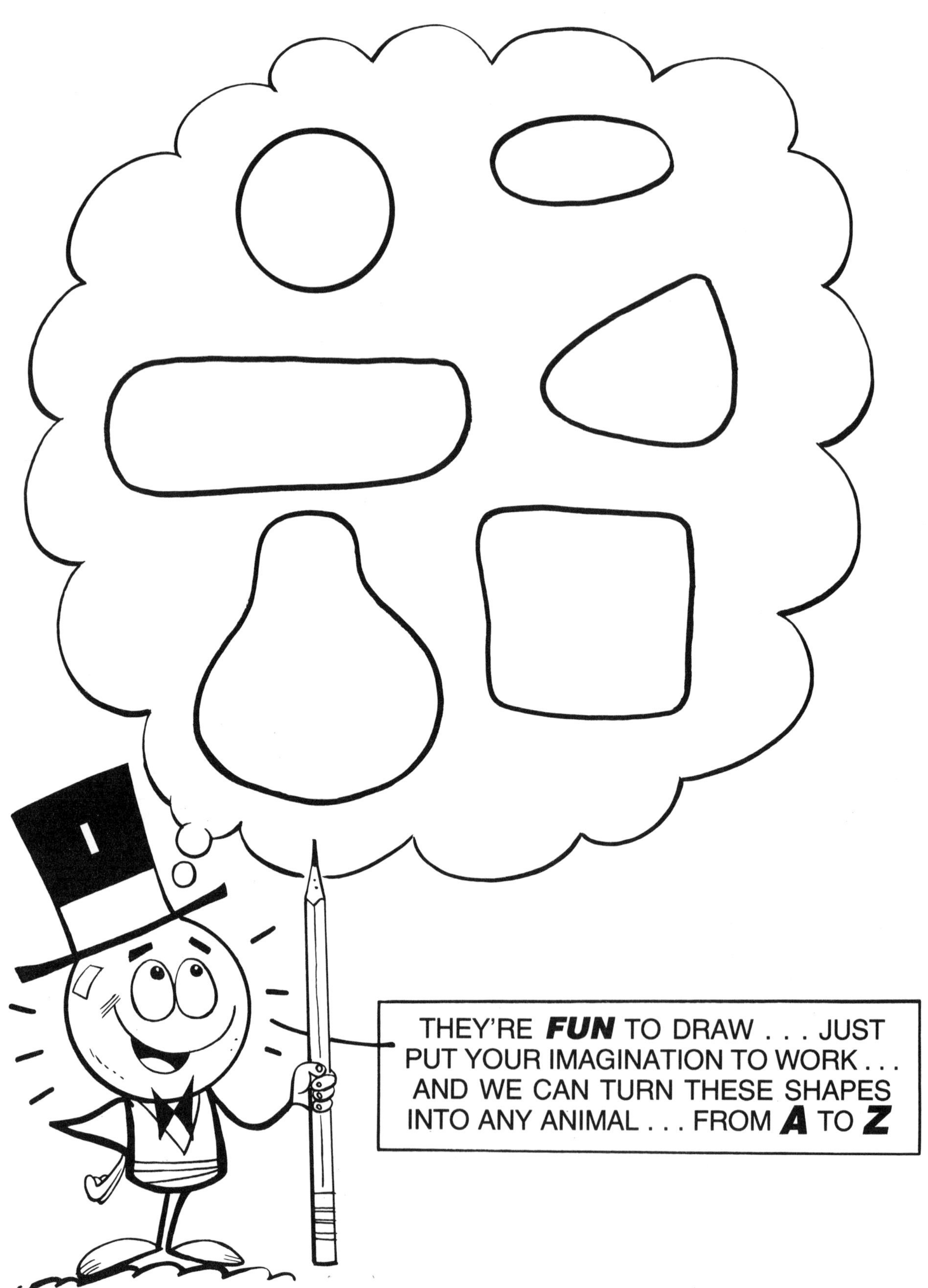
THEY'RE **FUN** TO DRAW . . . JUST PUT YOUR IMAGINATION TO WORK . . . AND WE CAN TURN THESE SHAPES INTO ANY ANIMAL . . . FROM **A** TO **Z**

. . . OR . . . FROM ***APE***

HEAD CONSTRUCTION
CIRCLE AND OVAL
HEAVY
BROWS
HEAD SITS
LOW ON
SHOULDERS
PEAR-
SHAPED
BODY
LONG
ARMS
SHORT
LEGS

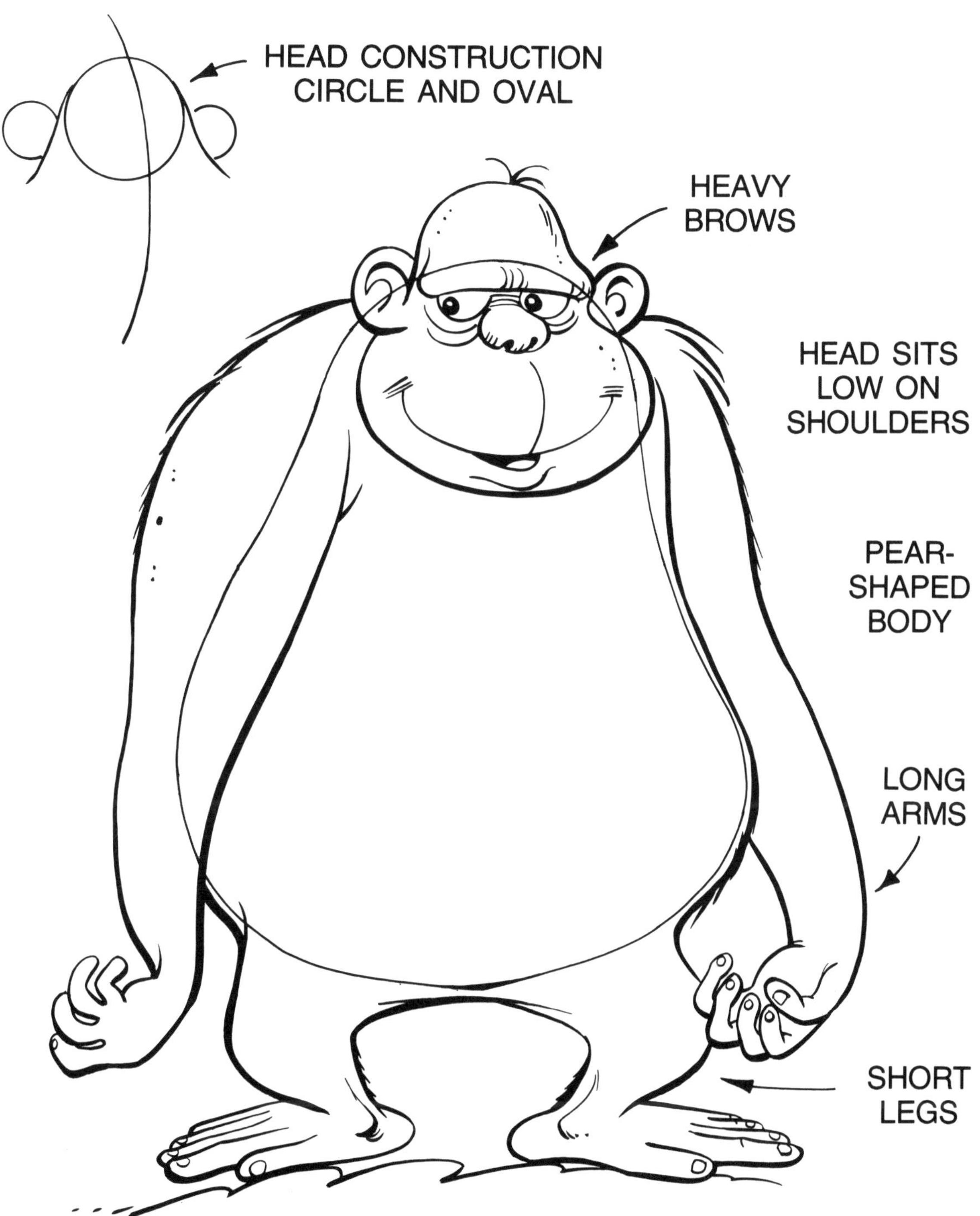

. . . TO ***ZEBRA*** . . . OR

HEAD SHAPE
(CIRCLE AND
OVAL AGAIN)
BODY
CAN BE SORT
OF EGG-
SHAPED

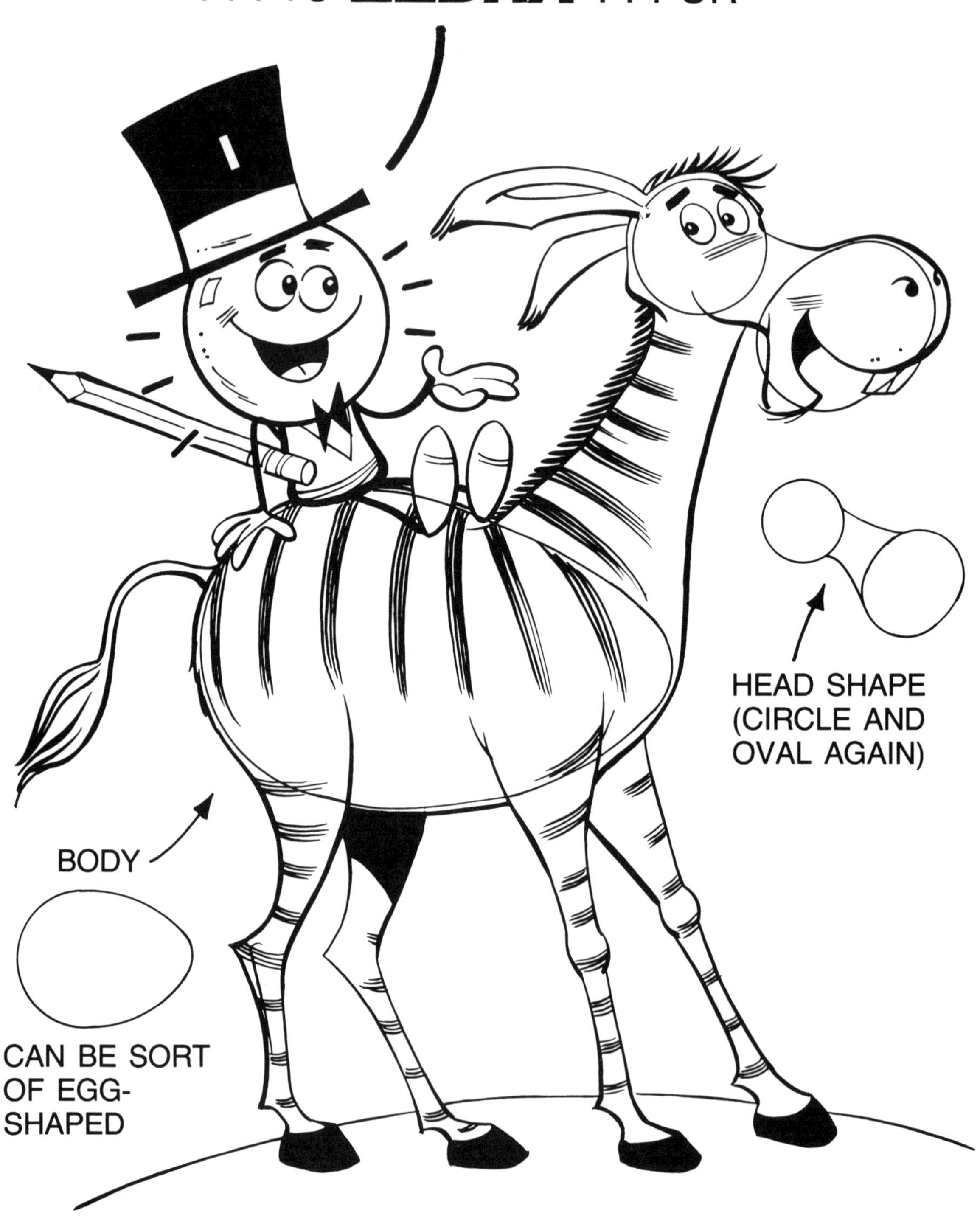

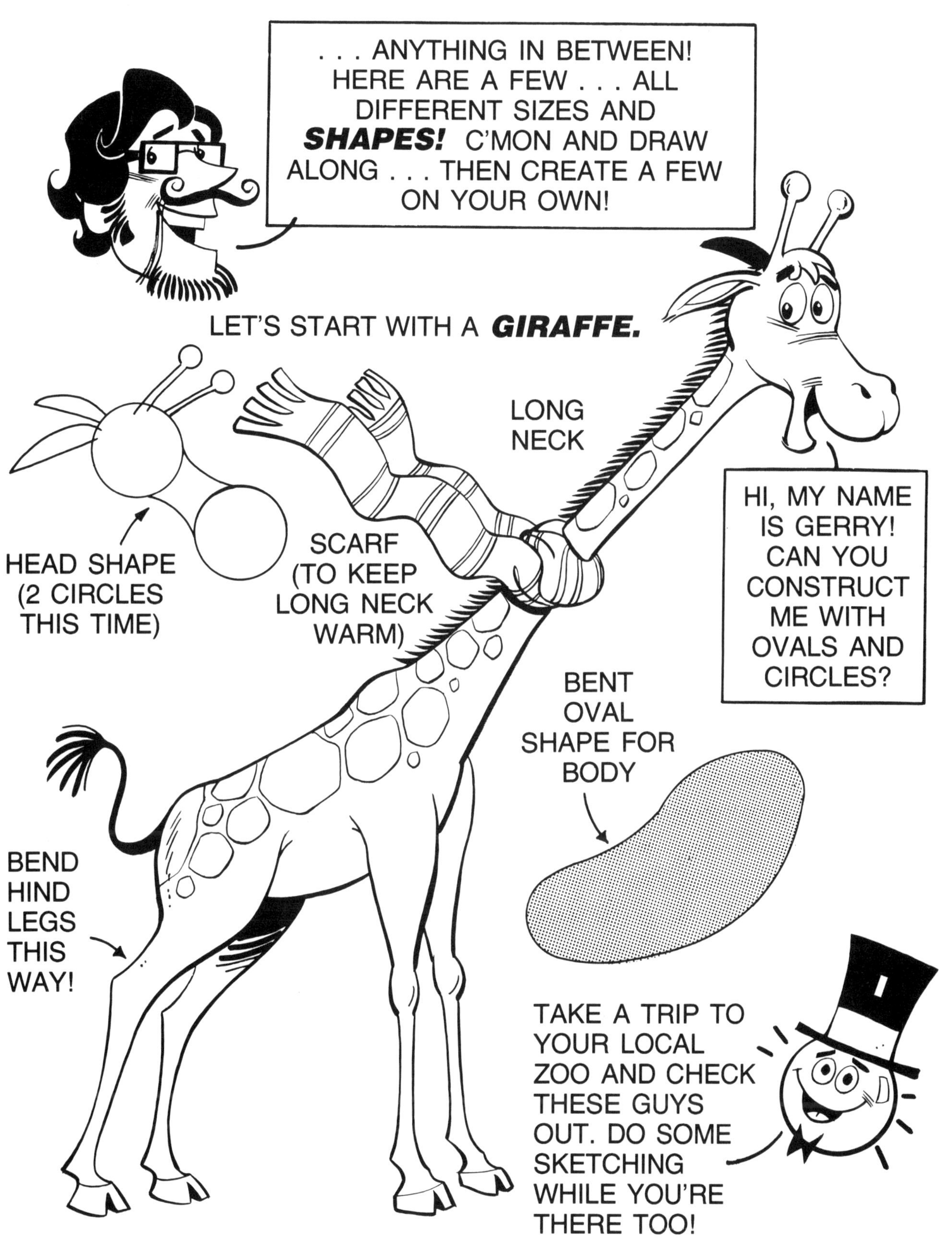
. . . ANYTHING IN BETWEEN! HERE ARE A FEW . . . ALL DIFFERENT SIZES AND **SHAPES!** C'MON AND DRAW ALONG . . . THEN CREATE A FEW ON YOUR OWN!
LET'S START WITH A ***GIRAFFE.***
HEAD SHAPE (2 CIRCLES THIS TIME)
SCARF (TO KEEP LONG NECK WARM)
LONG NECK
HI, MY NAME IS GERRY! CAN YOU CONSTRUCT ME WITH OVALS AND CIRCLES?
BENT OVAL SHAPE FOR BODY
BEND HIND LEGS THIS WAY!
TAKE A TRIP TO YOUR LOCAL ZOO AND CHECK THESE GUYS OUT. DO SOME SKETCHING WHILE YOU'RE THERE TOO!

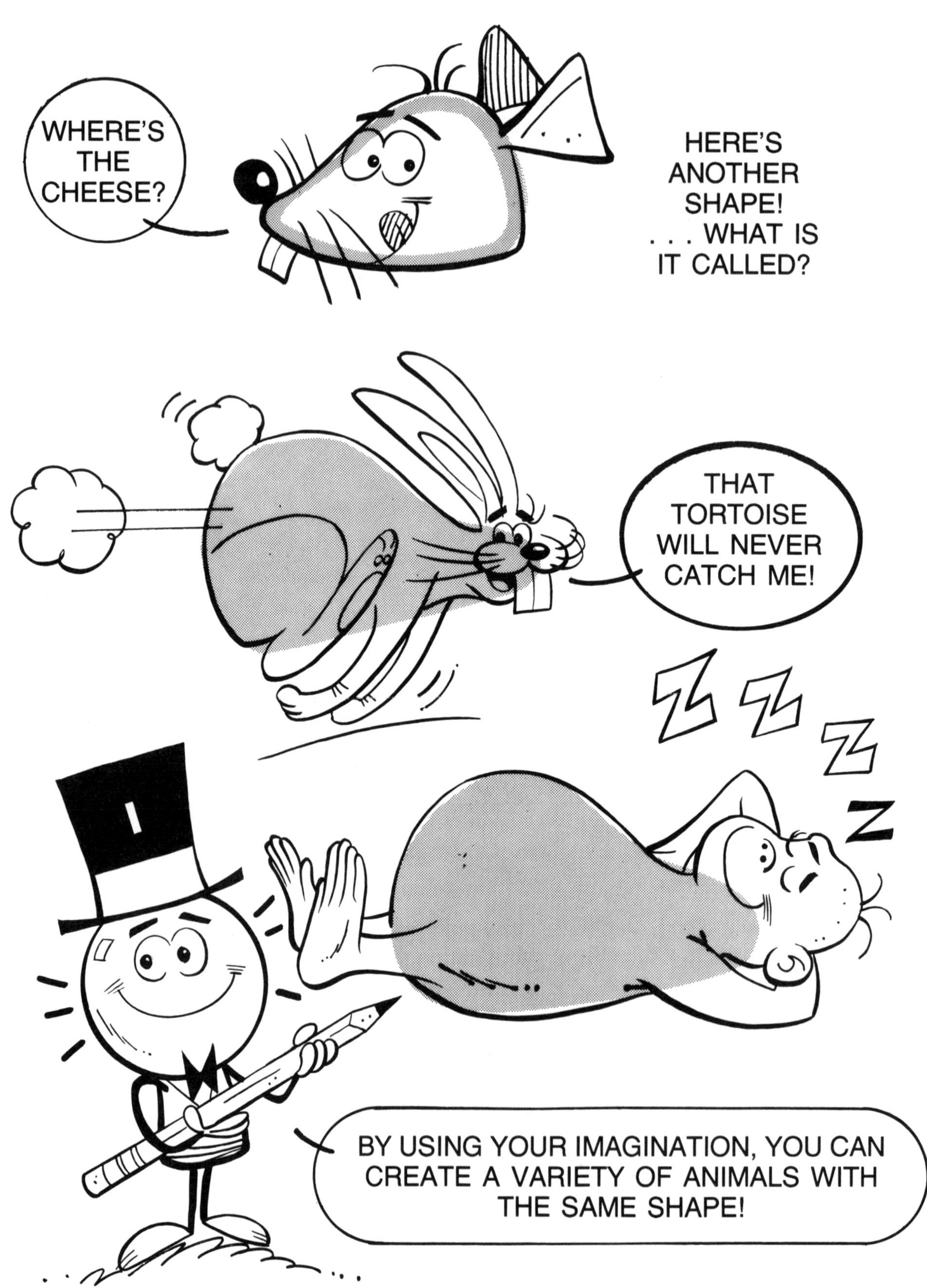
WHERE'S THE CHEESE?
HERE'S ANOTHER SHAPE! . . . WHAT IS IT CALLED?
THAT TORTOISE WILL NEVER CATCH ME!
Z Z Z Z
BY USING YOUR IMAGINATION, YOU CAN CREATE A VARIETY OF ANIMALS WITH THE SAME SHAPE!

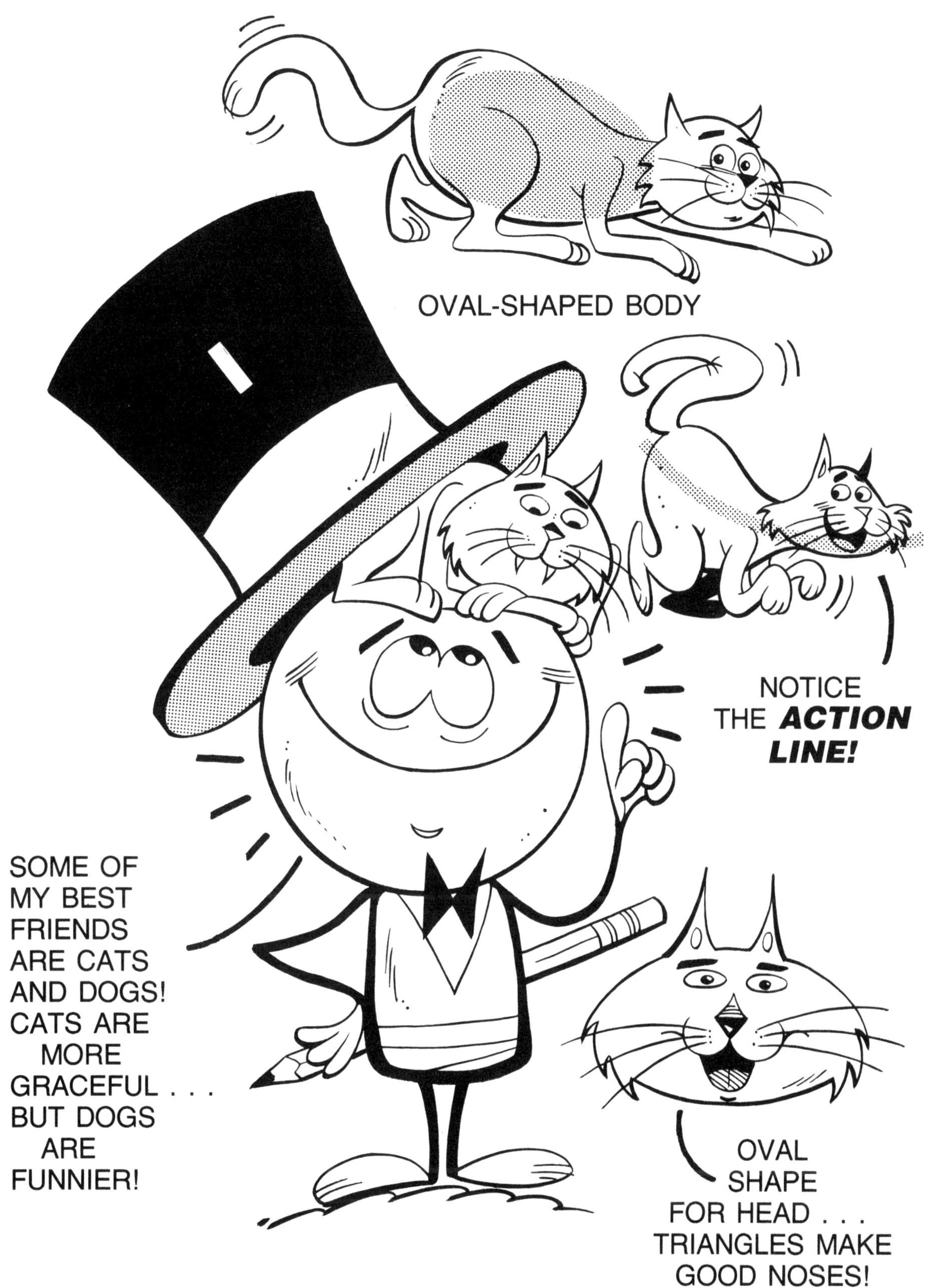
OVAL-SHAPED BODY
NOTICE THE **ACTION LINE!**
SOME OF MY BEST FRIENDS ARE CATS AND DOGS! CATS ARE MORE GRACEFUL . . . BUT DOGS ARE FUNNIER!
OVAL SHAPE FOR HEAD . . . TRIANGLES MAKE GOOD NOSES!

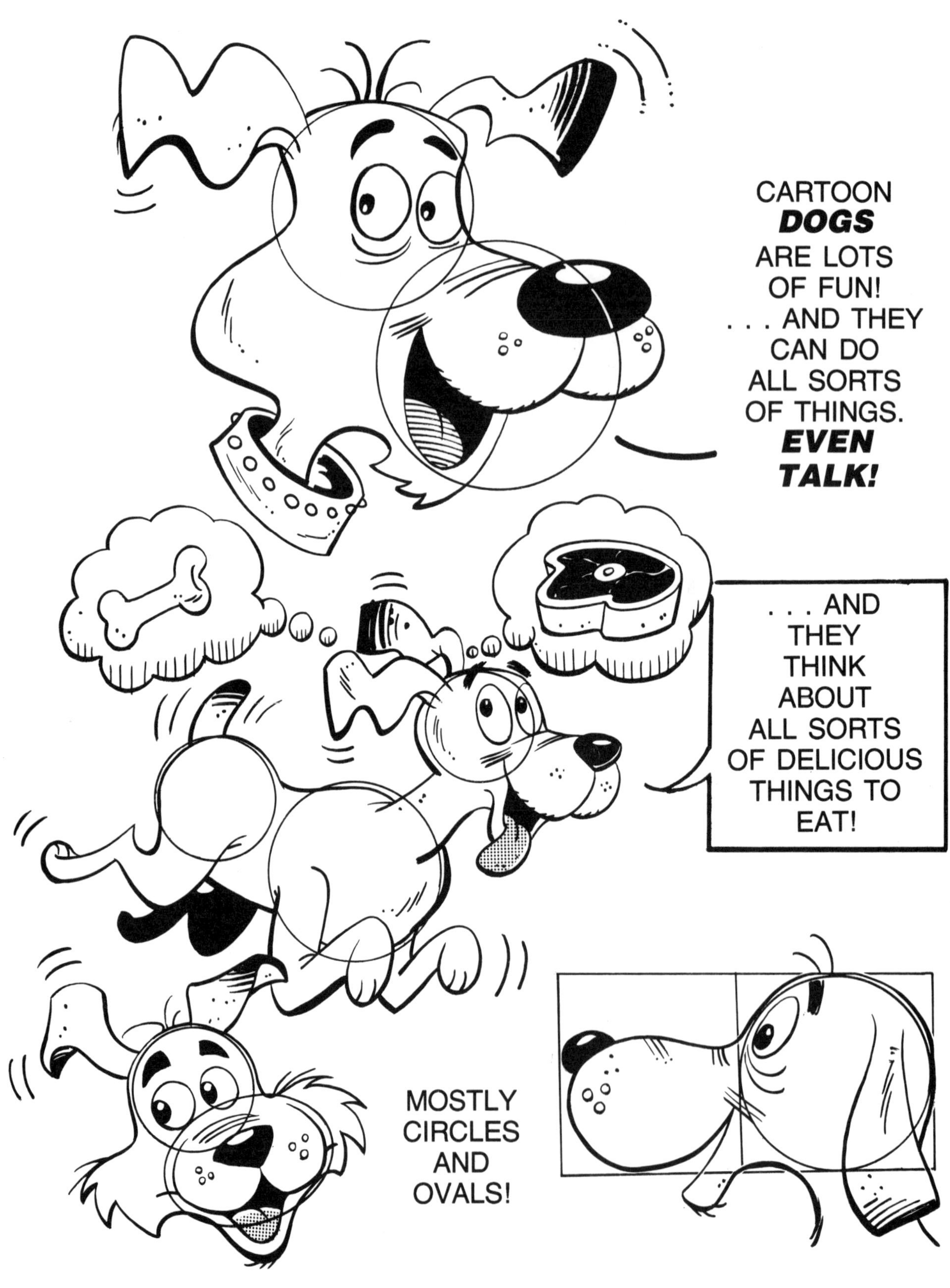
CARTOON **DOGS** ARE LOTS OF FUN! . . . AND THEY CAN DO ALL SORTS OF THINGS. ***EVEN TALK!***
. . . AND THEY THINK ABOUT ALL SORTS OF DELICIOUS THINGS TO EAT!
MOSTLY CIRCLES AND OVALS!

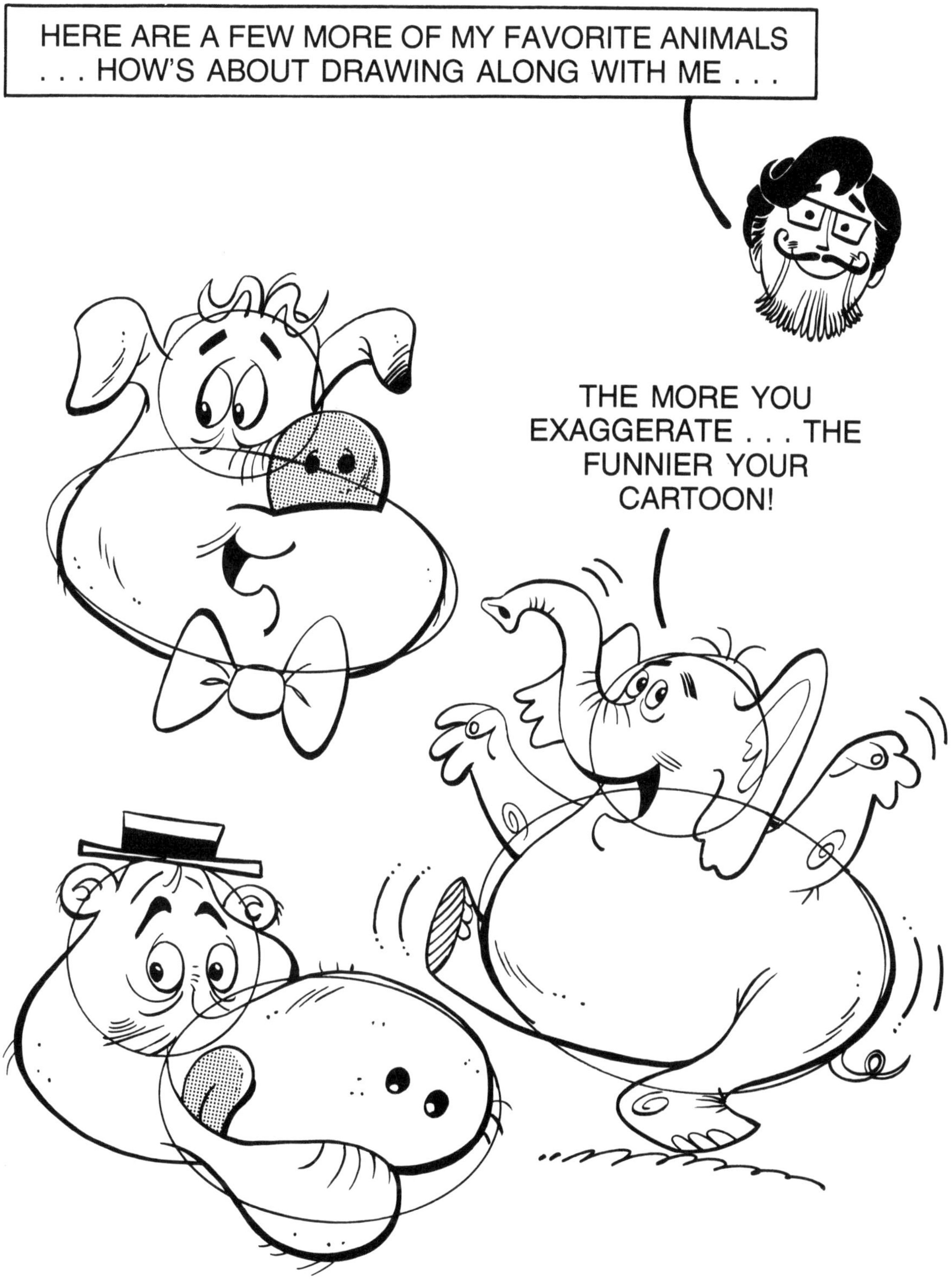

HERE ARE A FEW MORE OF MY FAVORITE ANIMALS
. . . HOW'S ABOUT DRAWING ALONG WITH ME . . .

THE MORE YOU
EXAGGERATE . . . THE
FUNNIER YOUR
CARTOON!

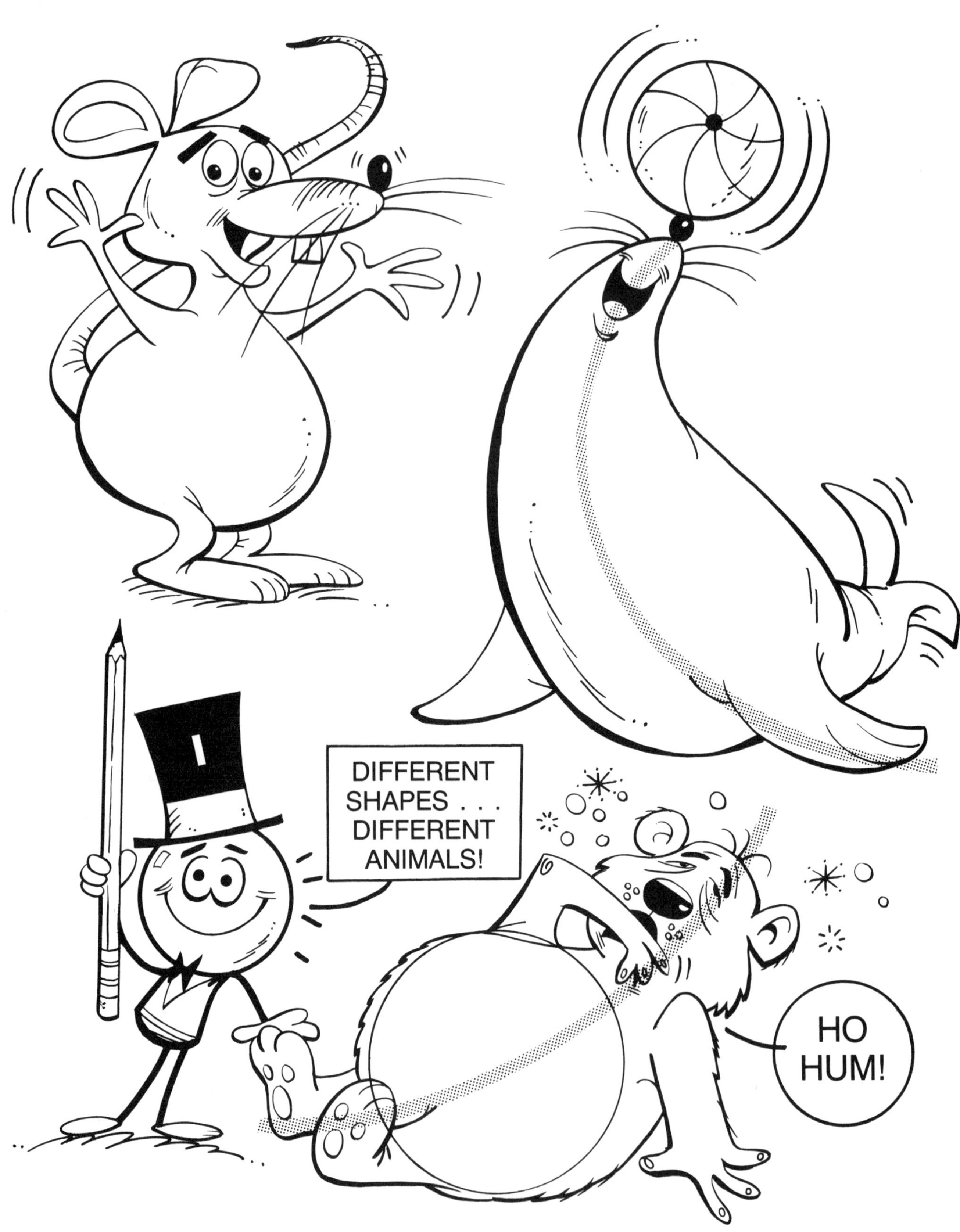
DIFFERENT SHAPES . . . DIFFERENT ANIMALS!
HO HUM!

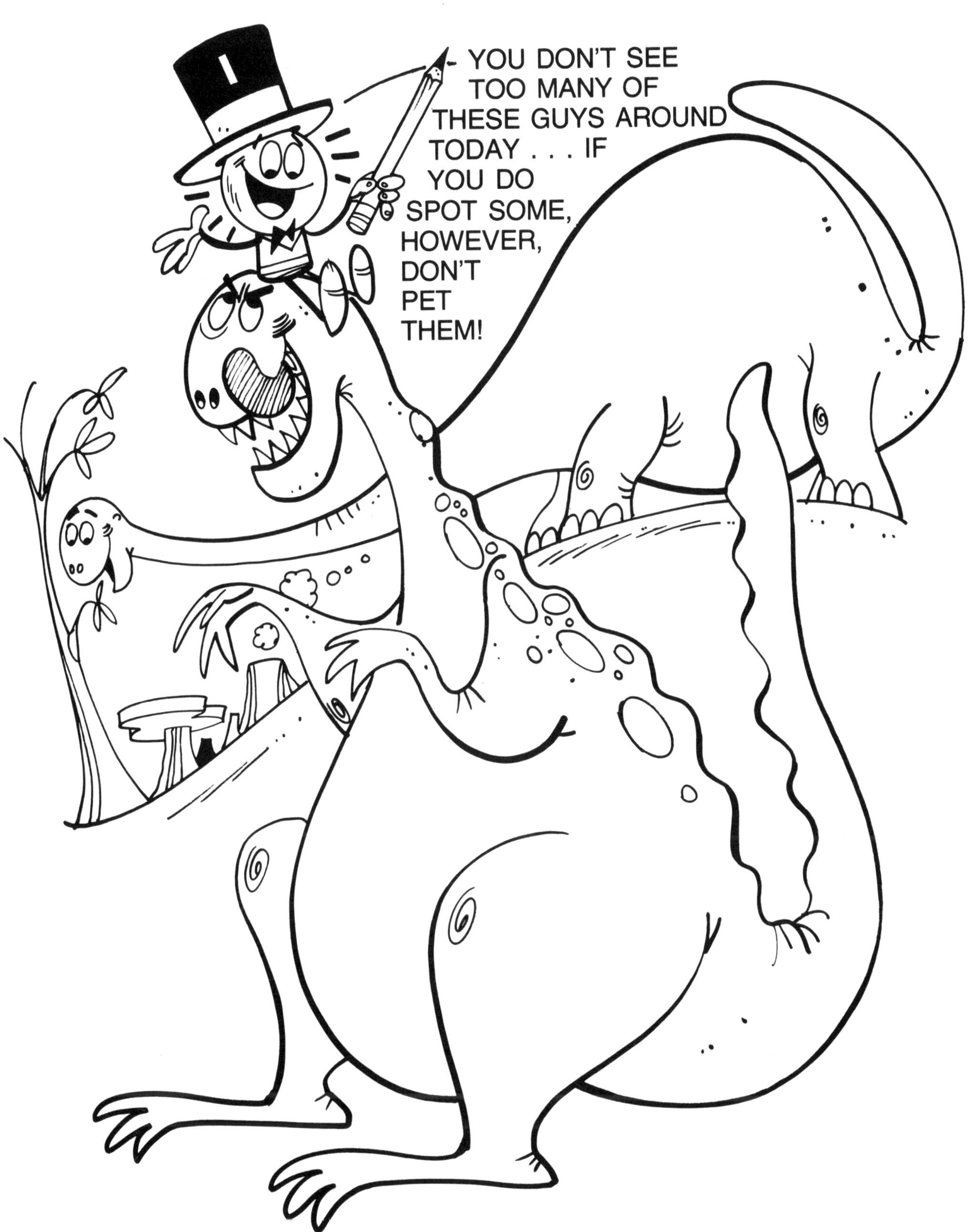
YOU DON'T SEE TOO MANY OF THESE GUYS AROUND TODAY . . . IF YOU DO SPOT SOME, HOWEVER, DON'T PET THEM!

HERE'S A QUICK PROJECT FOR YOU TO COMPLETE . . . JUST DRAW THESE CARTOONS, FILL IN THE MISSING PARTS, THEN GIVE THEM BODIES WHERE THEY ARE NEEDED!

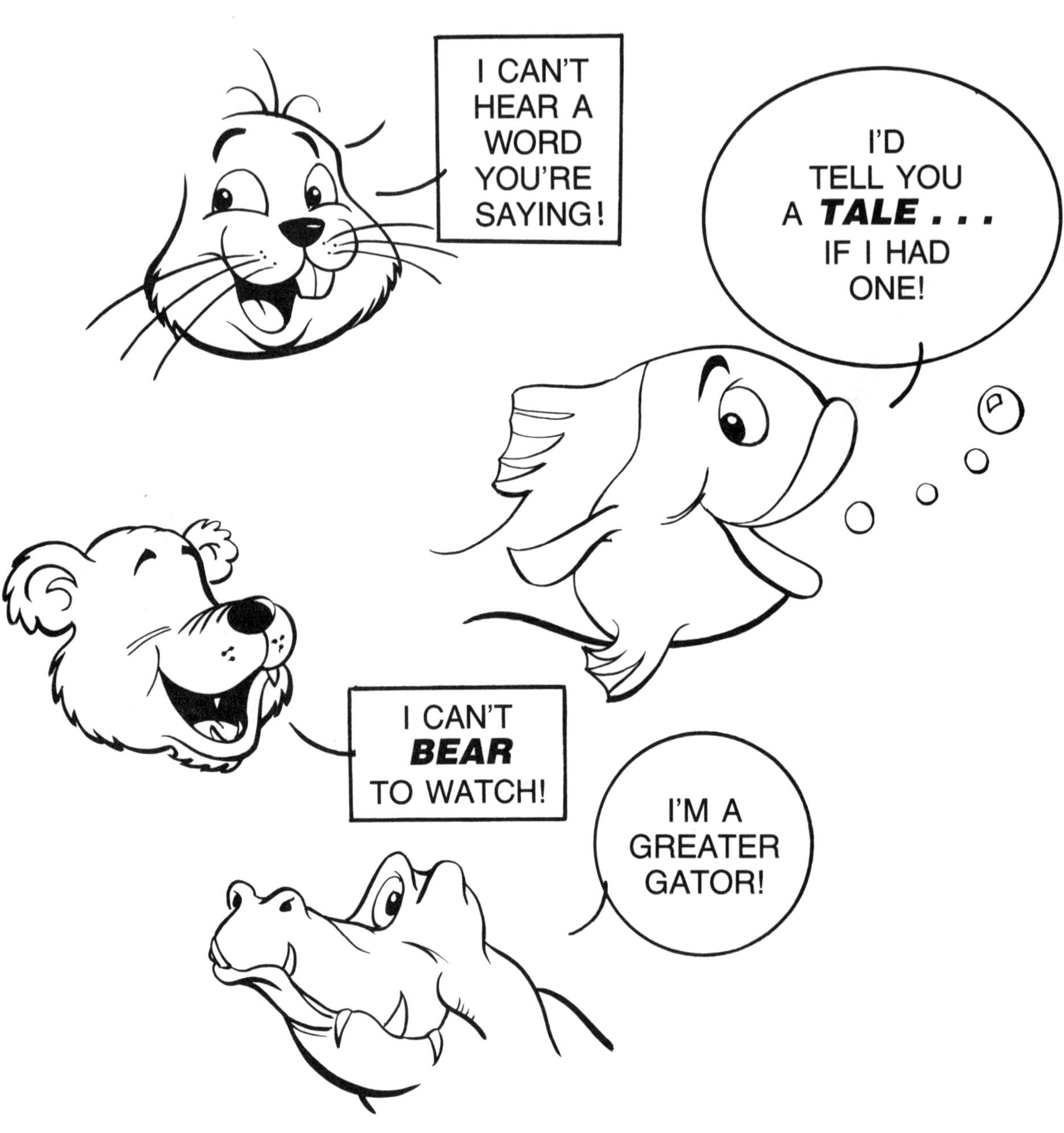

REMEMBER THE ADVICE YOU RECEIVED ON PAGE 84? WELL, HERE'S AN ***ASSIGNMENT*** FOR YOU! . . . SPEND A PLEASANT FEW HOURS WITH SOME VERY NICE ANIMALS AT THE ZOO. TAKE ALONG A SKETCH PAD AND DO SOME SKETCHING.

STUDY THE ANIMALS; THEY'RE GREAT SUBJECTS TO DRAW . . . AND IF YOU DON'T GET A GOOD LIKENESS, THEY WON'T EVEN COMPLAIN. THEN EXAGGERATE YOUR SKETCHES AND TURN 'EM INTO CARTOONS! MEANWHILE, HOW ABOUT COPYING THESE SHAPES?

. . . AND SEE WHAT KIND OF ANIMALS ***YOU*** CAN CREATE!

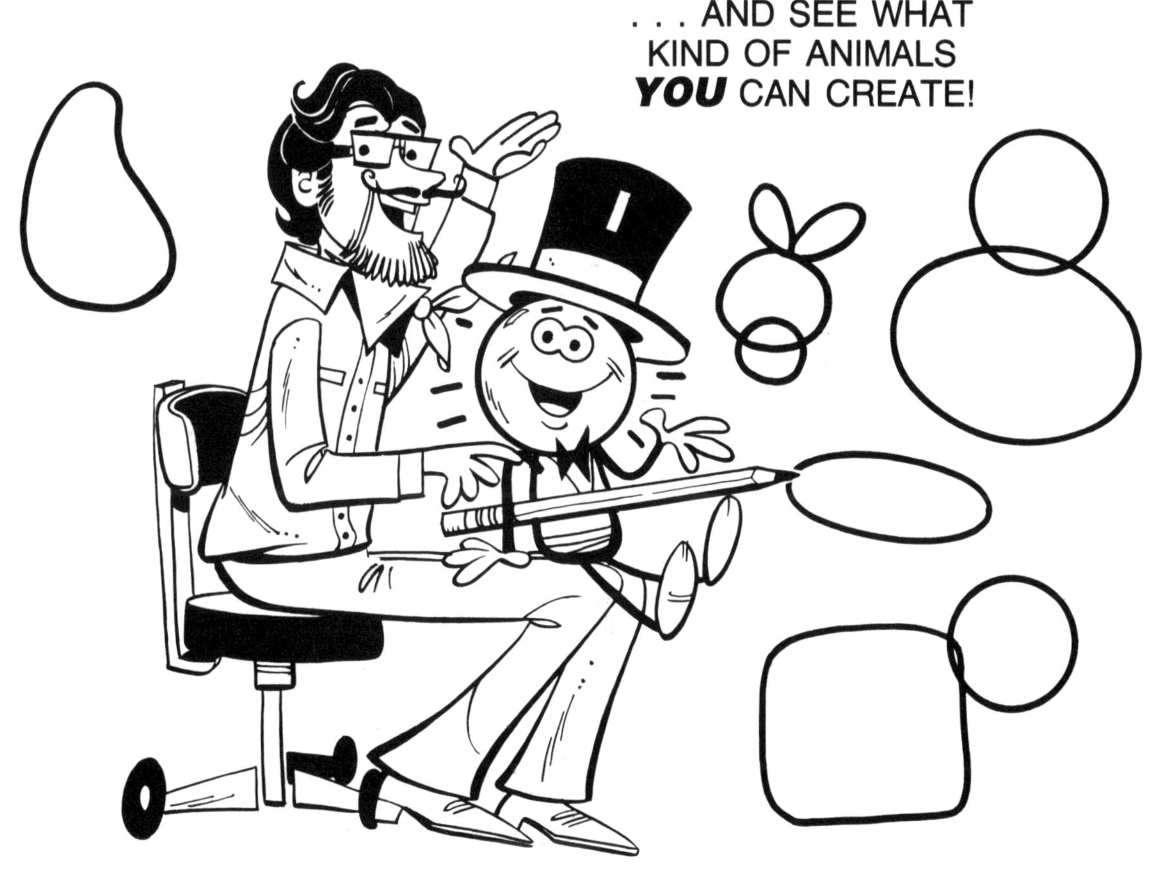

WELL, WE'VE LEARNED HOW TO CONSTRUCT CARTOON PEOPLE AND CARTOON ANIMALS . . . WE'VE ALSO LEARNED HOW TO MAKE 'EM MOVE AND GIVE THEM EXPRESSIONS! BUT, WE STILL HAVE A VERY IMPORTANT SUBJECT TO TACKLE . . . WE HAVE TO CREATE AN ENVIRONMENT IN WHICH THESE PEOPLE AND ANIMALS CAN FUNCTION!

. . . IT'S CALLED ***ATMOSPHERE!***

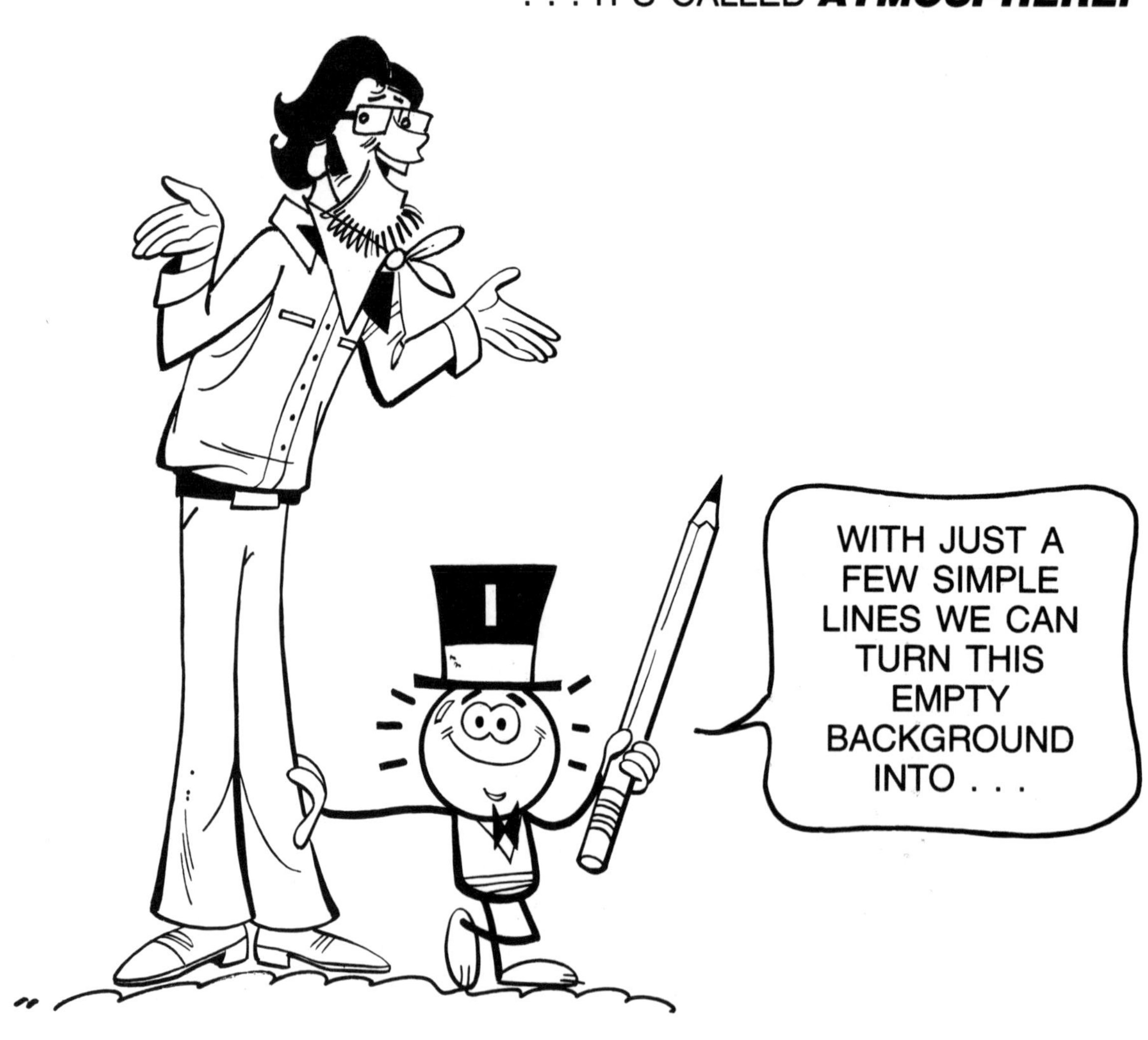

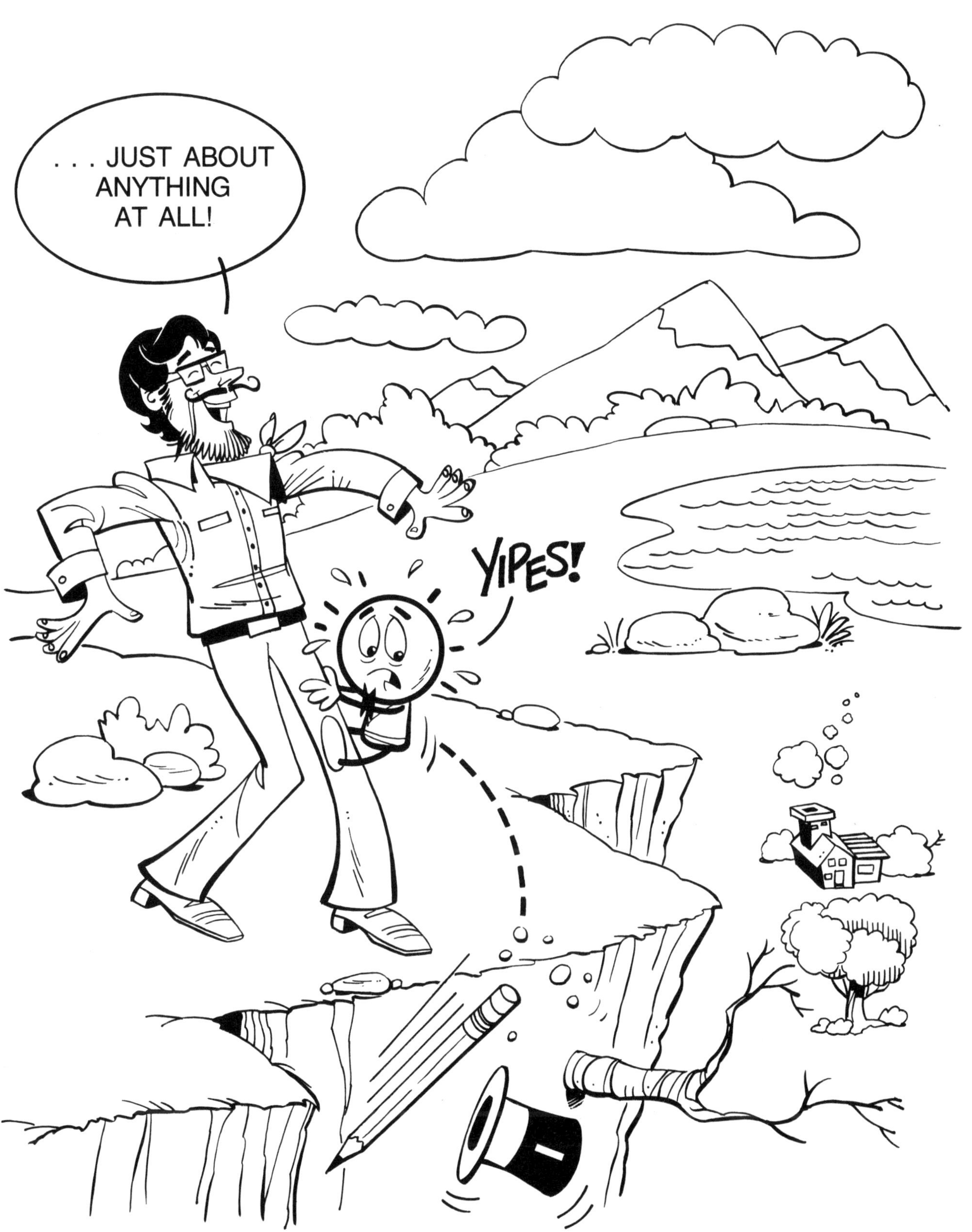
. . . JUST ABOUT ANYTHING AT ALL!
YIPES!

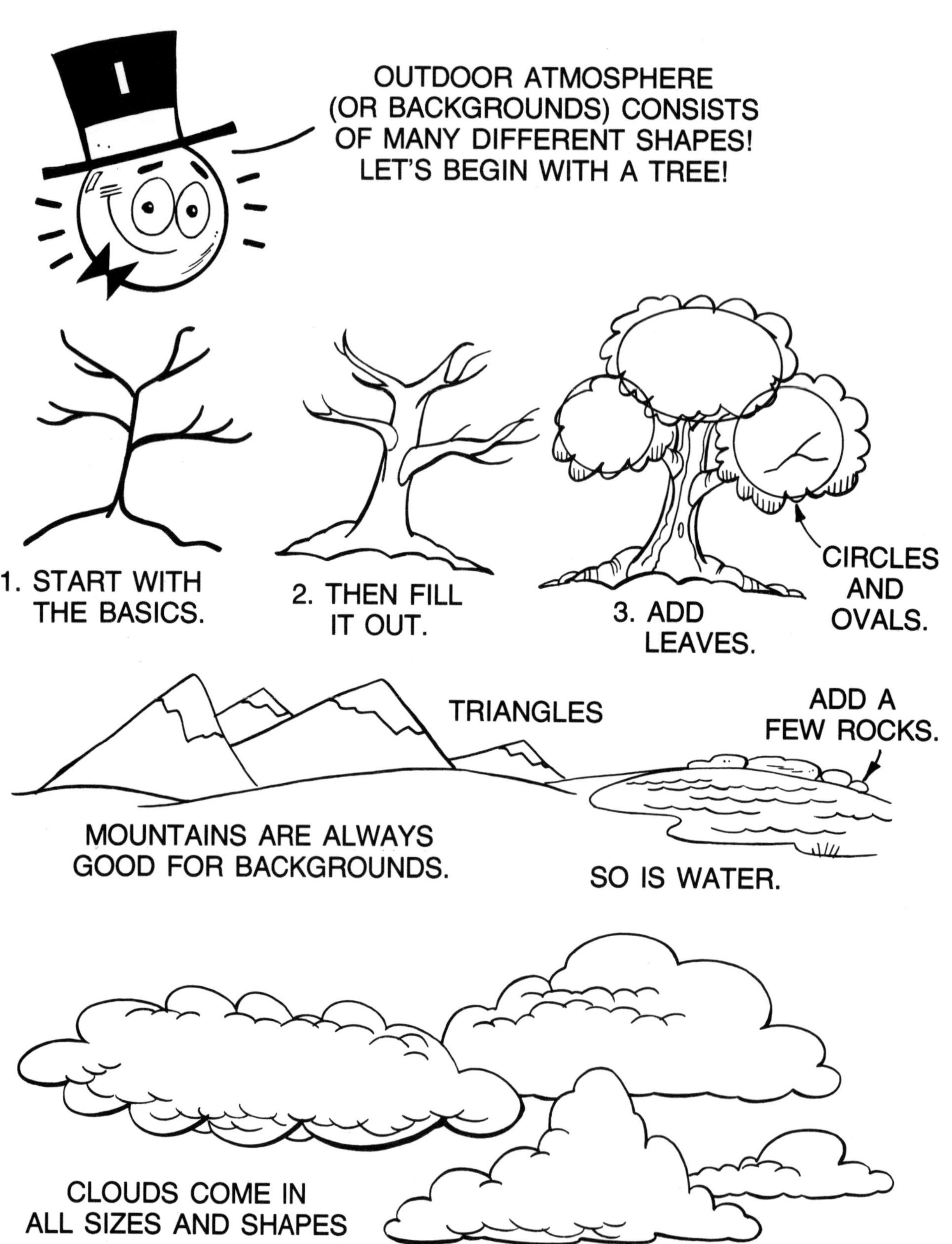
OUTDOOR ATMOSPHERE
(OR BACKGROUNDS) CONSISTS
OF MANY DIFFERENT SHAPES!
LET'S BEGIN WITH A TREE!
1. START WITH
THE BASICS.
2. THEN FILL
IT OUT.
3. ADD
LEAVES.
CIRCLES
AND
OVALS.
TRIANGLES
ADD A
FEW ROCKS.
MOUNTAINS ARE ALWAYS
GOOD FOR BACKGROUNDS.
SO IS WATER.
CLOUDS COME IN
ALL SIZES AND SHAPES

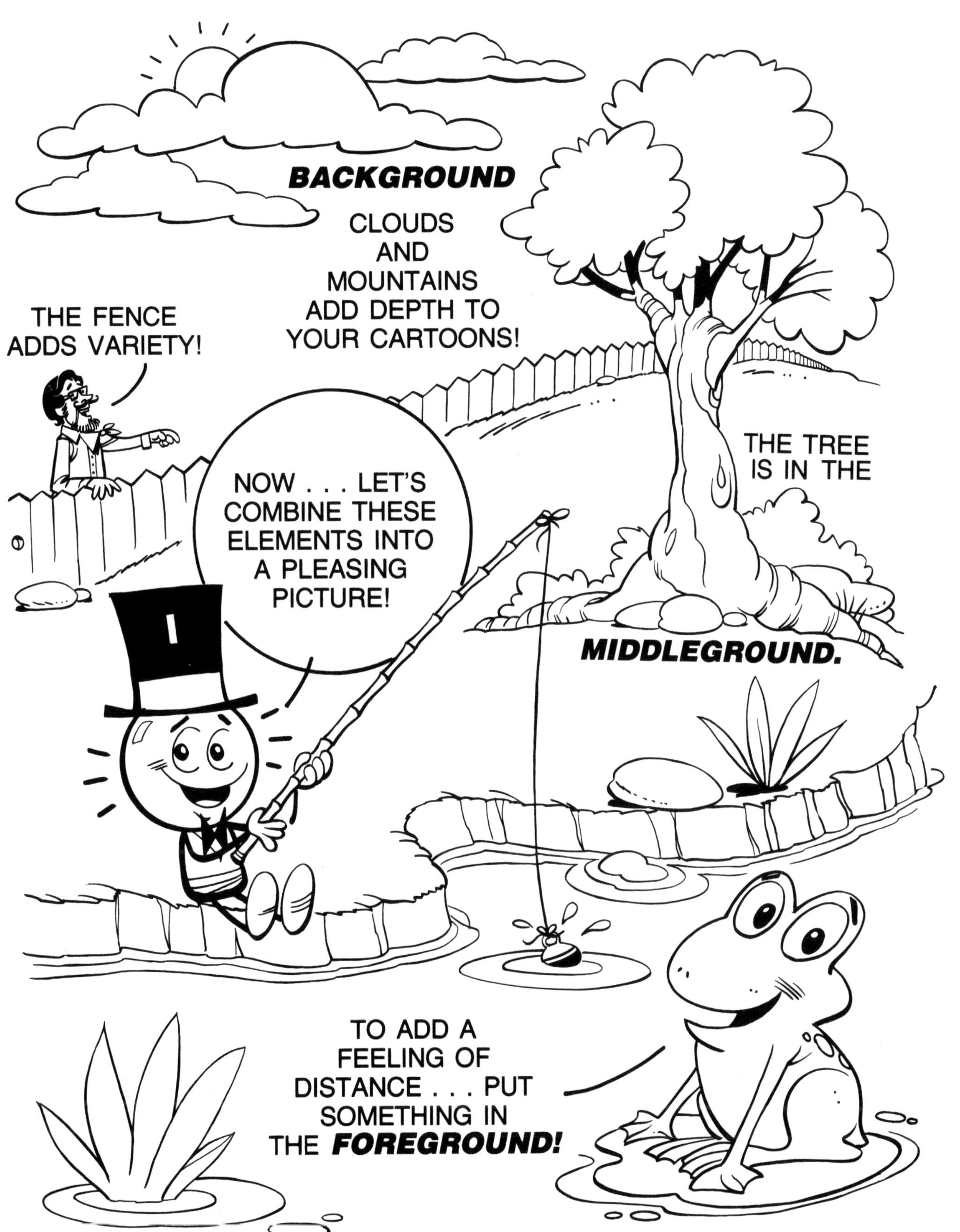
BACKGROUND
CLOUDS AND MOUNTAINS ADD DEPTH TO YOUR CARTOONS!
THE FENCE ADDS VARIETY!
NOW . . . LET'S COMBINE THESE ELEMENTS INTO A PLEASING PICTURE!
THE TREE IS IN THE
MIDDLEGROUND.
TO ADD A FEELING OF DISTANCE . . . PUT SOMETHING IN THE FOREGROUND!

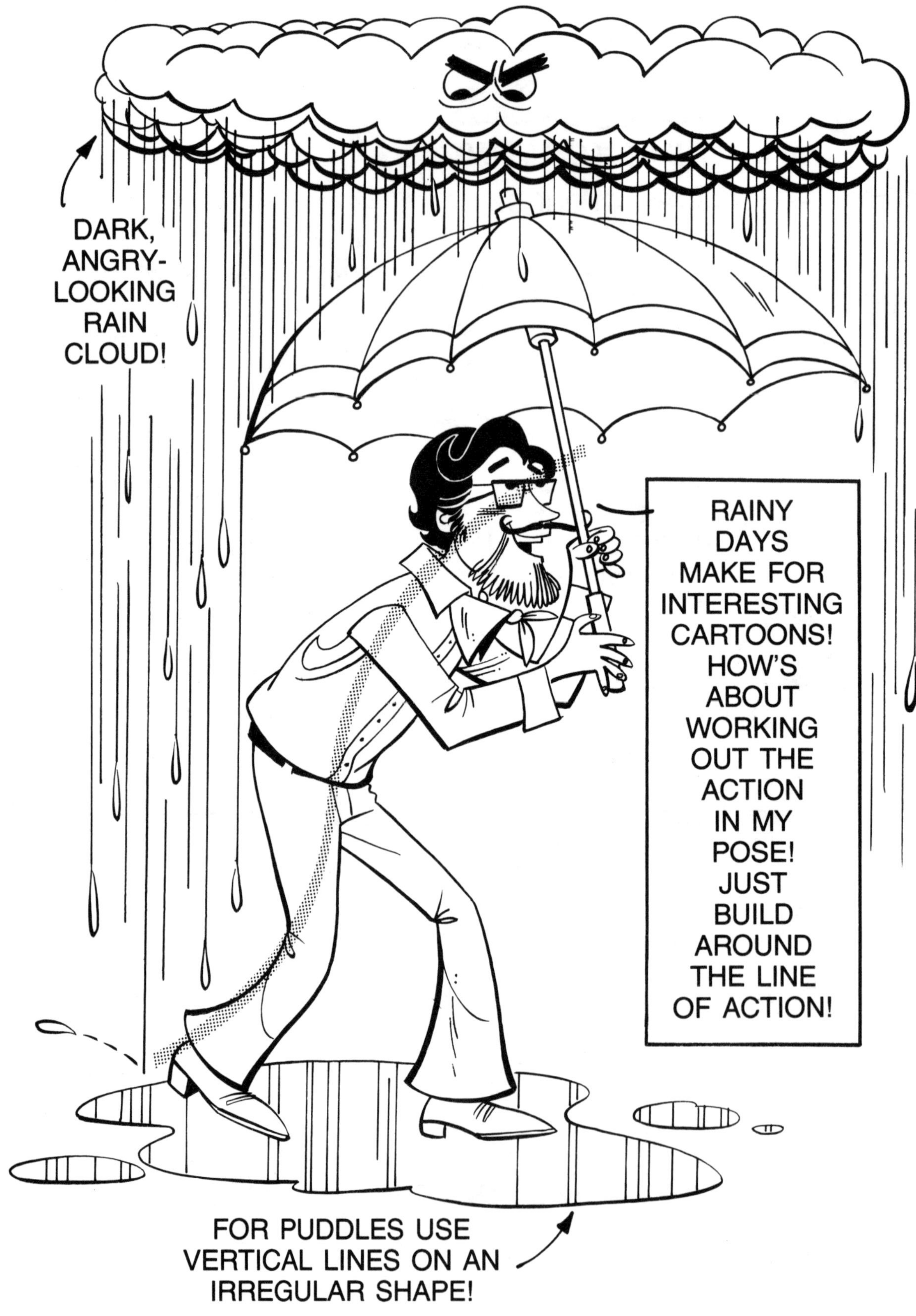
DARK, ANGRY-LOOKING RAIN CLOUD!
RAINY DAYS MAKE FOR INTERESTING CARTOONS! HOW'S ABOUT WORKING OUT THE ACTION IN MY POSE! JUST BUILD AROUND THE LINE OF ACTION!
FOR PUDDLES USE VERTICAL LINES ON AN IRREGULAR SHAPE!

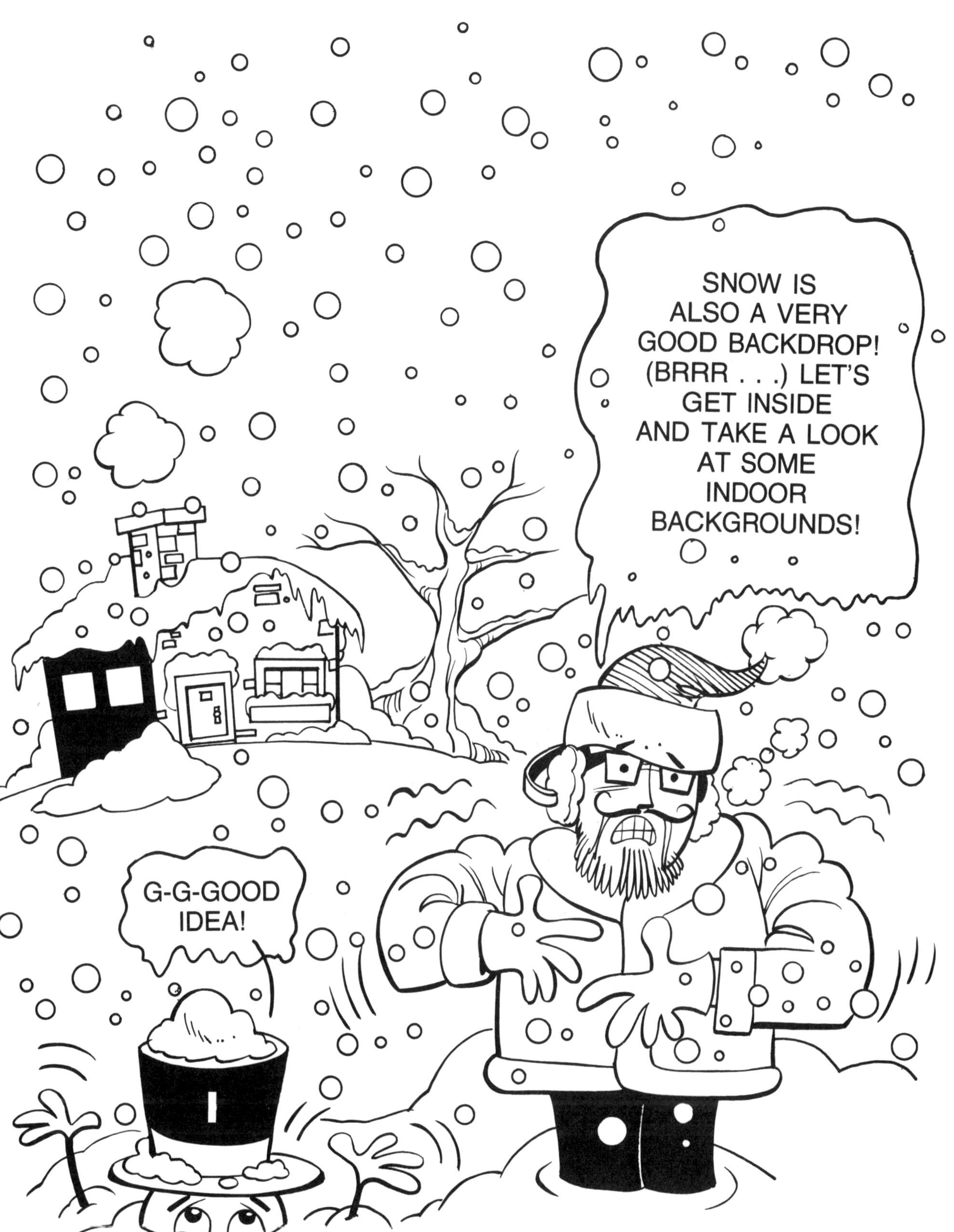
SNOW IS ALSO A VERY GOOD BACKDROP! (BRRR . . .) LET'S GET INSIDE AND TAKE A LOOK AT SOME INDOOR BACKGROUNDS!
G-G-GOOD IDEA!

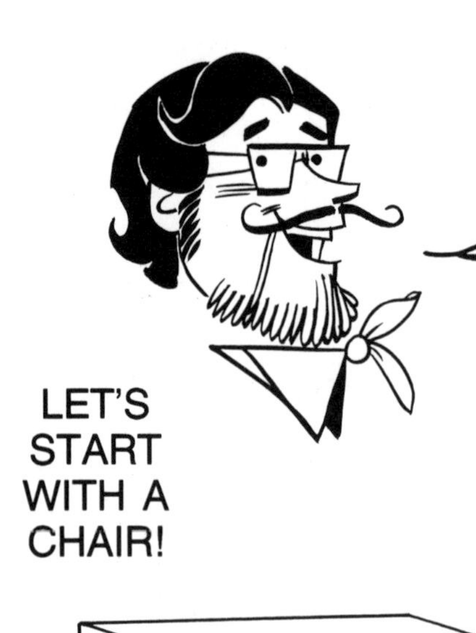

AHH . . . THIS IS MUCH BETTER . . . AND TO MAKE OURSELVES EVEN MORE COMFORTABLE, HELP ME TO DESIGN SOME FAMILIAR INDOOR ARTICLES.

LET'S START WITH A CHAIR!

BEGIN WITH A CUBE!

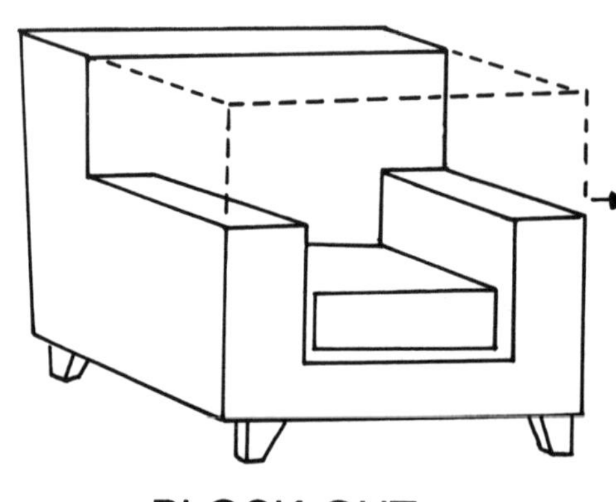

BLOCK OUT THE FORM

TO CHANGE THIS CHAIR INTO A COUCH, SIMPLY ***STRETCH*** IT OUT ABOUT TWICE AS LONG. (TRY IT!)

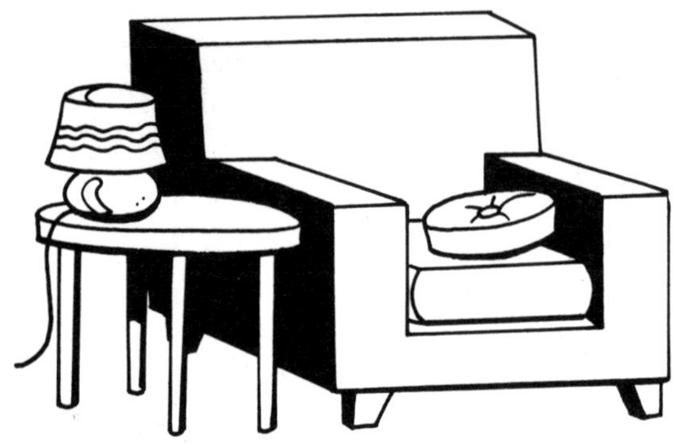

FINISH IT OFF AND ADD A TABLE, LAMP, PILLOW, ETC. WHAT SHAPES WERE USED TO CONSTRUCT THESE ITEMS?

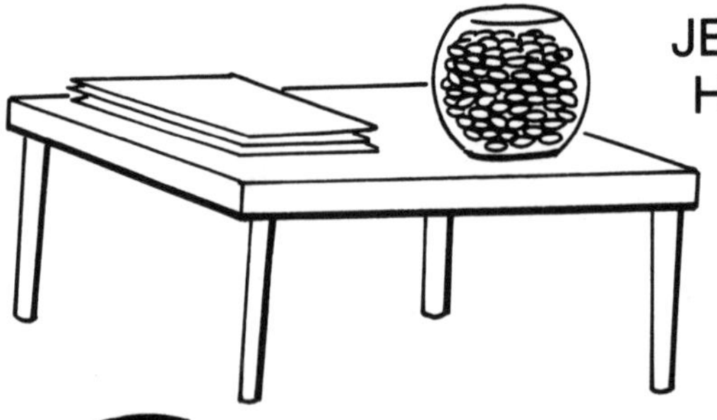

JARS ARE GREAT JELLYBEAN HOLDERS.

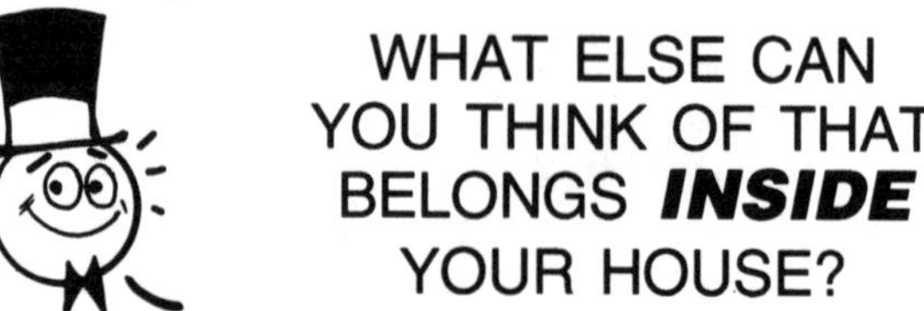

WHAT ELSE CAN YOU THINK OF THAT BELONGS ***INSIDE*** YOUR HOUSE?

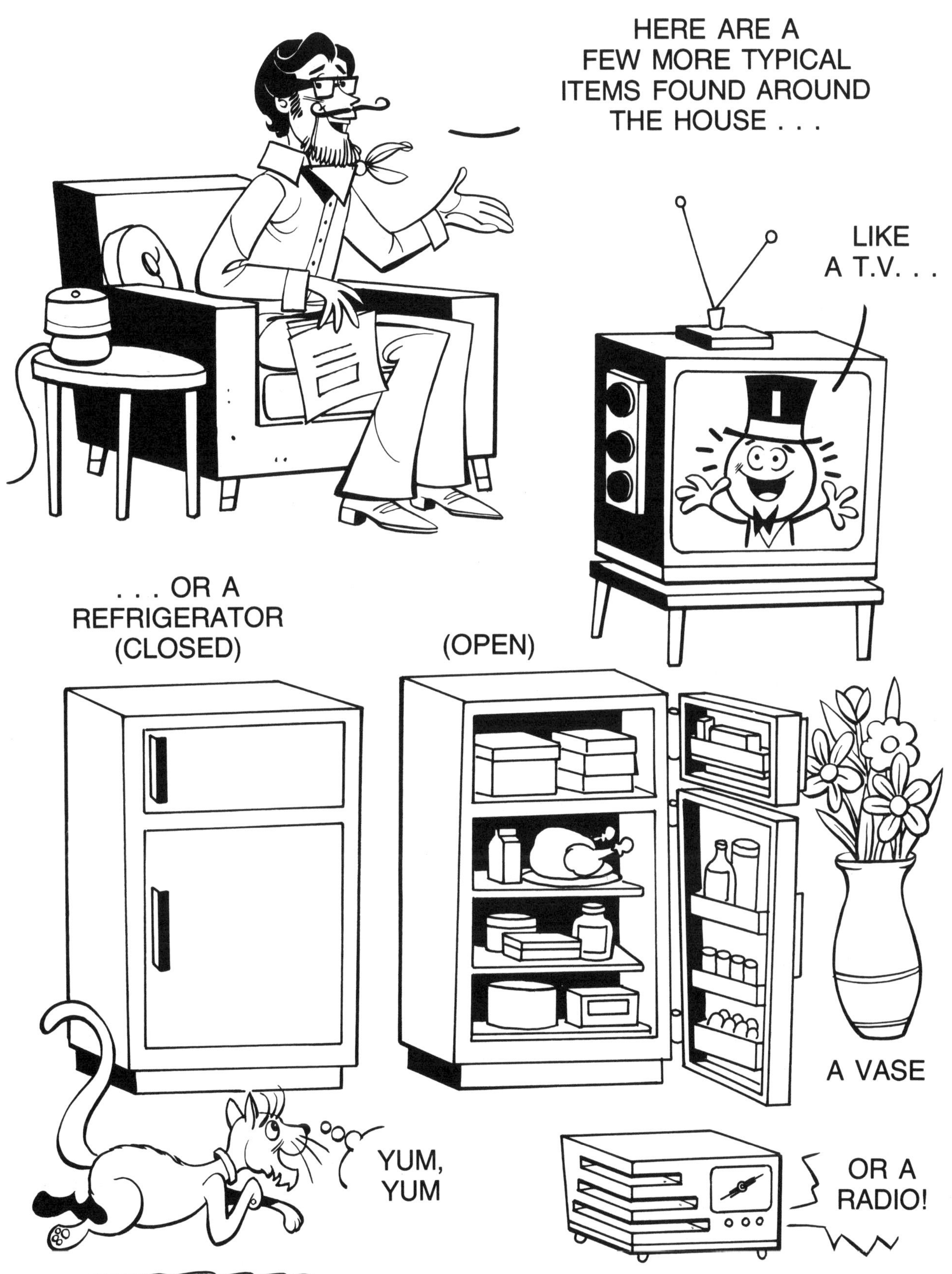
HERE ARE A
FEW MORE TYPICAL
ITEMS FOUND AROUND
THE HOUSE . . .
LIKE
A T.V. . . .
. . . OR A
REFRIGERATOR
(CLOSED)
(OPEN)
A VASE
YUM,
YUM
OR A
RADIO!

NOW, LET'S PUT IT ALL TOGETHER!

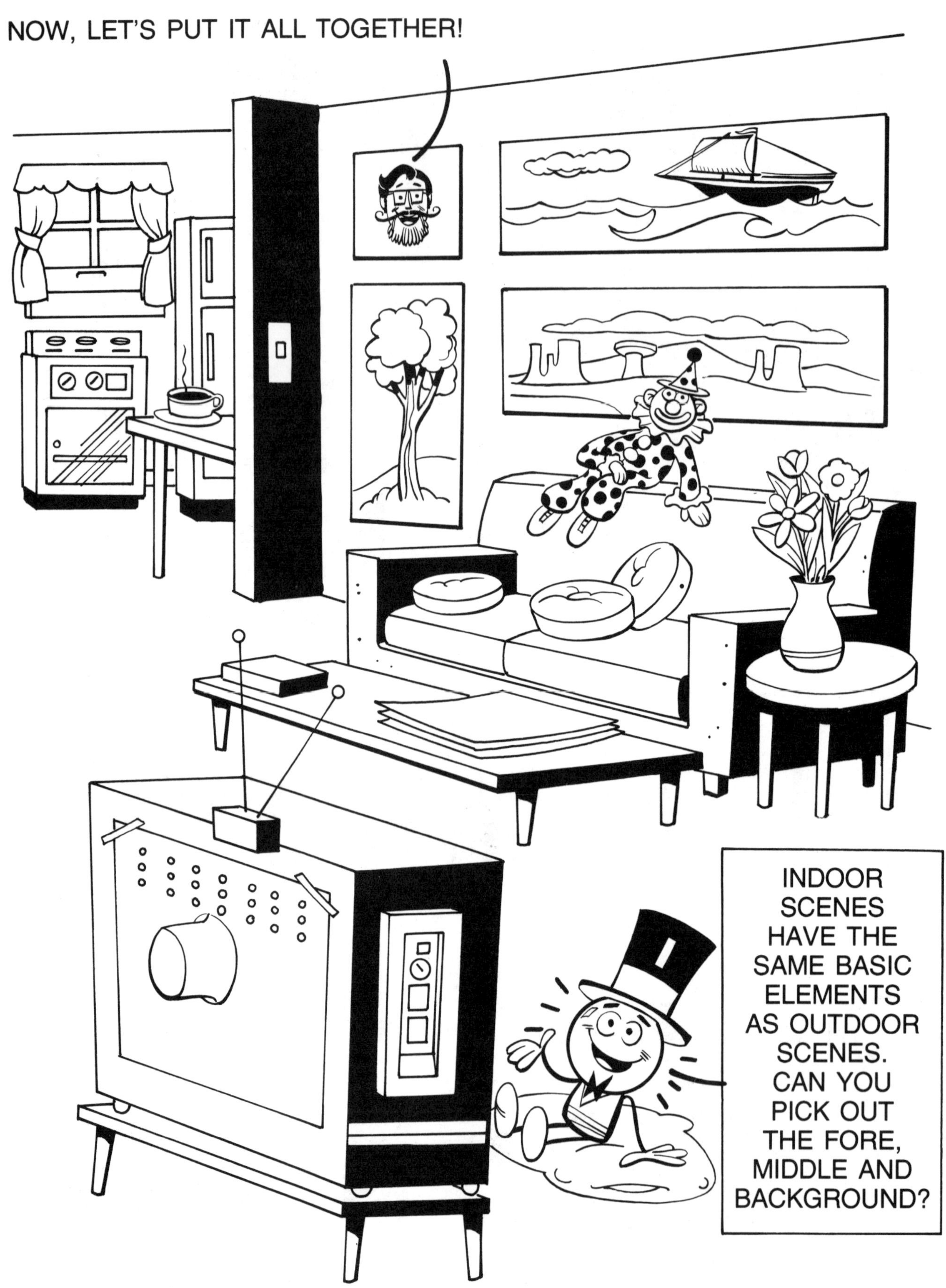

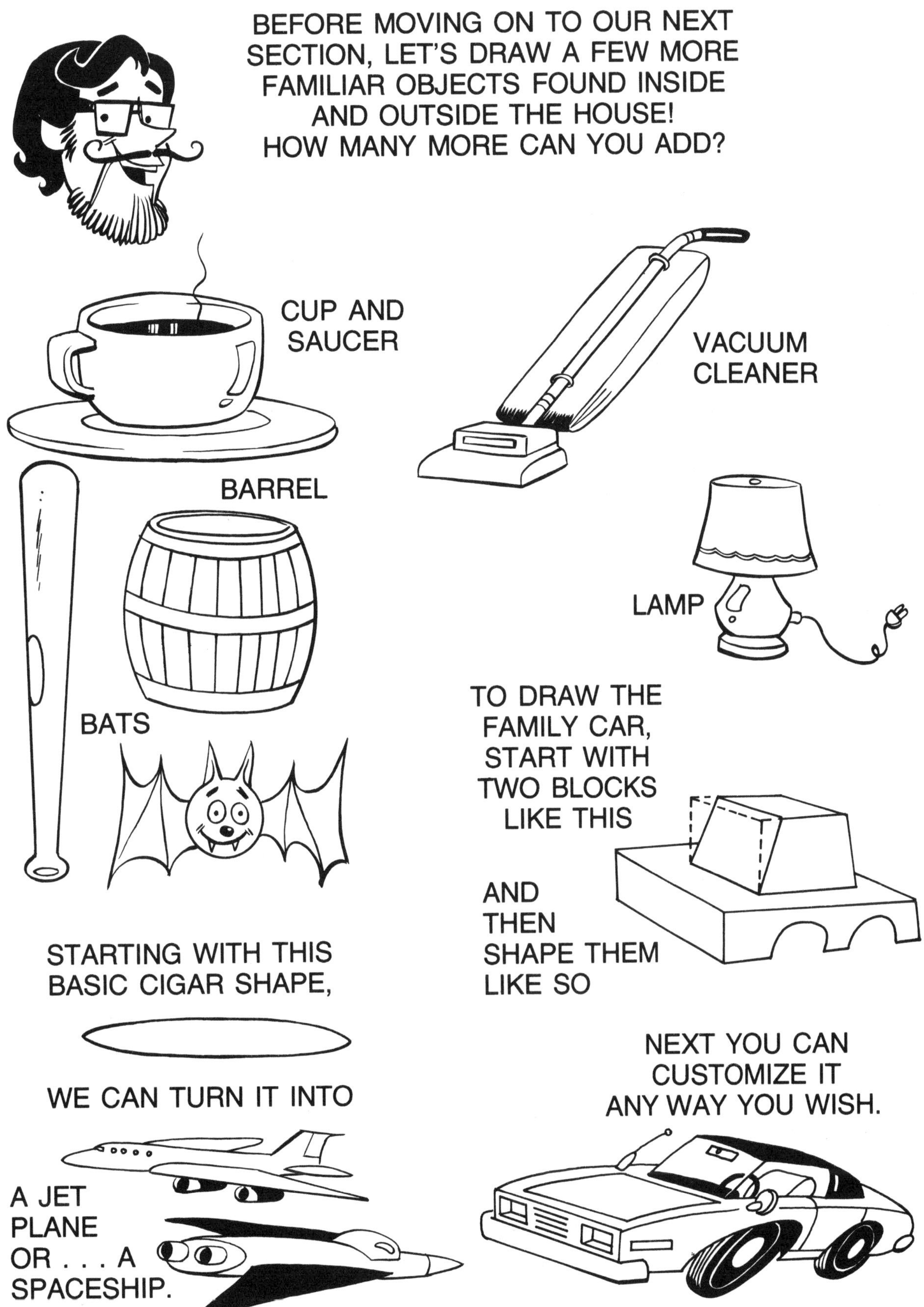

NOW THINK UP SOME ON YOUR OWN . . . THEN DRAW 'EM!

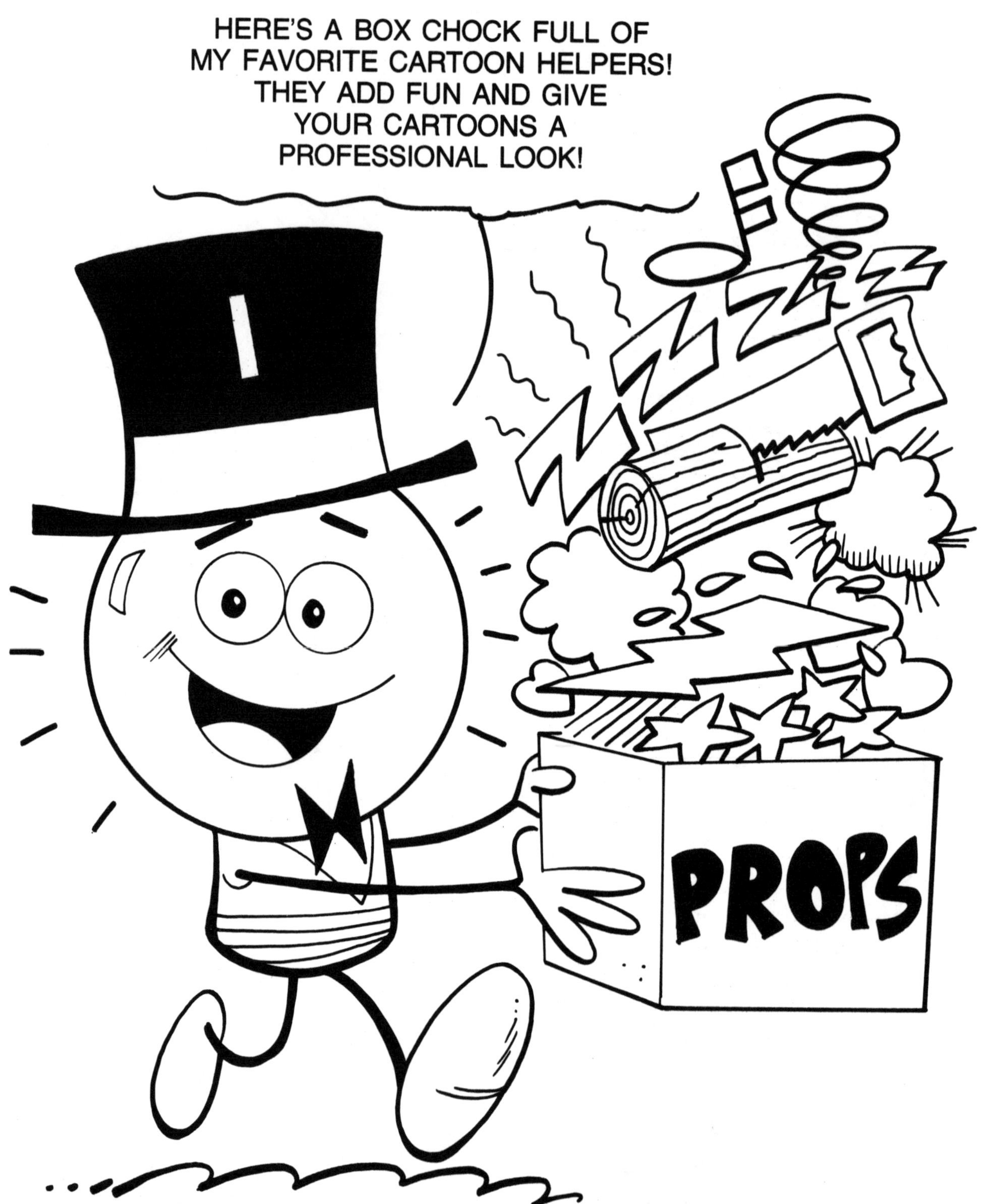
HERE'S A BOX CHOCK FULL OF
MY FAVORITE CARTOON HELPERS!
THEY ADD FUN AND GIVE
YOUR CARTOONS A
PROFESSIONAL LOOK!
PROPS

CARTOON PROPS ARE VERY HELPFUL IN SHOWING EXPRESSION. JUST BY ADDING A FEW LINES, WE CAN SHOW HOW OUR CARTOON CHARACTERS WILL REACT IN A GIVEN SITUATION!

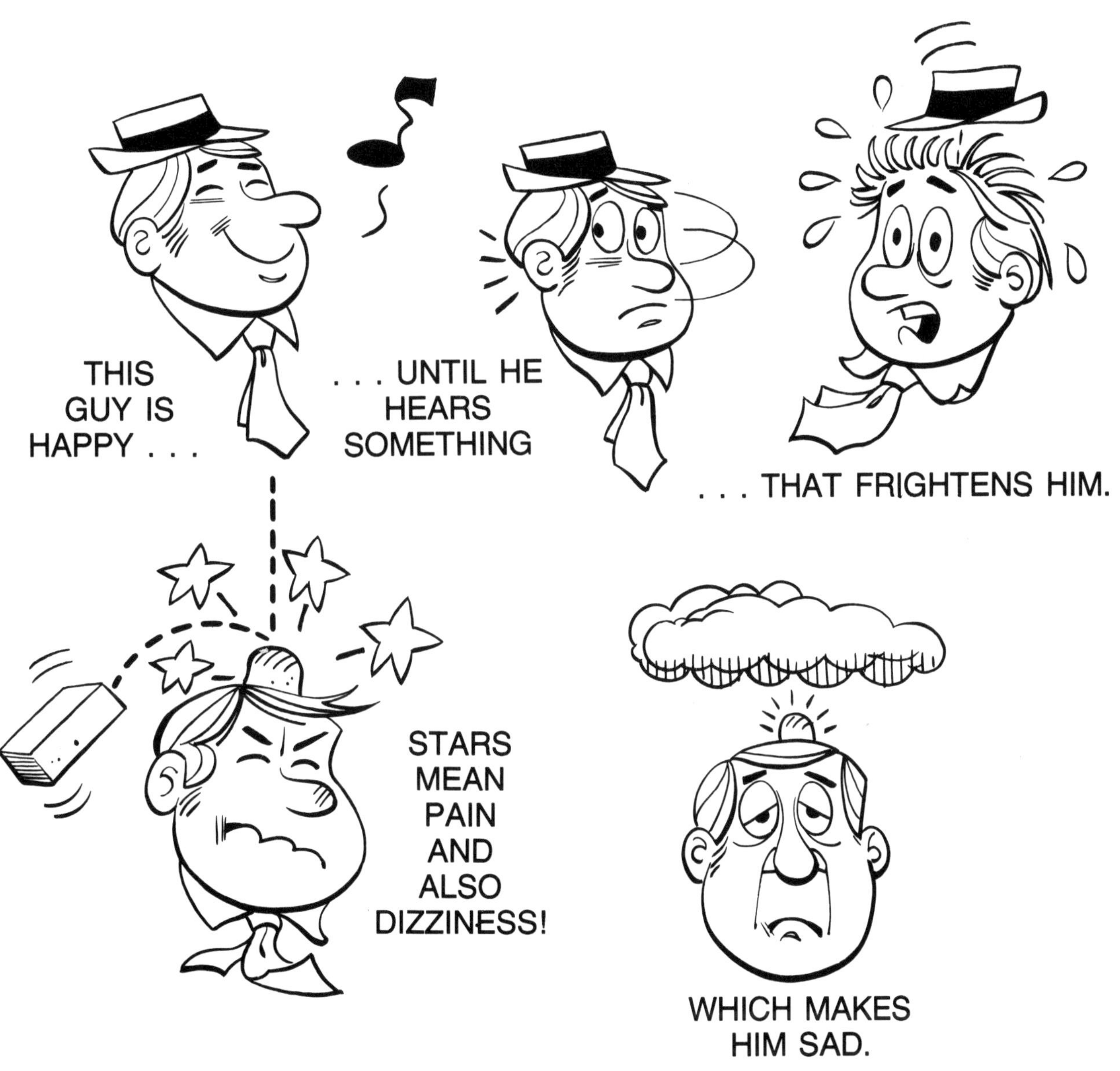

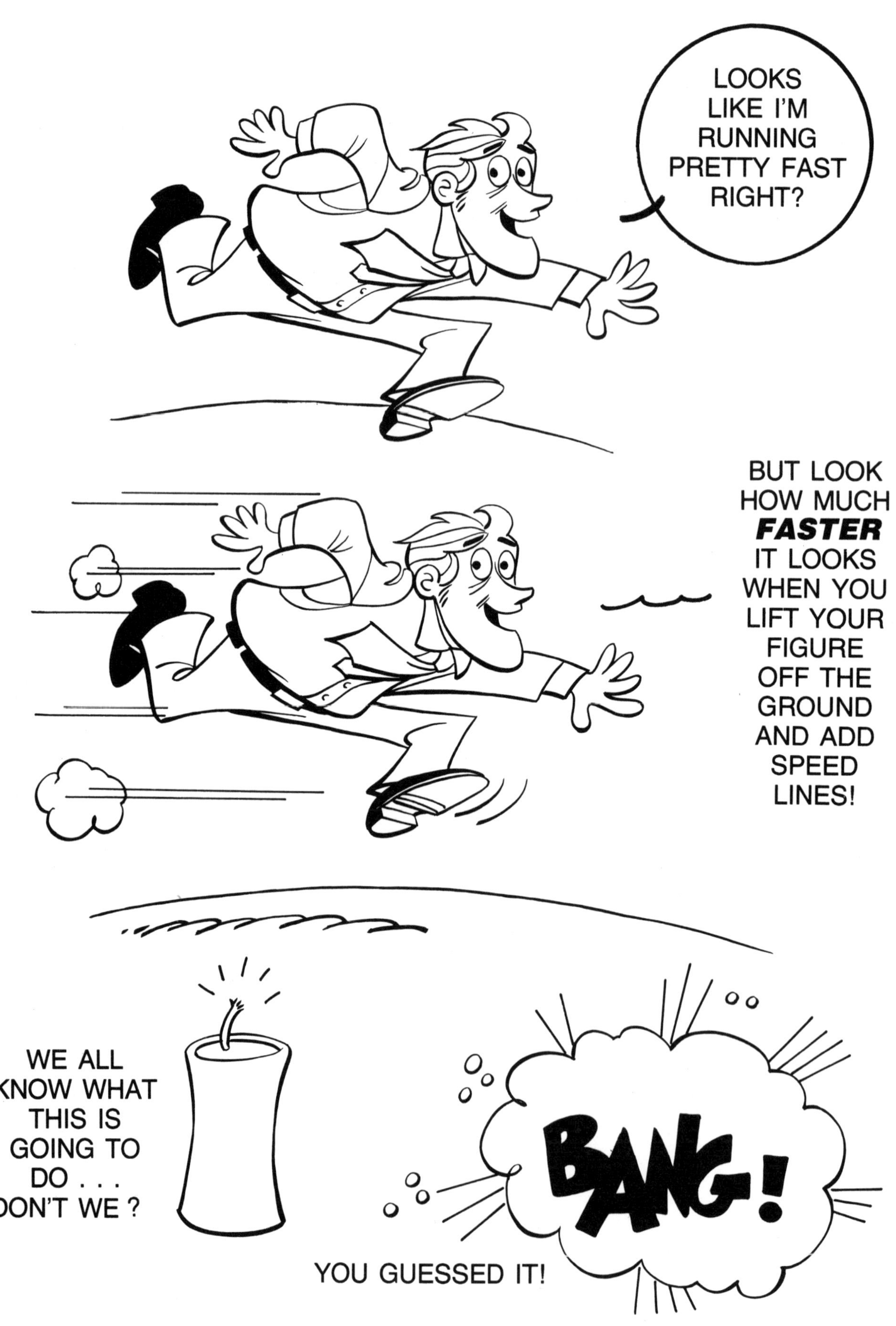
LOOKS LIKE I'M RUNNING PRETTY FAST RIGHT?
BUT LOOK HOW MUCH **FASTER** IT LOOKS WHEN YOU LIFT YOUR FIGURE OFF THE GROUND AND ADD SPEED LINES!
WE ALL KNOW WHAT THIS IS GOING TO DO . . . DON'T WE ?
BANG!
YOU GUESSED IT!

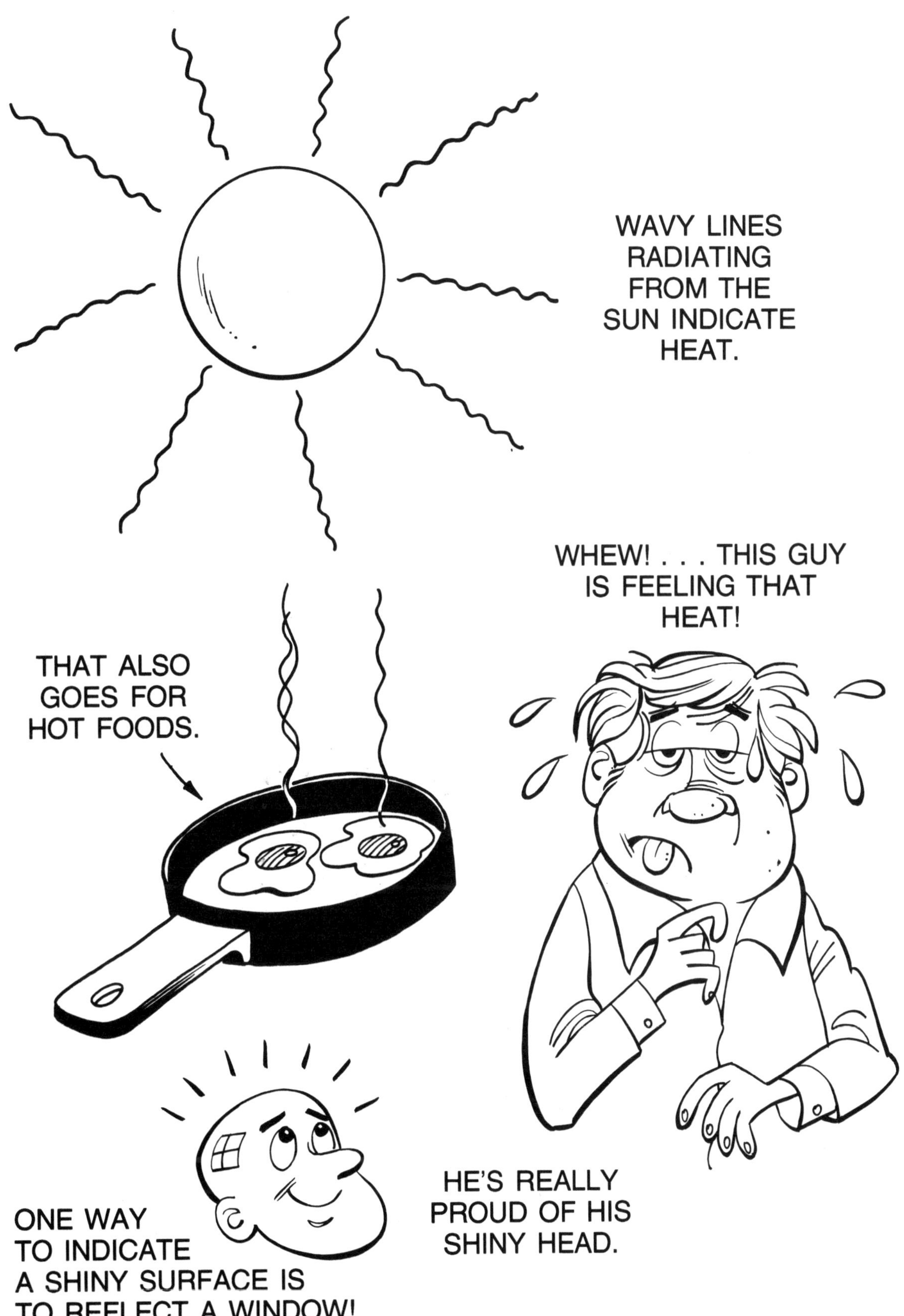
WAVY LINES
RADIATING
FROM THE
SUN INDICATE
HEAT.
WHEW! . . . THIS GUY
IS FEELING THAT
HEAT!
THAT ALSO
GOES FOR
HOT FOODS.
HE'S REALLY
PROUD OF HIS
SHINY HEAD.
ONE WAY
TO INDICATE
A SHINY SURFACE IS
TO REFLECT A WINDOW!

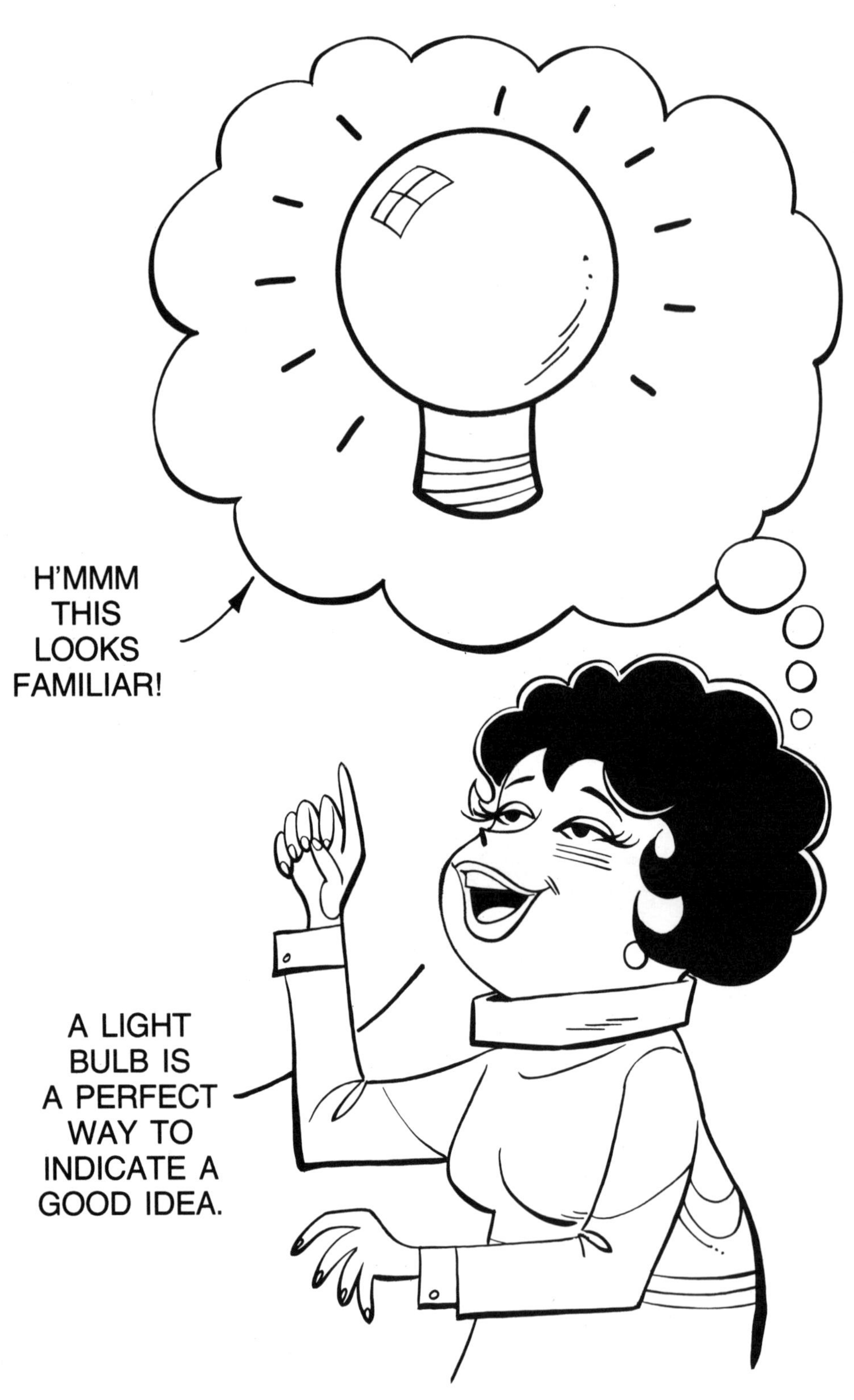
H'MMM
THIS
LOOKS
FAMILIAR!
A LIGHT
BULB IS
A PERFECT
WAY TO
INDICATE A
GOOD IDEA.

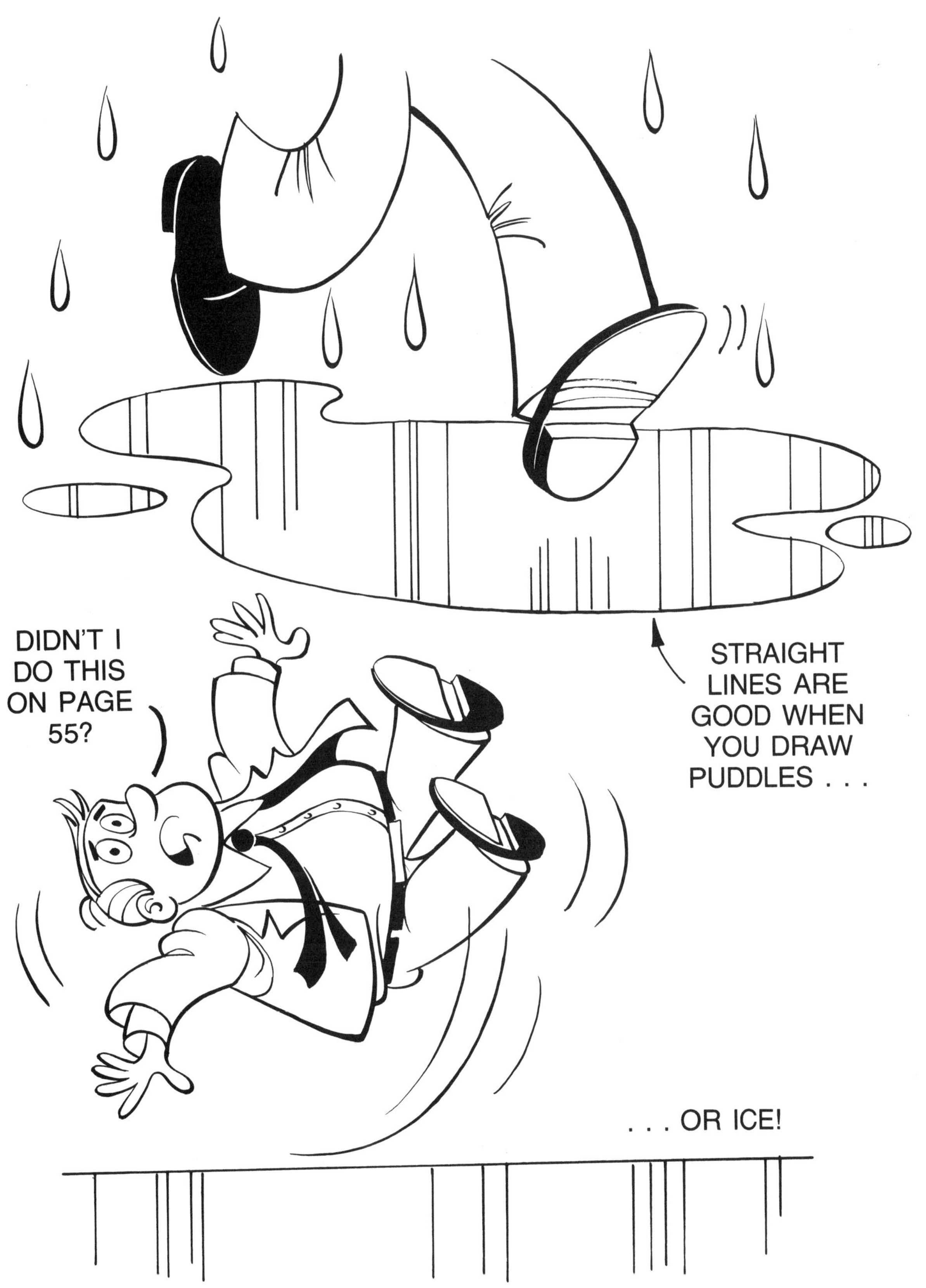
DIDN'T I
DO THIS
ON PAGE
55?
STRAIGHT
LINES ARE
GOOD WHEN
YOU DRAW
PUDDLES . . .
. . . OR ICE!

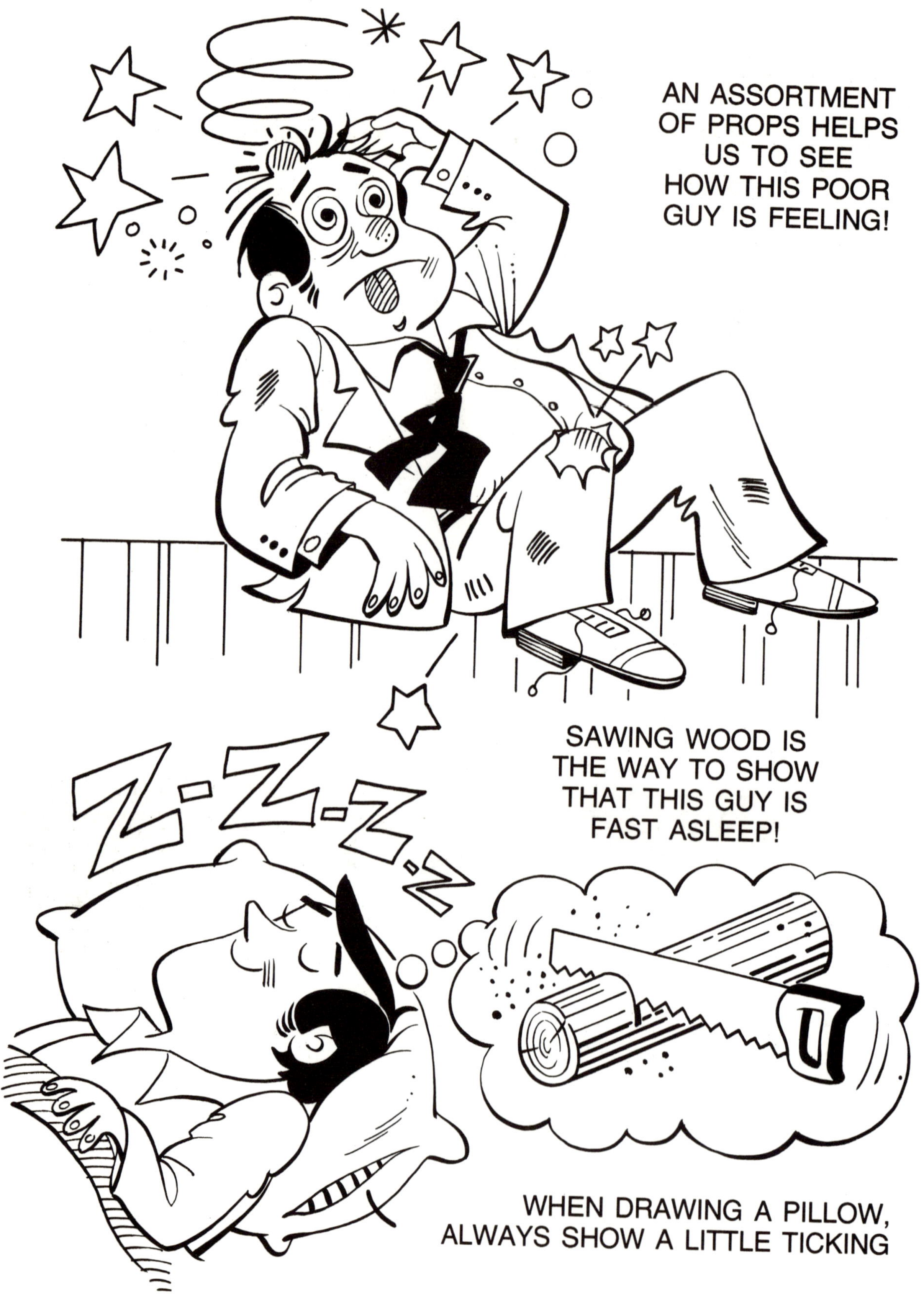

AN ASSORTMENT OF PROPS HELPS US TO SEE HOW THIS POOR GUY IS FEELING!

SAWING WOOD IS THE WAY TO SHOW THAT THIS GUY IS FAST ASLEEP!

WHEN DRAWING A PILLOW, ALWAYS SHOW A LITTLE TICKING

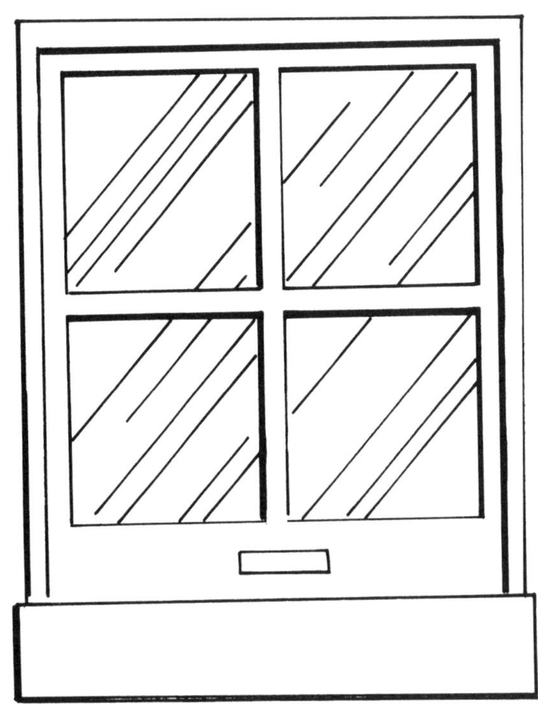

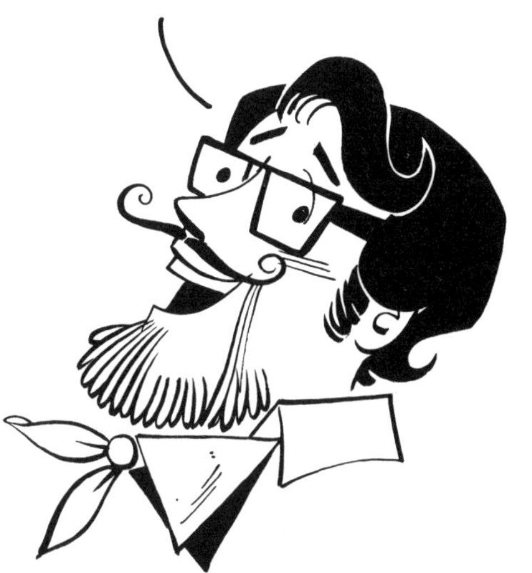
USING SLANTED LINES IS A GOOD WAY TO INDICATE GLASS . . . WHETHER A WINDOW . . .

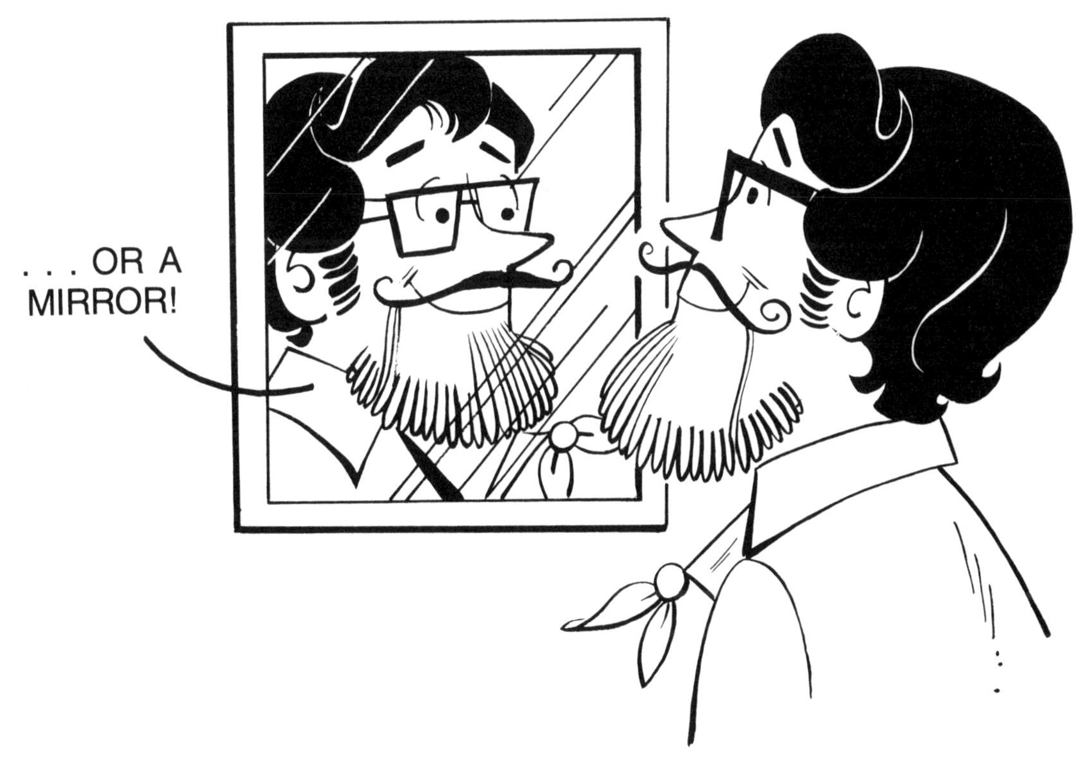
. . . OR A MIRROR!

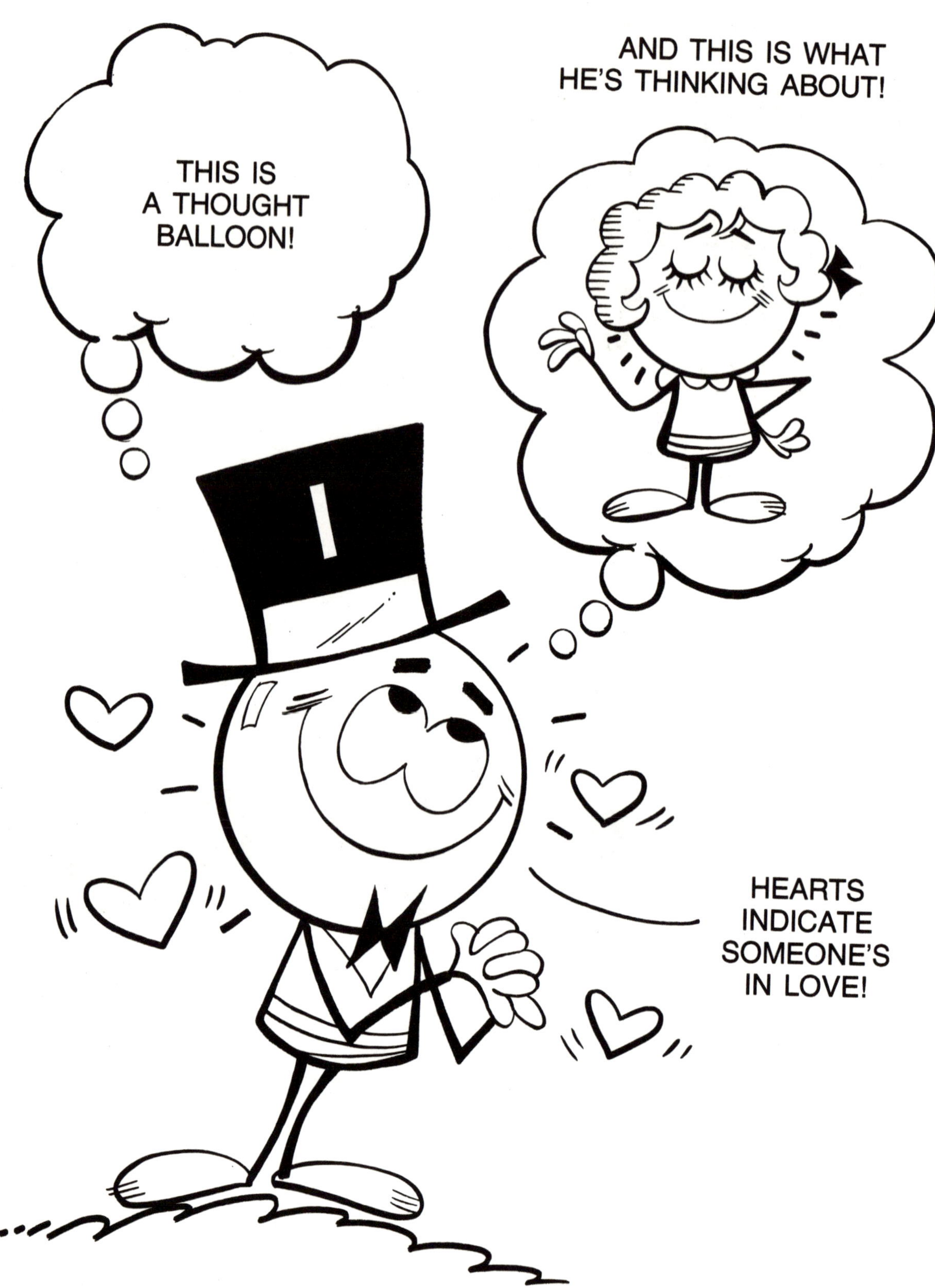
THIS IS
A THOUGHT
BALLOON!
AND THIS IS WHAT
HE'S THINKING ABOUT!
HEARTS
INDICATE
SOMEONE'S
IN LOVE!

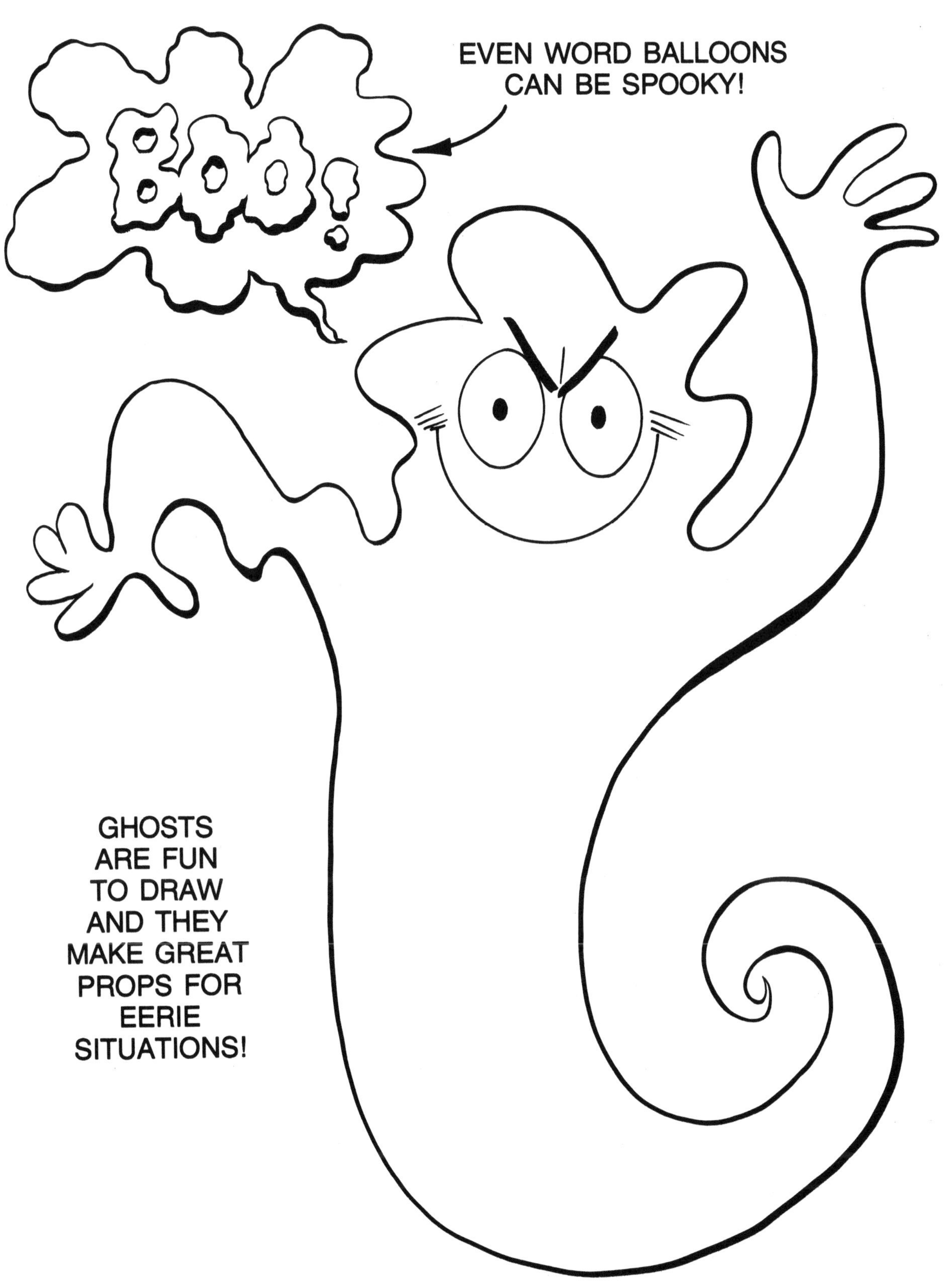
BOO!
EVEN WORD BALLOONS CAN BE SPOOKY!
GHOSTS ARE FUN TO DRAW AND THEY MAKE GREAT PROPS FOR EERIE SITUATIONS!

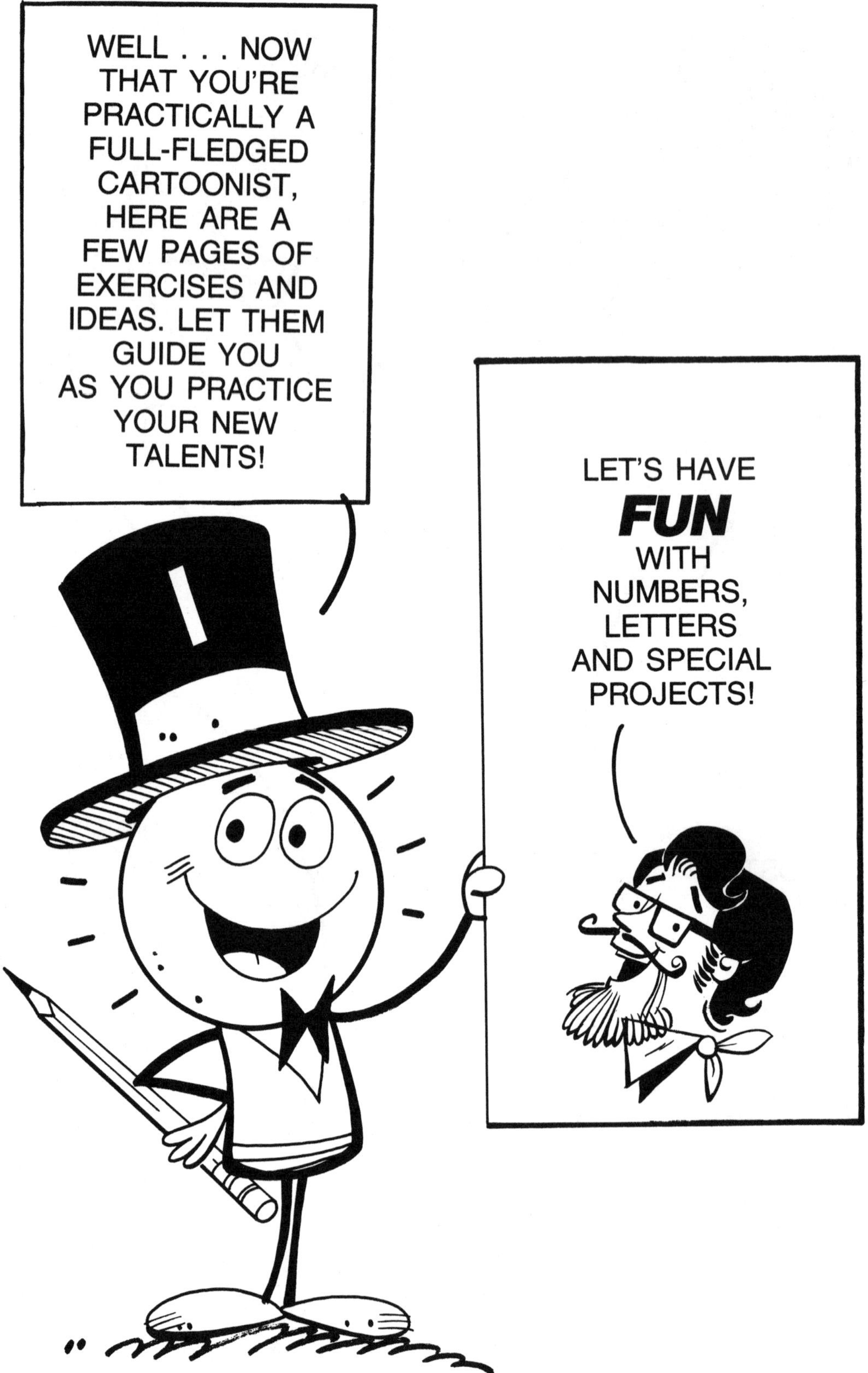
WELL . . . NOW THAT YOU'RE PRACTICALLY A FULL-FLEDGED CARTOONIST, HERE ARE A FEW PAGES OF EXERCISES AND IDEAS. LET THEM GUIDE YOU AS YOU PRACTICE YOUR NEW TALENTS!
LET'S HAVE **FUN** WITH NUMBERS, LETTERS AND SPECIAL PROJECTS!

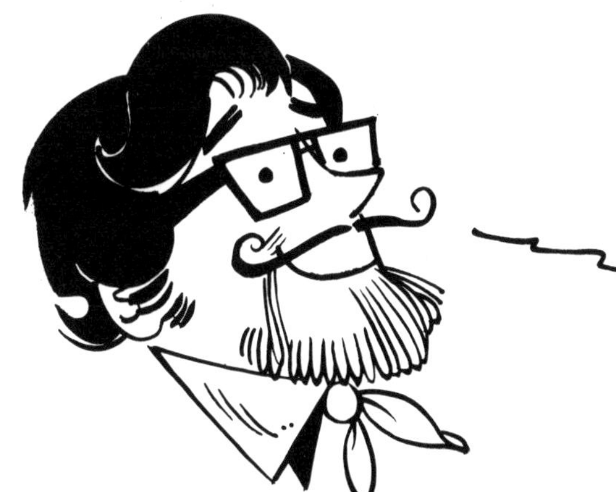

LET'S BEGIN WITH
SOMETHING FAMILIAR
TO ALL OF US . . .
NUMBERS!
. . . CAN YOU DRAW A
CARTOON USING THESE
NUMBERS AS A BASE?

1 2 3

4 5 6

7 8 9

0

USE THE CARTOONS
ON THE NEXT PAGE AS
A GUIDE . . . THEN TRY
A FEW ON YOUR OWN!

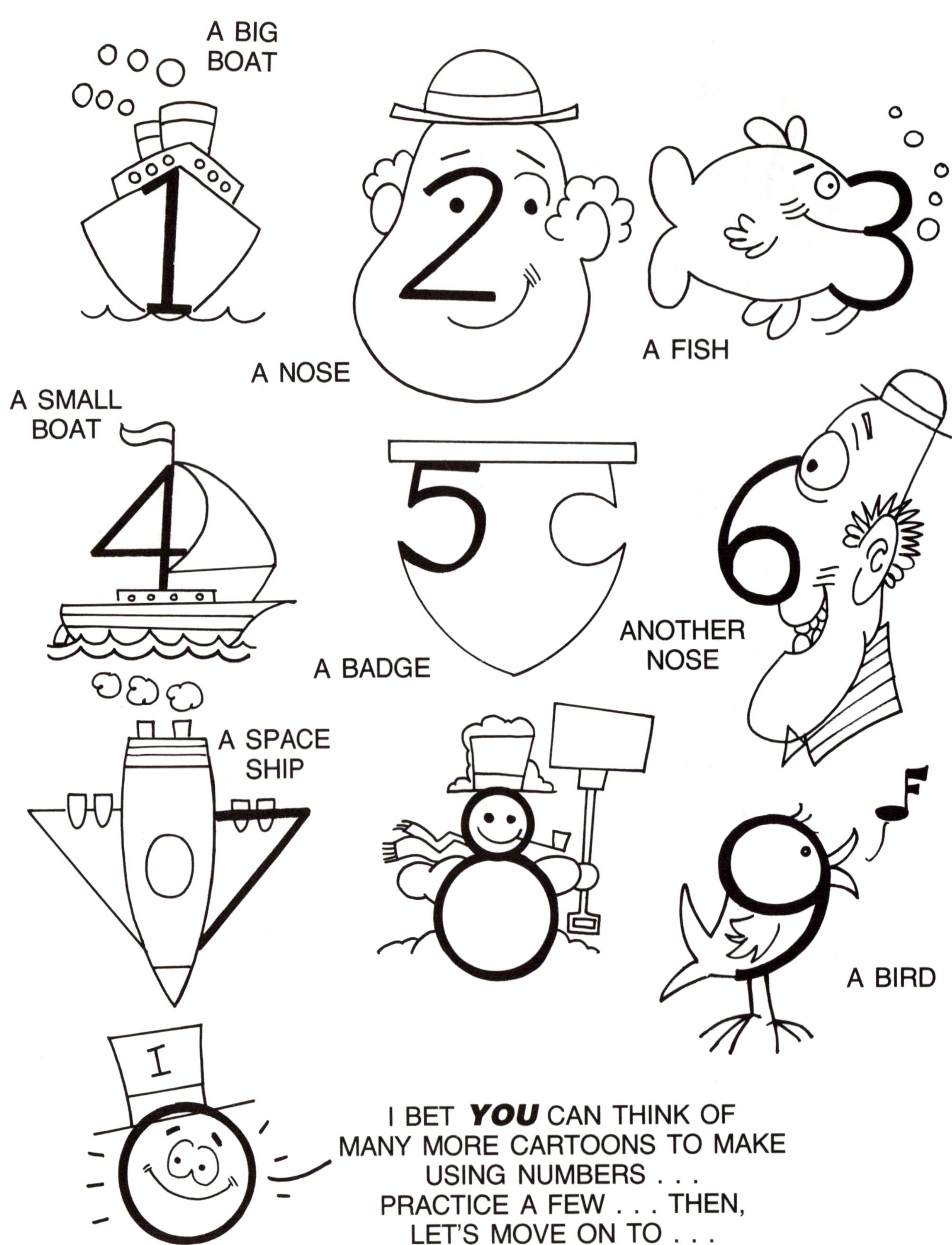

I BET ***YOU*** CAN THINK OF MANY MORE CARTOONS TO MAKE USING NUMBERS . . . PRACTICE A FEW . . . THEN, LET'S MOVE ON TO . . .

LETTERS

A B C

D E F

LET'S TRY THE
SAME THING WITH
LETTERS! ***I'LL*** HELP
YOU WITH THESE . . .
THEN . . . ***YOU***
WORK ON THE REST
BY YOURSELF!

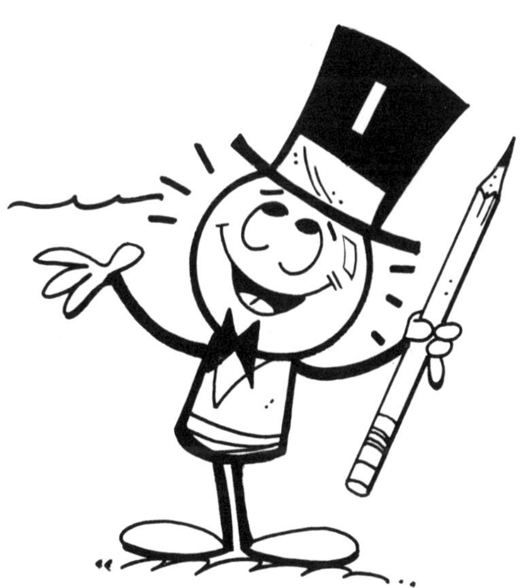

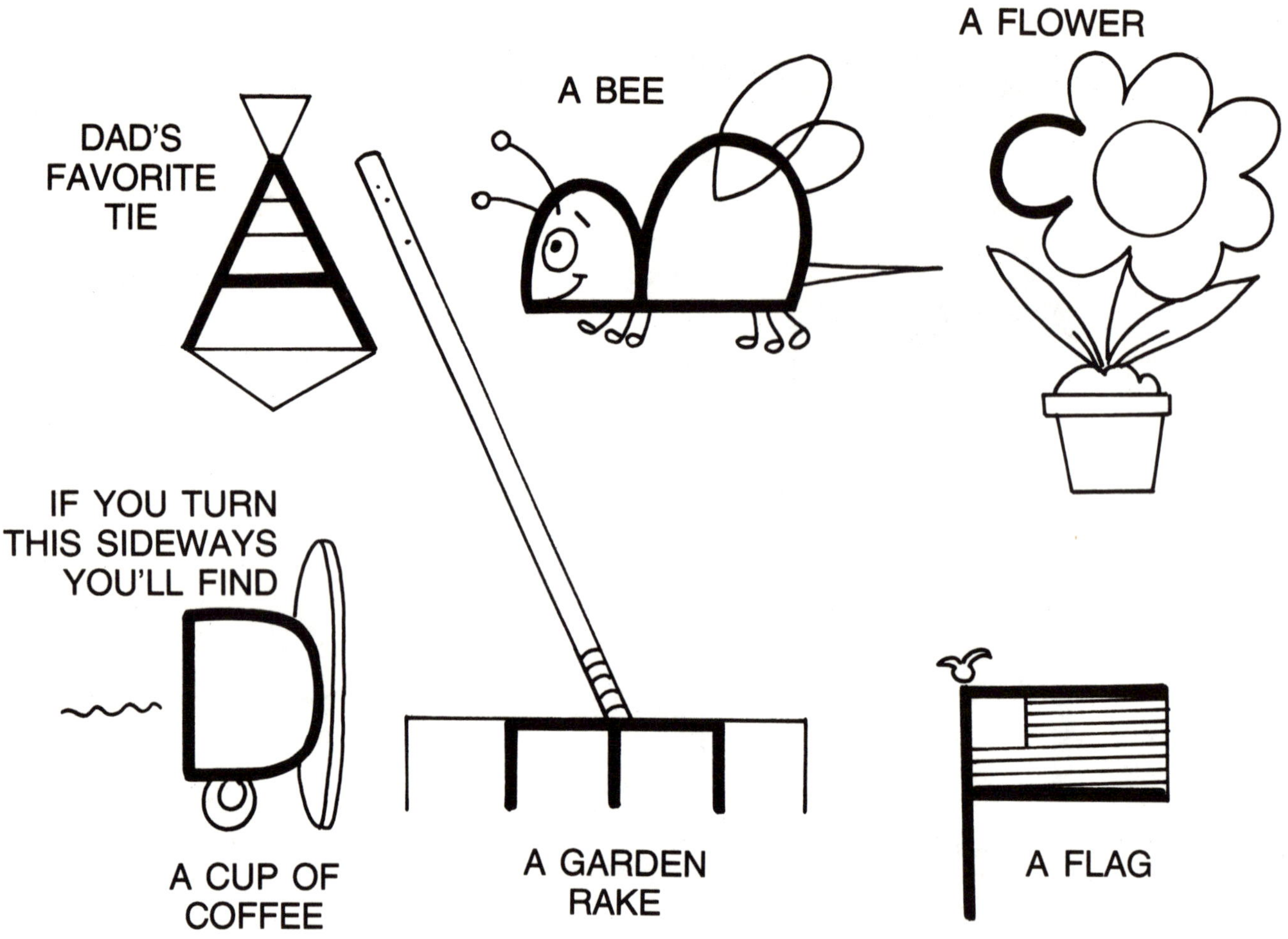

A FLOWER

A BEE

DAD'S
FAVORITE
TIE

IF YOU TURN
THIS SIDEWAYS
YOU'LL FIND

A CUP OF
COFFEE

A GARDEN
RAKE

A FLAG

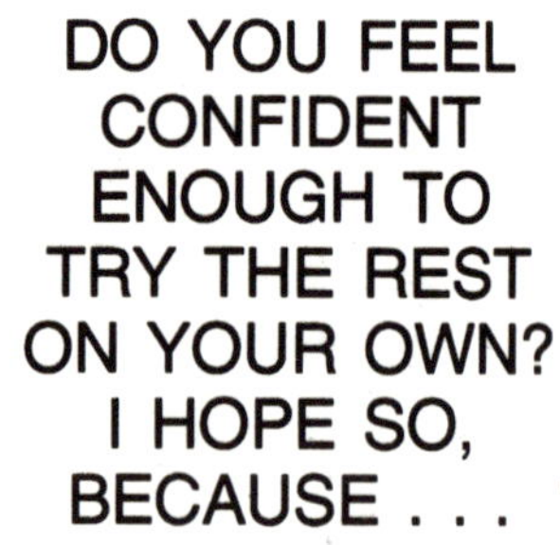

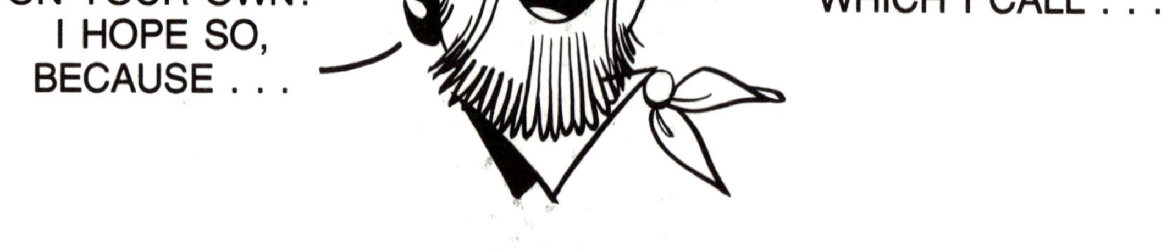

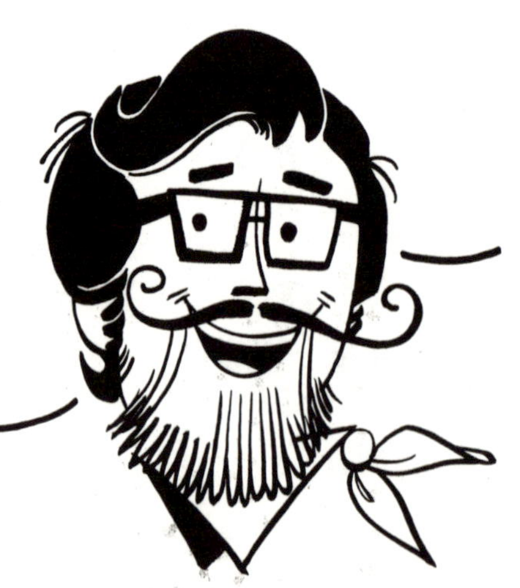

DRAW YOUR OWN CONCLUSIONS!

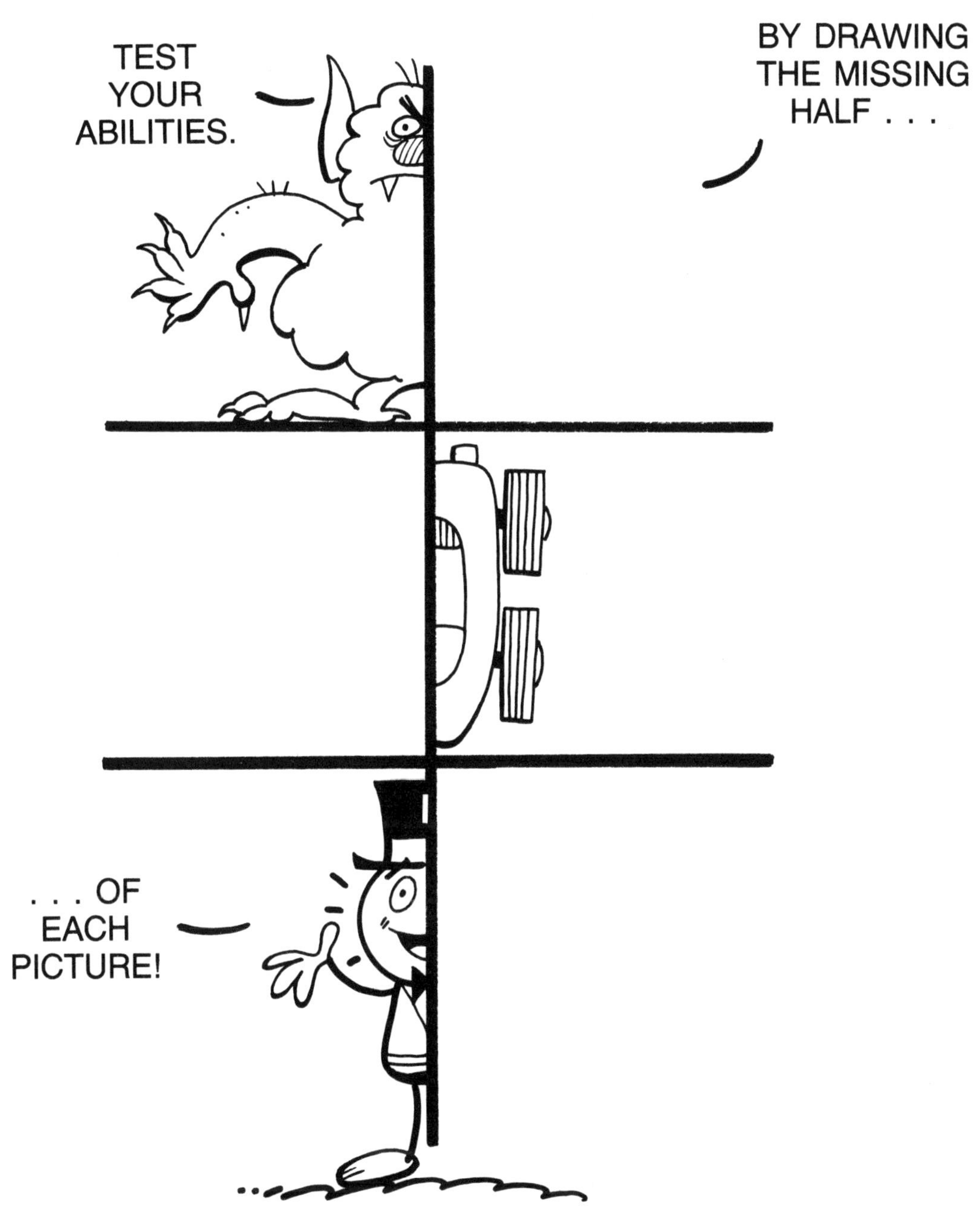

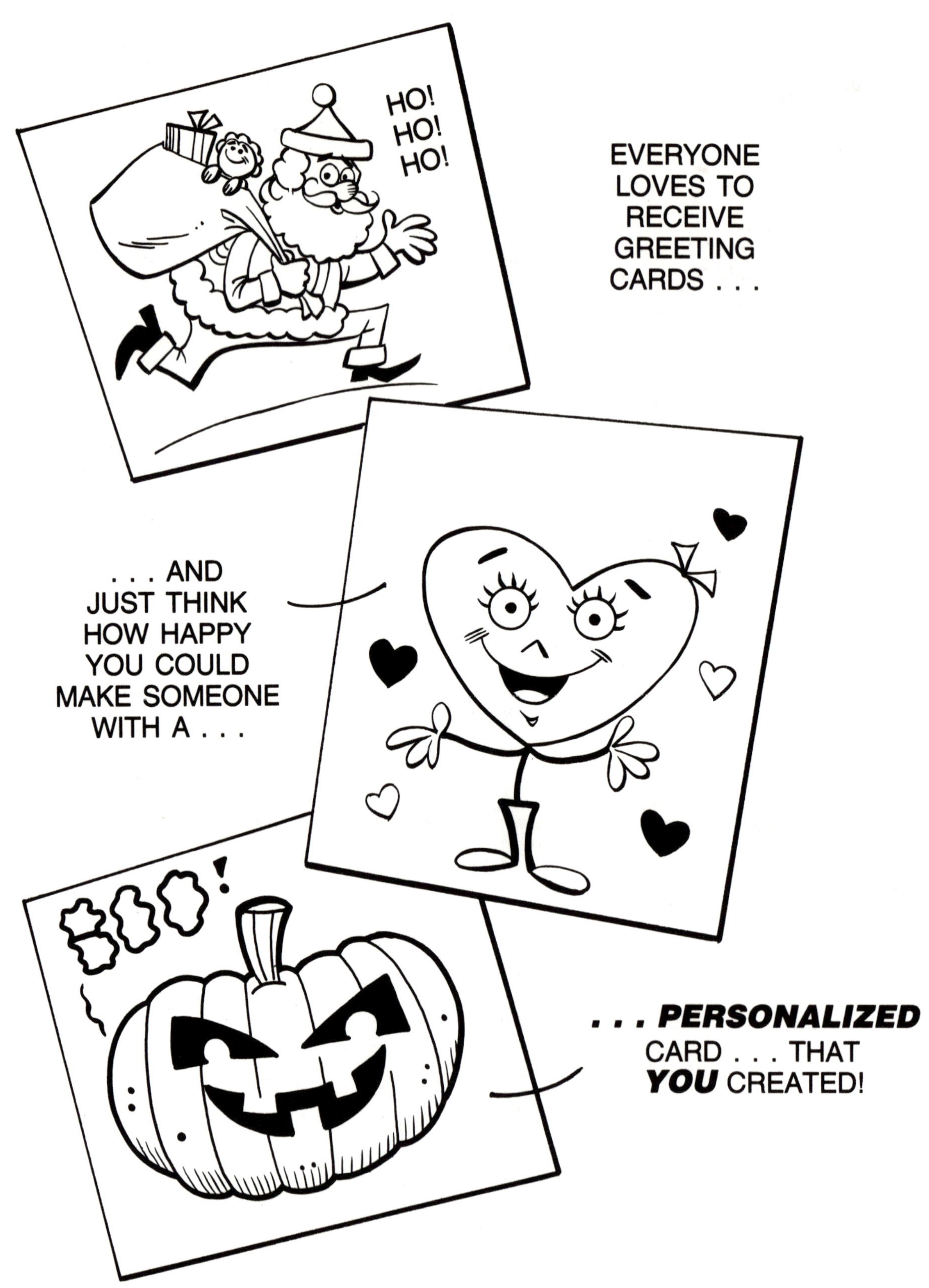
HO!
HO!
HO!
EVERYONE
LOVES TO
RECEIVE
GREETING
CARDS . . .
. . . AND
JUST THINK
HOW HAPPY
YOU COULD
MAKE SOMEONE
WITH A . . .
BOO!
. . . PERSONALIZED
CARD . . . THAT
YOU CREATED!

HERE ARE A FEW MORE

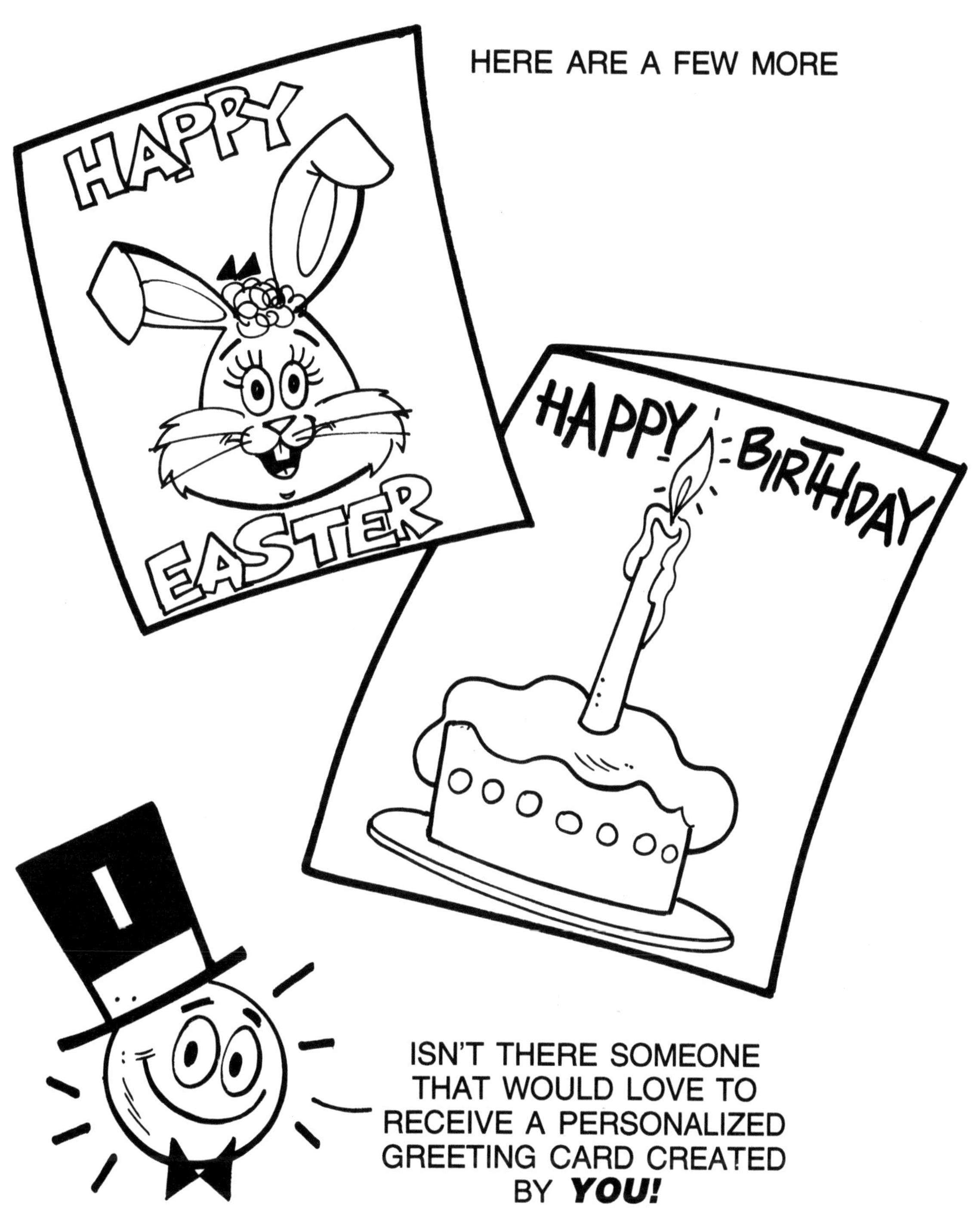

ISN'T THERE SOMEONE
THAT WOULD LOVE TO
RECEIVE A PERSONALIZED
GREETING CARD CREATED
BY ***YOU!***

YOU CAN ALSO USE YOUR NEW TALENT TO EARN SOME EXTRA MONEY BY CREATING SIGNS OR DRAWINGS FOR NEIGHBORHOOD STORES, OR BY DESIGNING ADS FOR LOCAL MERCHANTS.

HERE ARE JUST TWO EXAMPLES OF HOW TO USE YOUR CARTOONING ABILITY . . .

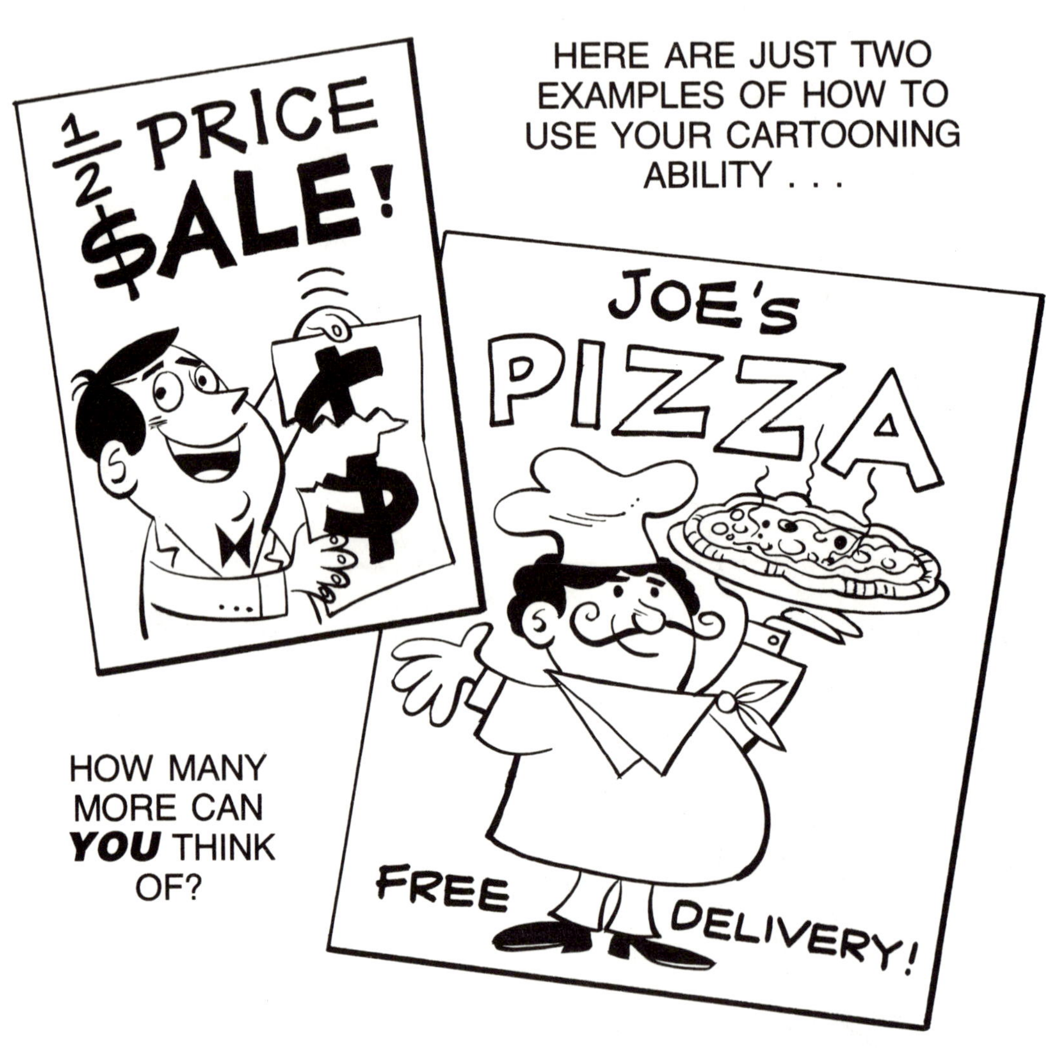

HOW MANY MORE CAN ***YOU*** THINK OF?

WELL . . . SO MUCH FOR THE BASICS. WE'VE COVERED A GOOD DEAL OF GROUND AND YOU HAVE LEARNED MANY THINGS . . . NOW IT'S UP TO ***YOU*** TO FOLLOW THROUGH! TO DRAW CARTOONS WELL YOU WILL HAVE TO WORK AT IT. THE BENEFITS TO BE DERIVED FROM ANYTHING WORTH HAVING ARE DIRECTLY PROPORTIONAL TO THE EFFORTS EXTENDED IN OBTAINING IT. PRACTICE WHAT YOU'VE LEARNED SO FAR . . . THERE IS STILL MUCH MORE TO LEARN . . .

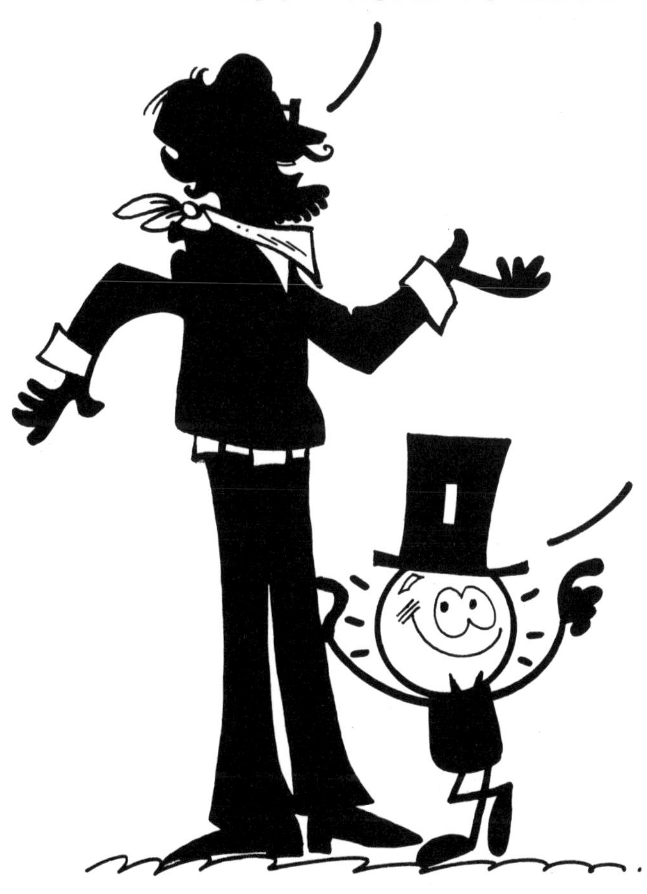

. . . SUCH AS, BASIC ANATOMY, PERSPECTIVE, LAYOUT, LETTERING, DIFFERENT KINDS OF CARTOONS, WORKING WITH INK, DEVELOPING YOUR OWN STYLE, AND SO ON . . .

. . . BUT ALL OF THAT, AND MORE,
CAN BE LEFT FOR FUTURE STUDY!
FOR NOW, ***LEARN THE BASICS,***
AND REMEMBER, IT'S THE CARTOONISTS
OF THE WORLD THAT BRING ZEST
AND HUMOR TO OUR LIVES.
DRAWING CARTOONS CAN BE A REWARDING
HOBBY, A FULFILLING, CREATIVE
PROFESSION . . . AND MOST IMPORTANT
OF ALL . . . A LOT OF FUN!
SO . . . TAKE PENCIL TO PAPER,
EXERCISE YOUR IMAGINATION,
THINK OF THAT CLEVER IDEA
AND . . .

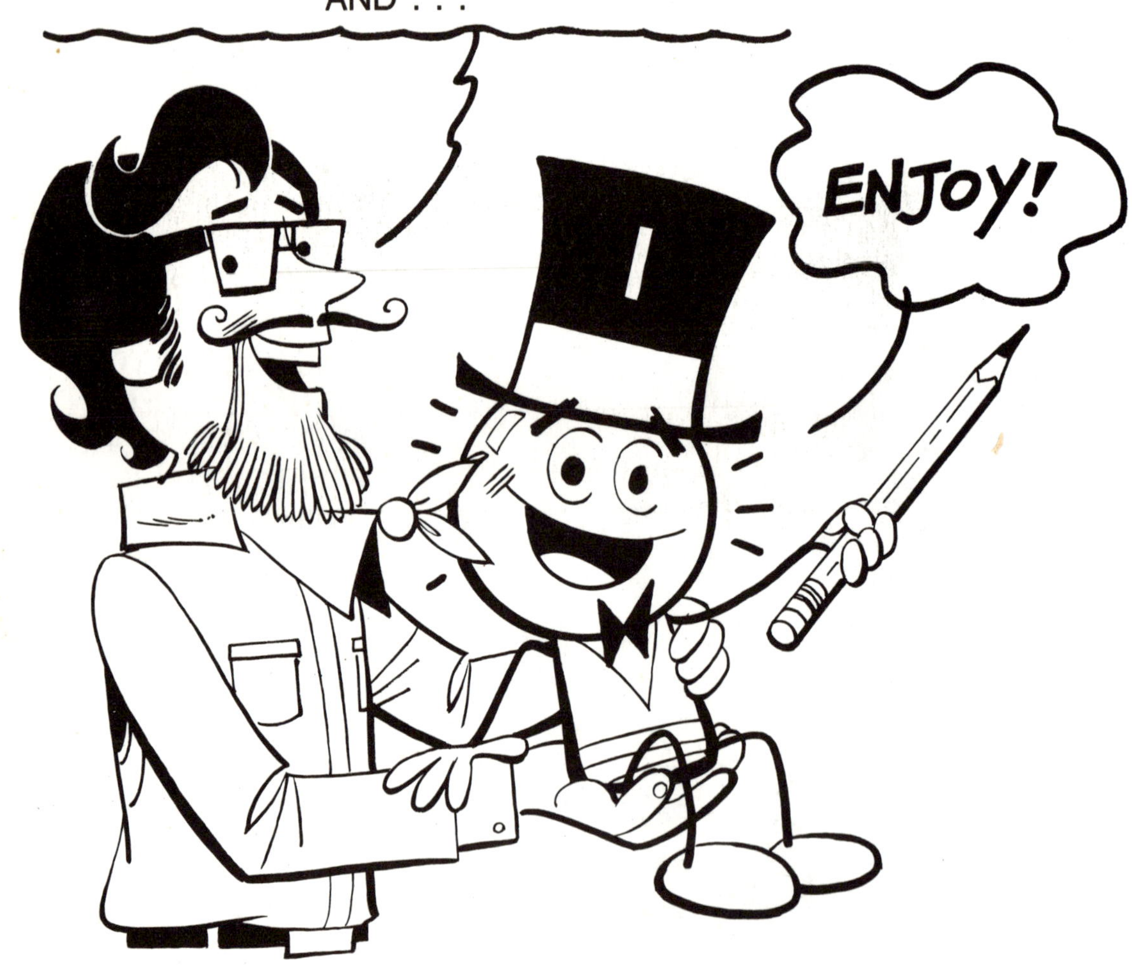